WOODWORKERS BUYER'S GUIDE TO POWER TOOLS

JM PUBLICATIONS, INC.
HENDERSONVILLE, TENNESSEE

Designed and Printed by Parthenon Press

Machine text by Frank Pittman

Electrical text by Tom Miller

Back Cover illustrations and design by Jennifer Chiles

Front Cover photography by Ron Benedict

Front Cover courtesy of William Warren, Tennessee Machinery
Co., Inc., Nashville, Tennessee

Published by JM Publications, Inc.
13 Walton Mall, P. O. Box 1408
Hendersonville, TN 37077-1408

Distributed by Sterling Publishing Co., Inc.
Two Park Avenue
New York, NY 10016

ISBN 0-9615844-0-8

Printed in The United States of America

CONTENTS

INTRODUCTION

We hope this 1986-87 edition of The Woodworkers Buyer's Guide to Power Tools will provide a service to each of those who read its pages. The guide is an attempt to provide enough information to the tool purchaser to enable him/her to make sound, logical decisions as to what type of equipment should be purchased.

Each chapter of the Guide represents an individual machine. Each chapter is presented in three basic parts: a written text, a comparison chart, and a photograph of most machines listed. The written text will give the consumer general guidelines to follow. The comparison chart will allow a first hand look at the individual statistics of each machine. Some machines appear to be similar until a photograph is presented. Obvious differences can be detected by examining each one. Finally, in each chapter, there are sections showing the special features and options of each machine.

There are a few machines that do not lend themselves to comparison because they are too highly specialized or too unusual. These machines have been listed in the rear of the book in the Miscellaneous section. The address of each manufacturer and importer represented is also listed at the back of the Guide.

When buying almost anything, one of the first items most people will consider is the price. It should certainly be a major consideration, but not the only one. If a person was fortunate enough to purchase whatever was required, irregardless of price, other requirements would still have to be considered. One does not buy a $200,000 sports car to use for hauling wood. A pick-up truck is cheaper and does a much better job. The same is true at the other end of the spectrum. Good oats are expensive. Once they have been run through the horse, they become less expensive, but, of course, the quality suffers somewhat. Each person must first define his/her own present and future needs. Only then can one begin any reasonable selection of tools.

GENERAL PURCHASING GUIDELINES

The thought process involved in purchasing woodworking machines is not very much different from the process you would use when purchasing any major item for your home. You must consider the manufacturer's reputation, guarantee, service, accessories available, where to buy, and how much to pay.

It is always best to purchase machines manufactured by companies with well established reputations for quality and service. An excellent way to help narrow your choice is to talk to people who own and use these machines already.

Try your best to understand the warranty or guarantee on the machine you are buying. Sometimes they are hard to figure out. Every reputable machine manufacturer will have one, and there is usually a specific time limit concerning repair and replacement. A common time limit on the warranty is one year. It is certainly best to understand the warranty when purchasing, rather than waiting until you experience problems.

The availability of replacement parts and the location of recognized service centers is another important item. Reputable manufacturers will have well established service centers and keep good inventories of replacement parts.

Where should you buy and how much should you pay? There is much to be said for seeing something before buying it. Few people today buy a family car without seeing or driving it. It is best in machine buying to not only see the item but to actually use it before buying, if you can. This is, unfortunately, not always possible

with large machines. Buying "sight unseen" really bothers most people. Be leery of machines which are sold by dealers who set up for a two day stay at a local motel. Their prices look good, but they will be gone if you need help. Buy from an established dealer with a good reputation. Woodworking machines, like automobiles, have a suggested retail price and an actual selling price. The selling price can be significantly less than the suggested retail price. It sure doesn't hurt to try to bargain a bit on price.

Good, used machines are available occasionally and may prove to be excellent investments. Many woodworkers prefer some of the older, heavier, cast iron machines over some of the newer models. If you are considering a used machine, inspect it carefully. Check the tables for cracks and warped castings. Remove belts from arbors and turn them through by hand, checking for side and end play. If you feel rough spots or notice side or end movement, the bearings need to be replaced. Inspect the condition of all adjustments, being sure that they function properly. Check the condition of miter gauges, fences, and other important accessories. Be sure to turn on the machine and listen to it. Unusual sounds or excessive vibration can indicate serious problems. A smooth running machine, new or used, should pass the "nickel test." This simple test involves placing a nickel on its edge on the machine table while the machine is running. The coin should remain stationary without falling over. If your machine passes this simple test, it is running smoothly. Finally, use the machine; put it under full load and see if it performs well. If a used machine passes all of these inspection points, it may well be an excellent buy.

You can encounter problems with some old machinery when it comes to replacement parts and accessories. If you are in doubt, check to see if parts are still available. This can be done by writing to the manufacturer. Be sure to include the model number and serial number of the machine in any correspondence with manufacturers.

In recent years, imported Taiwanese woodworking machines have hit the American market. Apparently these people have copied some of the better known woodworking machines—to the point that many times parts are even interchangeable. The imported copies are priced considerably less than the real thing. Generally these imports vary greatly in quality from one manufacturer to another and even within the same company. Before you decide to buy one of these machines, be sure to inspect it carefully for quality and take a close look at the warranty.

ELECTRICAL SYSTEMS ON WOODWORKING MACHINERY

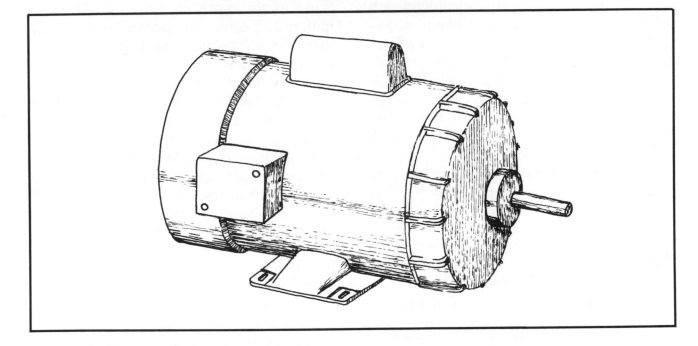

Woodworkers tend to have a far greater understanding of the power tools required for woodworking than they do the electrical requirements of those power tools. Consequently, we have electrical shocks and overloads, burned out motors, and even occasionally someone purchasing a machine that will not even work on his electricity!

Let's examine some of the electrical requirements that woodworkers may encounter:

THREE PHASE VS. SINGLE PHASE

All industrial and some commercial locations receive three-phase electricity from the power company. Everyone else, including residential users, have 220 volt single-phase electricity. It is MOST IMPORTANT that the voltage and type (phase) of electricity be determined prior to setting up shop in a new location. (See pictures of single-phase and three-phase panel boxes.)

Three phase is a tremendous advantage for electric motors only and nothing else. All other uses of electric current, resistance heat, lights, etc., still use plain old single

---

Used single-phase machinery always brings a premium because there are so many people who need it and can only use single phase.

---

phase anyway. Three phase electric motors are more efficient, cost less, and have no brushes so that they have lower maintenance costs. Much larger motors can be run on three phase than can be run on single phase. Because of these tremendous advantages, three phase is certainly worth the problems it creates if any one of the following apply: motors 5 HP or larger are going to be used; motors are going to be running nearly full time; used machinery may be purchased. If none of the above apply, then stick with single phase—it's much simpler.

Three-phase electricity is actually the two lines of 220 volt single-phase electricity with a third line added. This third line is said to cycle 120° out of cycle of the other two lines and is about 180 volts across ground. Therefore it is called the "high leg". A three-phase service entrance will yield the traditional 220 volts single phase by just not using the high leg and 220 volts three phase by using all three lines.

With three phase it is even more important to get an actual voltage reading than it is

---

Most small stationary woodworking machines and practically all portable power tools are single phase.

---

with single phase. Three phase comes from the power company in the following voltages: 208, 220, 440, and 550.

Woodworkers who are trying to build up a serious hobby shop, or maybe are thinking of working full time eventually, should give very serious consideration to going three phase for the following reasons:

1. *Motors are less expensive:* Three-phase motors, 3 HP or larger, usually cost about half the amount of a comparable single-phase motor.

2. *Larger HP available:* Single-phase motors usually don't get any larger than 3 or 5 HP, and on some woodworking machines, air compressors, planers, etc., it is nicer to have more power available.

3. *Lower maintenance costs:* Three-phase motors do not have the maintenance prob-

lems associated with the brushes burning out.

4. *More machinery options:* Used single-phase machinery always brings a premium because there are so many people who need it and can only use single phase. New single-phase machinery costs more than the comparable three-phase machine does because of the more expensive single-phase motor. Therefore, the person who can use three phase can buy industrial equipment which is usually readily available and in a more balanced supply and demand situation. The best buys in used woodworking equipment are always three phase.

Standard household current is 110 volt or 220 volt single phase. Most small stationary woodworking machines and practically all portable power tools are single phase. Most single phase motors are 3 HP or less, but occasionally the limit is stretched up to 5 HP. Single-phase motors are more expensive to purchase and to maintain.

A quick way to tell the difference— single-phase motors have a capacitor somewhere on the housing, and the plug has two lines with ground. Three-phase motors have no capacitors, and the plug has three lines with ground.

PHASE CONVERTORS

Some people need three phase and only single phase is available. For these people, one of several types of phase convertors is the answer. One can be purchased in the size and type to suit the application, and they do just as their name suggests; they run on single phase and produce three-phase electricity of the same voltage. Some are small transformer-type convertors that are inexpensive (about $200, maybe less) and mount directly on the three-phase machine and are wired directly to that machine. Larger units use single-phase current to run a motor attached to a generator which actually generates the third line in the three-phase power supply. These "phase generators" cost more ($500—$1000 or more depending upon size/capacity) and can be wired to run an entire shop with various machines starting, stopping, and running at the same time.

Phase convertors are just the ticket for the person with a basement shop who hopes one day to go full time and run his woodworking

---

"Rated horsepower" is derived in a very curious way, something like measuring fog. A ten amp motor, for example, will be working at full load and drawing exactly ten amps.

---

business in a commercial location. From the very beginning, he can buy three-phase equipment instead of buying "hobbiest" type machines only to replace everything after moving. Time and expense is saved initially by getting three phase, and again by not having to replace everything. An added advantage pops up if the shop is eventually moved to a location that is wired three phase and the convertor is sold. Convertors bring a premium on the used market because everyone wants one! Even if three phase is available from the power company, it may be less expensive to use a convertor instead of paying for another service entrance if the shop may be moved to another location in a year or two. (You can take the convertor with you, but you can't move a service entrance!)

RATED HORSEPOWER VS. TRUE HORSEPOWER

The laws of nature prevent what some portable power tool manufacturers try to convince you that their tools are able to do. Power-in equals power-out, less a little for loss in the system—and the loss is practically the same for all makes of power tools. No

tools are able to "create" energy. Since amperage is the measure of power going in, then power available for use from a ten amp motor will be greater than for an eight amp motor and less than for a twelve amp motor.

"Rated horsepower" is derived in a very curious way, something like measuring fog. A ten amp motor, for example, will be working at full load and drawing exactly ten amps. However, if you stall the motor, momentarily before it stalls, it will draw about 28 amps and then kick the breaker. Small tool manufacturers conclude that any motor drawing 28 amps in this case is doing the work of a 2½ HP motor, and they rate it as such. The ten amp motor in this example can only do ½ HP worth of work on a continuous basis so the 2½ HP rating is of absolutely no value.

Amperage is inversely proportional to voltage; when the voltage is double, the amperage is cut in half. When comparing the amperage of various motors, be sure to compare at the same voltage. Three-phase motors will draw less amps for the same

---

The laws of nature prevent what some portable power tool manufacturers try to convince you that their tools are able to do.

---

power rating than will single phase, so be sure that you compare motors of the same phase.

The Europeans and most of the rest of the world avoid the problems that Americans run into with the "horsepower" measurement by using instead a "KW", meaning kilowatt, rating. Their power rating measures the number of kilowatts consumed in an hour and avoids HP/volts/amps altogether. However, one can still look at the motor nameplate and get an amperage rating for comparison.

The sooner American consumers catch on

to the "Rated Horsepower" game, the sooner we will see manufacturers switch to another designation, maybe a KW rating, just as auto manufacturers switched to cubic inches from HP ratings for cars some years ago.

CONTROLS AND SWITCHES

A very important, but often overlooked component of a woodworking machine, is the switch or control that starts and stops it. It can vary anywhere from a simple toggle

---

Magnetic controls get their name from the electromagnetic coil up inside the control that closes the contacts and keeps them closed when energized.

---

switch to a low-voltage magnetic control with all the wiring in solid conduit. Operator safety as well as protection for the motor can be gained by going to one of the more sophisticated types of controls. Let's look at the advantages of each, starting with the simplest.

Manual Switch—A manual switch may be a simple toggle switch, pushbutton switch (where the buttons stay in when they are depressed until the other button is depressed), or a disconnect. There is no motor protection, and it will restart after an electrical interruption just like an electric light. This is the least expensive switch and is used on portable power tools and stationary machinery with motors of less than one HP.

Manual Switch with Overload—This switch is just as described above except it contains "heaters" which are nothing more than circuit breakers that are exactly matched to the amperage draw of the motor. The full voltage to run the motor passes through the switch. The overload will trip when the

motor overloads before the motor burns up. It can be reset when it cools down which is much easier than replacing a burned-out motor.

Magnetic Controls—Magnetic controls get their name from the electromagnetic coil up inside the control that closes the contacts and keeps them closed when energized. This is the same type of control as the ignition switch on an automobile. When the electricity is interrupted (or the car stalls), it won't restart again until someone pushes the start button and re-energizes the coil. Full electrical power to run the motor is going through the magnetic control and only enough power to energize the coil is actually going through the switch. Therefore, there is a much greater degree of safety for the operator at the switch.

With magnetic controls, start/stop stations or emergency stop stations can be located at as many remote locations as is desirable, all operating the same control. Magnetic controls usually cost between $100 and $300 complete and also contain heaters that exactly match the amperage draw of the motor. These controls can be used on any motor but are a necessity on motors 3 HP or larger because of the amount of electricity involved and as an insurance policy for motor burnout.

MOTORS

When purchasing a new machine or a new replacement motor, you will run into designations about the motor frame size and means of cooling. The frame size numbers (56T, 145TC, 182T, etc.) are simply identification numbers for a particular set of specifications about the arbor size, mounting hole configuration, etc., so that motors with the same frame number will fit interchangeably.

The other motor designation denotes the means of cooling: open, ODP, or TEFC.

Open, which is very seldom seen anymore, has very large holes in the end to allow easy access of air (and anything else in the atmosphere) into the motor windings. The open type motor has largely been replaced by the motor labelled ODP for Open Drip Proof. This type motor still has openings in the ends, but they are shielded. Water and dust from above cannot fall or 'drip' directly into the motor housing. This motor is widely

---

To change a three-phase machine to single phase, you always have to replace the motor.

---

used in all but very dusty, dirty conditions today. These dirty conditions call for a TEFC motor, meaning Totally Enclosed Fan Cooled. A TEFC motor has no openings in the housing for cooling, but instead, has a shrouded fan on the end opposite the shaft. This fan is mounted on the end of the motor shaft and flows air through the shroud and down along the sides of the motor all the time that the motor runs. TEFC motors cost a little more, but they save a lot of trouble under dirty conditions such as table saws, bandsaws, lathes, etc.

MAKING CHANGES

From time to time everyone has to change something electrical on their woodworking machine. When changing motors, it is important to get the right RPM and frame size, or else you will end up redrilling mounting holes or buying new pulleys and maybe belts. If you suspect that the motor is not original, it would be good to check the motor RPM, the pulley diameters and figure out the speed the machine is actually running. It may be necessary to change motor RPM or pulleys to arrive at the correct running speed.

When changing controls, the amperage of the motor at the operating voltage must be known to get the correct size overload heaters. Remember, if the heater rating is too high, then you have absolutely no overload protection!

To change a three-phase machine to single phase, you always have to replace the motor, but sometimes, you can use the same controls with the correct size heaters. Changing single phase to three phase involves replacing the motor and the controls.

A Note of Caution: Whenever starting any three-phase machine for the first time, whether the motor was replaced or not, always remove any arbor nuts, blades, wheels, etc., that may go flying off if the machine starts up in reverse. Unlike single phase, there is no way of prewiring it to always run in one direction; there is a 50-50 chance that it will turn backwards, and two leads need to be reversed for it to run the other way. Once connected and running correctly, it will always run that direction until it is rewired for some reason.

IN CONCLUSION . . .

It is best to look at the whole picture before making decisions about types of electricity. Where and how will these machines be used five years from now? How many hours a day will they be used? What type of electrical service is now available?

When looking at the controls or switch on a machine, ask, "Is it adequate for that size motor?" "Does it protect the operator?" "Does it protect the motor from burnout?"

The wrong electrical system on a woodworking machine can make it unsafe, difficult or impossible to run, just as the correct electrical system will give you the peace of mind to concentrate on what you are doing instead of thinking about what might be going wrong with the electrical system.

13

TABLE SAW

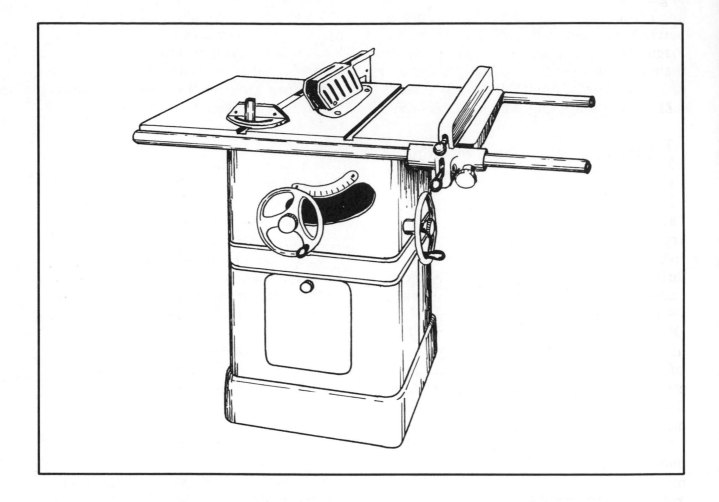

A good table saw is an important machine to serious woodworkers. These versatile machines are used most for conventional ripping and crosscutting, but they can be used for mitering, resawing, tenoning, grooving, dadoing, core box sawing (cove cutting with a conventional blade), box joint work, moldings (with special molding heads), splining, feathering, and a host of other special operations.

You should analyze your present and future woodworking plans in order to justify the purchase of a table saw. You may not need this machine at all. For example, if you are involved in figure carving or wood turning only, a band saw may suffice. If your interests include furniture and cabinet construction, a table saw is a must.

If your interests seem to justify a table saw, the next problem is selecting the best machine. You will find that there are many saws on the market to choose from. If woodworking is a new hobby for you, your project work is generally small, and your space and budget are limited, maybe a small bench model is your best bet. Bench models usually have small tables and are generally lighter in design and construction. They are certainly not designed for heavy duty use. While it is possible to do good work on a bench model saw, you will probably find that it is easier on a heavier floor model. Floor models have larger tables and generally their long term accuracy is better.

Table saw prices range from approximately $70.00 to over $2,000.00. As you can imagine, there is quite a difference in quality.

SIZES

The size of a table saw is commonly referred to in terms of the largest blade diameter the machine will take. A 10" saw will take a blade up to 10" in diameter. Some machines are designed to allow for slightly larger blades, but generally, this isn't the case. You, for example, could use an eight or ten inch blade but generally not a twelve inch blade on a 10" table saw.

Table saw sizes range from 4" to 16" with 10" probably being most common. Ten inch machines are popular because they have sufficient capacity for most work, occupy less floor space, and the machine and related blades are not as expensive as larger machines.

Smaller blades usually run more quietly than larger ones. This fact may seem fairly insignificant, but if you spend many hours around your saw, the noise level can become very significant. Frequently, owners of large machines will run smaller than maximum

---

The size of a table saw is commonly referred to in terms of the largest blade diameter the machine will take.

---

blades simply because of the noise reduction. Noise level is also influenced by blade design; some tooth configurations are simply louder than others.

The blade diameter will determine the

depth cutting capacity of the machine. A 10" machine will have a maximum 90 degree depth of approximately 3⅛" and a maximum depth of 2⅛" at 45 degrees. The capacity increases to 4⅛" maximum 90 degree depth and 2⅞" at 45 degrees for a 12" machine. When selecting a saw, analyze the kind of work you will do most often in terms of cutting depth required and choose accordingly.

BLADES

You could own the most accurate table saw in the world and still produce poor work if the blade used is badly chosen and poorly maintained. Most new machines are supplied with one conventional, chisel tooth combination blade. This type of blade will do a fair job of ripping and a relatively poor job of crosscutting. When buying a new machine you should probably invest in a good quality carbide tipped blade at the same time. A combination saw blade is one that can be used for both crosscutting and ripping operations and is the best choice if you want to invest in only one blade. There are several types of combination blades on the market, and they produce varying degrees of quality. Many woodworkers use "planer type" combination blades. These blades have a raker tooth followed by four scoring or crosscut teeth. This tooth configuration seems to yield acceptable quality for most woodworking. You may later want to purchase special crosscutting or ripping blades and a dado head.

TABLE

The size and construction of the working surface or table is another important consideration in saw selection. Many manufacturers supply the machine with a solid basic table and table extensions to increase the overall width of the surface. Larger tables are needed when your work involves cutting large panels. Sliding tables are also available on some machines. The sliding table feature makes the handling of large panels easier, but it also adds to the machine's cost.

The material used to make the table has a lot to do with its long term accuracy. Cast iron has been used for many years as a primary table material. Today, however, you will also find aluminum, steel, and even plastic being used. Cast iron is still considered to be the best choice. It is heavier, harder, and generally more accurately machined than other materials.

One of the first things you should do in evaluating a table saw is examine the table closely for cracks and warped castings. Don't buy a machine with either of these flaws. The table should also be smoothly finished on the top surface.

The table insert which surrounds the blade is a part which some woodworkers complain about. This part is removed for blade replacement and can be replaced with special inserts for dado head set-up. Inserts are usually made from a softer material than the rest of the table to prevent blade damage if it should deflect to the side. Inserts frequently have built-in leveling screws so they can be adjusted flush with the rest of the table. It's not possible, however, to level the insert to the table if the insert itself doesn't have a flat top surface. You will find that

---

The table insert which surrounds the blade is a part which some woodworkers complain about.

---

many inserts are not flat. If this is the case, it is virtually impossible to align these parts. Make sure that you take a good look at the table insert accuracy and its leveling features.

Saw tables usually have two milled slots for the miter gauge, one on either side of the blade. These slots should be smoothly machined and parallel to each other and the blade.

FENCE AND MITER GAUGE

Some woodworkers say that the quality of the rip fence and miter gauge is a good index to the overall quality of the machine. While this may or may not be true, these two items do certainly have a lot to do with the accuracy and safety of the machine.

Poor fence design has long been a complaint of woodworkers. Machinery man-

---

Since the rip fence is used so often and is adjusted repeatedly during the life of the saw, sturdiness of its design is important.

---

ufacturers have responded, and in recent years, fence designs have been greatly improved, especially on better machines. Table saws in the lower price range will still be subject to the same old complaints.

Fence problems include: warped fences or fences with surfaces that are not straight, fence face not at 90 degrees to table, fences which flex or deflect on the outfeed end, fences which do not move parallel with the blade when adjusted with a "fine tuning" knob, and fence locks which fail to be positive and gradually slip out of adjustment during long runs.

Since the rip fence is used so often and is adjusted repeatedly during the life of the saw, sturdiness of its design is important. Look at it carefully, checking for ease and accuracy of adjustment, locking features, straightness, squareness, and the type and length of the guide rails.

The miter gauges provided with some machines, especially the cheaper models, are almost a joke. It is hard to believe what some manufacturers call miter gauges. Stamped sheet metal or poor quality, warped injection molded plastic are examples of low quality. Whatever happened to cast iron or even cast aluminum gauges? Some manufacturers may consider this accessory to be a disposable part. You would do well to dispose of the cheaper ones. If you ever expect to get consistent, accurate performance from a miter gauge, follow these guidelines. It should be equipped with an accurate guide bar which fits the saw table slots without side play; have an accurate front face, one that is at 90 degrees to the saw's table; have a convenient adjusting knob which is large enough to be tightened with ease; have no play between the gauge and its guide bar when locked; be designed so extension boards can be easily installed on the face of the gauge for special operations; and have an accurate, easy to read degree scale. The miter gauge, like the rip fence, is an often used accessory. Evaluate its design carefully before you buy.

DRIVE MECHANISM & BLADE CARRIAGE

Table saws are either direct or belt driven. The saw blade on a direct drive machine is mounted to the arbor of the motor. Direct drive requires less space under the table, therefore, bench model machines are often of this design. Belt driven machines are very common. These drive systems utilize one or more v-belts to transfer the power from the motor to the arbor. Heavy duty machines will have two or three drive belts, while lighter duty models will have only one.

The rigidity and design of the blade carriage or the part of the machine which houses the arbor, bearings, motor, and raising/tilting mechanism is important in terms of a machine's long term accuracy and life. Better saws will have heavy cast iron assemblies while inexpensive models will have stamped steel parts. Look under the table and examine the carriage. The heavier the better.

BASE DESIGN

The best work will come from a table saw which is stable and securely fastened to the floor or a suitable base. If you purchase a bench model be sure to secure it to a heavy base. Floor models perform best if they are securely anchored to the floor. The machine certainly should not walk or move while it is being used. This could create a serious safety hazard.

ELECTRICAL INFORMATION

It is easy to become confused when you try to evaluate some of the electrical information pertaining to table saws. You will find that some models offer a wide variety of possible electrical components while others offer no choice. Consider the following items: phase (single or three), voltage, HP, RPM, and electrical controls.

Most home shops and many small cabinet shops do not have three phase current. The average woodworker, therefore, will be looking for single phase equipment. Single phase voltage is 115-220.

Motors used on most saws have an RPM range from 3450 up. Generally the smaller bench models have higher RPM. It is important to know what RPM your saw arbor has. There are saw accessories, molding heads for example, which are unsafe to operate at high speeds.

Most table saws, except for the very small bench models, will have at least a one horse power motor. Larger floor models will have 2 to 7½ HP units.

Electrical control options are possible on some models. Many of the smaller machines will have only a simple start-stop button. Others may include overload protection. The overload protection feature simply means that the starter is equipped with a device which will shut the motor off automatically before it heats up to the point of burning out.

BLACK & DECKER 8″
7708

BLACK & DECKER 10″
7755

BLACK & DECKER 10″
1732

BLACK & DECKER 10″
1736

BLACK & DECKER 10″
1738

CRAFTSMAN 8″
BENCH TOP
9 HT 22161

CRAFTSMAN 10″
FLEXIBLE DRIVE
9 HT 24169N

DELTA 10″
34-429

CRAFTSMAN 10″
ELECTRONIC
9 HT 22683N

DELTA 10″
CONTRACTOR'S
34-410

DELTA 10″
UNISAW®
34-764

THE FINE TOOL SHOP 10″
204-0023

THE FINE TOOL SHOP 10″
204-0027

HITACHI 12″
C12Y

GENERAL 10″
350

JET 10″
708512

JET 10″
708520

JET 14″
708577

KITY USA 10″
MODEL 617
7217

POWERMATIC 12″
MODEL 68

SKIL 8¼″
3102:02

STARTRITE 10″
TA 250

VEGA 12″
MODEL 12

WILKE MACHINERY CO. 12″
TSC-12S

TABLE SAW

BRAND *NO PHOTO AVAILABLE	Model Number	Size of Saw	Motor**	Special Features***	Options****	Table Size (Without extensions)	Maximum Depth of Cut	Maximum Cut at 45°	Maximum Cut to Right of Blade	Maximum Cut to Left of Blade	Maximum Width of Dado Cut	Overall Dimensions H x VV x D	Arbor Diameter	Speed of Saw Blade (RPM)	Motor Drive*****	Table Height	Shipping Weight	Suggested Retail Price
BLACK & DECKER (Mfg.-DeWalt)	7708	8"	1 HP / 17	4-47-51 / 73-74	39	15⅜x26¾	1¾"	1¾"	9½"	12¼	—	—	⅝"	—	D	—	38	$146
BLACK & DECKER (Mfg.-DeWalt)	7755	10"	2 HP / 1-5-15-17	4-47-51-65 / 73-75-76-77	—	20 x 27	3⅜"	2¼"	24"	—	—	—	⅝"	—	—	35"	135	621
BLACK & DECKER	1732	10"	1.6 HP / 17	4-47-51-73 / 78-79-80	—	17 x 20	3⅛"	2⅛"	24"	—	13/16"	—	⅝"	5,000	—	—	78	269
BLACK & DECKER	1736	10"	1.6 HP / 17	4-39-47-51 / 73-80-81-82-83	—	20 x 27	3¼"	2¼"	24"	—	13/16"	—	⅝"	5,000	D	—	130	429
BLACK & DECKER	1738	10"	2 HP / 15-17	39-47-84 / 85-86-87	—	17 x 20	2¼"	1 11/16"	15¾"	—	13/16"	—	⅝"	3,450	D	—	120	529
CRAFTSMAN	9 HT 22161	8"	.5 HP / 5	4-63-64-65	33-34-35-36	—	1¾"	1 11/16"	12¾"	13½	—		—	—	—	—	47	150
*CRAFTSMAN	9 HT 24173N	9"	1.6 HP / 5-15	4-66	—	—	2"	1⅞"	16"	11½	—	—	—	—	D	—	75	289⁹⁹
*CRAFTSMAN	9 HT 29805N	10"	2 HP / 5-15	4-67	—	—	2½"	2 5/16"	24"	—	—	—	—	—	D	—	130	389⁹⁹
*CRAFTSMAN	9 HT 22664N	10"	2 HP / 5-15-16	4-39-51	—	20 x 40	2½"	2 5/16"	24"	—	—	—	—	—	—	—	153	399⁹⁹
CRAFTSMAN	9 HT 24169N	10"	1 1/16 HP / 5-15-16	4-68-69-78	37	—	3⅜"	2¼"	—	—	—	—	—	—	F	—	235	589⁹⁹
CRAFTSMAN	9 HT 22683N	10"	1 1/16 HP / 5-17	4-68-69 / 70-71-72	—	—	3⅜"	2¼"	—	—	—	—	—	—	B	—	265	689⁹⁹
*CRAFTSMAN	9 HT 2425N	12"	3.5 HP / 8-15-19	4-51-65 / 72	38	—	3 9/16"	2¼"	24"	—	—	—	—	—	D	—	228	649⁹⁹
DELTA	34-429	10"	1.5 HP / 17-20	4-51 / 94-95-96	40	20 x 27	3⅛"	2⅛"	25"	15½	13/16"	—	⅝"	4,000	—	33½"	302	1193
DELTA	34-410	10"	1.5 HP / 1-10-17-20	4-80-93 / 97-98	—	20 x 27	3⅛"	2⅛"	25"	15½	13/16"	34¼ x 45 x 39¾	⅝"	4,000	—	34¼"	265	1032

TABLE SAW

BRAND *NO PHOTO AVAILABLE	Model Number	Size of Saw	Motor**	Special Features***	Options****	Table Size (Without extensions)	Maximum Depth of Cut	Maximum Cut at 45°	Maximum Cut to Right of Blade	Maximum Cut to Left of Blade	Maximum Width of Dado Cut	Overall Dimensions H x W x D	Arbor Diameter	Speed of Saw Blade (RPM)	Motor Drive *****	Table Height	Shipping Weight	Suggested Retail Price
*DELTA	34-621	9″	1 HP 1-4-15-17	4-51-80 92-98-99	—	15 x 22	2¾″	2″	24″	24″	13/16″	34½ x 37½ x 36	⅝″	3,800	—	34½″	152	$710
*DELTA	SUPER 10	10″	1 HP	4-47-51 77-92-100-101	—	22 x 24	2 9/16″	1 13/16″	24″	—	13/16″	38 x 41¼ x 32	⅝″	3,450	D	35″	152	597
*DELTA	34-695	10″	13 AMP 4-17	4-47-51-76 77-92-100-102	—	22 x 17	3¼″	2⅛″	24″	—	13/16″	39 x 42 x 22	⅝″	5,500	—	34½″	119	349
*DELTA	34-580	9″	13 AMP 4-17	4-47-51-77 92-100-110	—	22 x 17	2″	1⅝″	15″	15″	13/16″	38 x 32 x 17	⅝″	3,450	—	33½″	110	314
*DELTA	31-205	8″	9.5 AMP 4	4-50-51-76 92-103	41	16 x 26	2 1/16″	1⅞″	10¾″	—	½″	13⅞ x 26 x 17¼	⅝″	3,450	—	32½″	35	206
DELTA	34-764	10″	3 HP 2-12-14-20-21	4-27-51-104 105-106-107-108	42-43	20 x 27	3⅛″	2⅛″	25″	15½″	13/16″	—	⅝″	4,000	B-Q3	34″	464	1871
*ELEKTRA BECKUM	110301	12″	3 HP 1-3	4-46-47	9-10-11-12	29½ x 24	3½″	—	—	—	—	—	1″	3,360	D	31½″	110	410
FINE TOOL SHOP (Mfg.-King Feng Fu)	204-0023	10″	.75 HP 5	4-51-73-77 92-119	—	26 x 17¼	3″	2½″	—	—	—	—	⅝″	5,000	—	—	39	189⁹⁵
FINE TOOL SHOP (Mfg.-King Feng Fu)	204-0027	10″	1.5 HP 5-15	4-10-39 122-123-124	—	—	3⅛″	2 3/16″	—	—	—	—	—	4,150	—	—	286	499
*GRIZZLY	G1022	10″	1.5 HP 1-9	39-40-41-42 43-44-45	7-8	—	3⅛″	2⅛″	—	—	—	—	⅝″	—	B	37″	220 Net	325
*GRIZZLY	G1023	10″	3 HP 1-6	46-47	—	—	—	—	—	—	—	—	⅝″	—	B	—	500	795
HITACHI	C12Y	12″	see option #5 1	9- 20 thru 29	6	20 x 27	4⅛″	2⅞″	25″	15½″	—	40 x 49 x 41	1″	3,800	B	34¼″	330 Net	2160
J. PHILLIP HUMFREY, LTD. (Mfg.-General)	350-24	10″	see option #54	4-12-39-53 61-92-125	55 thru 60	28 x 36	3⅛″	2⅛″	25″	15½″	1″	—	⅝″	4,000	B-Q2	34″	390 Net	1253⁶⁰ w/o motor
JET	708512	10″	1.5 HP 1-10-13	1-2-3-4-5	—	20 x 27	3⅛″	1⅞″	25″	—	—	27 x 40 x 37	⅝″	—	B	—	248	470

TABLE SAW

BRAND *NO PHOTO AVAILABLE	Model Number	Size of Saw	Motor**	Special Features***	Options****	Table Size (Without extensions)	Maximum Depth of Cut	Maximum Cut at 45°	Maximum Cut to Right of Blade	Maximum Cut to Left of Blade	Maximum Width of Dado Cut	Overall Dimensions H x W x D	Arbor Diameter	Speed of Saw Blade (RPM)	Motor Drive *****	Table Height	Shipping Weight	Suggested Retail Price
JET	708520	10″	3 HP 1-10-14	2-4-6 thru 12 14-16-17-26	1-3	20 x 27	3″	2⅛″	26″	15½″	13/16″	36½ x 46 x 40	⅝″	4,200	B-Q3	34″	485	$1399
*JET	708575	12″	3 HP 1-10	2-4-6 thru 12 16-17-19-26	2-3	24 x 30	3¾″	2⅝″	32″	19″	13/16″	36½ x 52⅜ x 35¾	1″	4,000	B-Q3	34″	570	1899
JET	708577	14″	7.5 HP 2-12	2-6 thru 10 13-14-15-17-18-26	4	28 x 38	5⅛″	3″	36″	16″	2″	34 x 64½ x 41½	1″	3,750	B-Q4	34″	950	2990
KITY USA	Model 617 7217	10″	—	4-51-92 116	45-46-47 48-49-50	31½ x 21½	2¼″	—	24″	24″	—	—	—	3,300	—	—	32	828[30]
*POWERMATIC	Model 66 1660010	10″	2 HP 1-7-20	4-27-92 109 thru 113	44	—	3⅛″	2⅛″	25″	—	13/16″	—	⅝″	4,000	B-Q3	34″	500	2136
POWERMATIC	Model 68 1680010	12″	3 HP 1-7-14	4-27-51-92 112-113-114	44	—	4⅛″	2⅞″	30″	24″	13/16″	35 x 23⅞ x 25⅜	1″	—	B-Q3	35″	775	3443
SKIL	3102:02	8¼″	2 HP	4-51-65 117 thru 121	51-52-53	16 x 27	2 1/16″	2″	—	—	—	27 1/16x17⅜x10⅛	—	5,500	—	—	41	194[99]
STARTRITE	TA 250	10″	3 HP 1-6	4- 48 thru 53	13-14-15-16 17-18-19	27¾ x 36¼	3⅛″	2⅛″	19⅝″	—	13/16″	39 x 32 x 41	⅝″	3,850	B	34″	450	2153
*SUNHILL (Mfg.-Rexon)	RXW-10	10″	1.5 HP 9-18	4-39-51 73-88	—	20⅛ x 27	—	—	—	—	—	—	—	4,500	—	—	286	499
*SUNHILL (Mfg.-Champ Fond)	TS-412	10″	3 HP 1-18	4-89-90-91 93	—	—	—	—	—	—	—	—	⅝″	4,000	—	—	450	1850

(ALL PRICES INCLUDE FREIGHT TO THE NEAREST TERMINAL OF OUR HOUSE CARRIER [SUNHILL])

BRAND *NO PHOTO AVAILABLE	Model Number	Size of Saw	Motor**	Special Features***	Options****	Table Size (Without extensions)	Maximum Depth of Cut	Maximum Cut at 45°	Maximum Cut to Right of Blade	Maximum Cut to Left of Blade	Maximum Width of Dado Cut	Overall Dimensions H x W x D	Arbor Diameter	Speed of Saw Blade (RPM)	Motor Drive *****	Table Height	Shipping Weight	Suggested Retail Price
VEGA	12	12″	see option #20	4 54 thru 62	21 thru 32	19¾ x 29	4⅛″	—	—	—	—	—	⅝″	—	B	34″	500 Net	2775
WILKE MACHINERY CO.	TSC-12S	12″	2 HP 1-17-20	4-36-39-51 83-92	—	20 x 27	4¼″	4⅛″	24″	19⅞″	—	—	⅝″	3,400	—	—	297	589[95]

***MOTOR*
1. Single phase
2. Three phase
3. 110 V
4. 115 V
5. 120 V
6. 220 V
7. 230 V
8. 240 V
9. 110/220 V
10. 115/230 V
11. 220/440 V
12. 230/460 V
13. Manual overload reset
14. Magnetic control
15. Capacitor start
16. Sleeve bearing
17. Ball bearing
18. Sealed bearings
19. Actual HP not given; develops 3.5 HP
20. TEFC
21. 24 V pushbutton station

******MOTOR DRIVE*
B—BELT DRIVE
D—DIRECT DRIVE
F—FLEXIBLE DRIVE

Q2—TWO BELTS
Q3—THREE BELTS
Q4—FOUR BELTS

***SPECIAL FEATURES**

1. Prewired to 115V.
2. Prewired to 230V.
3. Mitre gauge permits cuts to 60°.
4. Blade guard with splitter and anti-kickback attachment.
5. 10" extension wings on both sides of the table.
6. Box type body is made of steel plate.
7. All moving parts are enclosed.
8. Spindle is supported by a one piece housing incorporating two enclosed precision ball bearings.
9. Spindle tilts 45°.
10. Rip fence can be used on either side of the saw blade.
11. 24V safety control system.
12. Mitre gauge and table insert are standard equipment.
13. Heavy duty cast iron table.
14. Saw arbor is changeable.
15. Wide selection of arbor extensions available to permit the use of many saw accessories.
16. Guide rail fastened to the front and rear of the table.
17. Front guide rail is calibrated.
18. Standard equipment includes dado insert, splitter with guard, 24V safety control system, spanners.
19. Standard equipment includes 3 HP motor w/cover, splitter with guard, two extension wings, 24V safety control system, spanners.
20. Cast iron rip fence.
21. Hand brake for instant stopping of blade.
22. Overload motor protection.
23. Sealed, lubricated for life ball bearings.
24. Dust collection duct.
25. Maximum rip capacity to 35" at right side by

shifting guide bars.
26. Standard equipment includes rip fence, mitre gauge, blade guard, and table insert.
27. Extension table included.
28. Spindle lock for easy, safe blade change.
29. Micro-set dial system to ensure accurate adjustment of rip fence.
30. Prewired to 110V.
31. All ball bearing arbor tilts using worm gear mechanism.
32. Cast iron table with slotted cast iron extensions.
33. Mounted on a steel stand.
34. Metal blade guard.
35. Blade insert.
36. Dado insert.
37. Extra long tubes can be added for extra large jobs.
38. Table size with extension wings is 41" X 27".
39. Cast iron table.
40. Table size with two extensions is 36.06" X 27.08".
41. One piece steel cabinet stand.
42. Extra large solid handwheels.
43. Magnetic safety switch.
44. All sealed ball bearings in the spindle and the motor.
45. Precision type rip fence with scales and locks.
46. Table is galvanized steel.
47. Thermal overload protection switch.
48. Includes TEFC motor and control, start/stop button, overload and no-volt protection.
49. Heavy duty two position rip fence, constructed of anodized aluminum.
50. Table insert.
51. Mitre gauge.

52. Saw blade tilts away from rip fence to prevent binding.
53. Extra heavy duty steel cabinet base.
54. Rolling table size is 18½" X 29".
55. Rolling table travel is 29¾".
56. Starter is fuse protected.
57. Rolling and fixed tables are made from ⅜" steel plate, precision ground after aging; each table weighs over 100 lbs.
58. Rolling table rides on a 1½" square steel bar; the Vee rollers utilize six sealed ball bearings.
59. Two position rip fence with "micrometer" adjustment.
60. The mitre gauge is a 27" long piece of extruded aluminum angle.
61. Arbor pulley mounted between ball bearings.
62. Front and side access doors for cleaning.
63. Aluminum table with two extensions is 17" X 35".
64. Aluminum mitre gauge; pick-off-type rip fence.
65. Switch with removable locking key.
66. Aluminum table with steel extensions gives 37" X 20" work area.
67. Aluminum table with steel extensions gives 40" X 27" work area.
68. Mitre gauge features a hold down clamp.
69. Quick-release, self-aligning pick-off-type rip fence.
70. Electronic saw raises and lowers blade by way of a front-mounted computerized panel, accurate to .005".
71. LED bevel display reads .1°, programmable for bevel, elevation and shut downs.
72. Cast iron extensions give a 40" X 27" work area.

***SPECIAL FEATURES

73. Self-adjusting rip fence.
74. Can crosscut finished stock up to 5" without sliding material over the blade. Push the blade handle down to cut the material.
75. Extensions give a 27" X 49" table surface.
76. Cast aluminum table.
77. Price includes stand.
78. Extensions give a 42" X 20" table surface.
79. Sealed ball bearing construction, iron-impregnated ferrolon™ table wears like iron, but is light weight and will not rust.
80. Steel stand included.
81. Extensions give a 45" X 27" table surface.
82. Exclusive slip clutch disengages blade from motor drive if work binds.
83. Totally enclosed drive mechanism.
84. Extensions give a 35" X 20" table surface.
85. Rack and pinion rip fence.
86. Table length mitre bar.
87. Grid aluminum extensions.
88. Two cast iron extension wings, 10⅛" X 27".
89. Milled aluminum 30" T-square style fence.
90. Micro-adjustment knob and single lever lock fence.
91. One piece cast iron frame.

92. Rip fence.
93. Table size with extensions is 27" X 40".
94. Table size with extensions is 36" X 27".
95. Self-aligning MICRO-SET® rip fence.
96. Table insert.
97. Jet-lock rip fence.
98. Contractor's saw.
99. Table size with extension wings is 30" X 22".
100. HOMECRAFT® saw.
101. Table size with extension wing is 22" X 37".
102. Table size with extension wings is 22" X 32".
103. Height with Option #41 is 36¼".
104. UNISAW®.
105. Table size with extension wings is 36" X 27".
106. Precision bored bearing seats, pre-loaded bearings, precision ground arbor, 24V safety control station on models with magnetic controls.
107. Jet-lock MICRO-SET® rip fence.
108. Transformer and three-leg overload protection.

109. Table size with extension wings is 28" X 38".
110. Box style precision ground rip fence.
111. Arbor is mounted in large, sealed ball bearings.
112. Arbor tilts away from the rip fence for safer operation.
113. Posi-track fence and rail system.
114. Table size with extension wings is 38" X 48".
115. All machines are performance tested before shipment.
116. Cuts 45° by tilting machine table.
117. All ball and needle bearing construction.
118. Cut steel helical gearing.
119. One piece die cast aluminum table.
120. 12" rip capacity.
121. Steel rip fence.
122. Free dado set and insert included.
123. Die cast aluminum extension wings.
124. Table size with extensions is 40½" X 27".
125. Includes steel base.
126. Motor recommended—1.5 HP to 3 HP, TEFC, 3600 RPM.

****OPTIONS

1. #708521, 3HP, three phase, 220/440V; prewired to 220V; $1,427.
2. #708576, 3HP, three phase, 220/440V; prewired to 220V, $1,899.
3. #708580, sliding table attachment, made from cast aluminum; table rides on a smooth bearing surface for easy cutting of 4 X 8 wood panels. Table folds down when not in use; has extension legs for added stability; sliding table size is 30" X 18"; overall table saw size w/attachment is 85" X 80" X 34" for the 10" saw, and 89" X 80" X 34" for the 12" saw; weight 158 lbs., $585.
4. #708579, same features as #708580; sliding table size is 30" X 34½"; overall table saw size w/attachment is 91" X 80" X 34" for the 14" saw; 161 lbs., $699.
5. Choice of motors available: 3.1 HP @ 112V or 3.8 HP @ 230V.
6. Machine is $1,850 without the motor.
7. #G1187, extension tubes, 70" long, $49.95 prepaid.
8. #G1193, cast iron extension wing, $39.95 prepaid.
9. 48" panel cutting attachment, $75.
10. Sliding carriage, $123.
11. Crosscut/mitre fence, $33.
12. Roller stand, $36.50.
13. A 2 HP, 110V, single phase motor available in place of 3 HP motor.
14. Saw available with 3 HP, 220/440V, three phase motor, $2,013.
15. #SM1571, right hand table extension, table board, and fence extension, $237.
16. #SM1575, 24V control, $255.
17. #SM1572, Dado hold down unit, $168.
18. #WID600, Dado set, $182.
19. See Dust Collection section for accessories.

20. Choice of motors available: 3 HP, TEFC, single phase, 240V or 3 HP, TEFC, three phase, 230/460V.
21. #7115, conventional mitre gauge, $35.75.
22. #7127, extension table, $125.
23. #7113, throat plate, $15.
24. #7114, throat plate insert for dado head, $15.
25. #7144, rigid overarm guard, $125.
26. #7502, fence extrusion, 29½", $55.
27. #7509, fence extrusion, 43", $75.
28. #70158, mitre gauge assembly, 27", $70.
29. #70185, mitre gauge assembly, 54", $85.
30. #70244, fixed and retractable mitre gauge, stop set (w/scale), $42.25.
31. #70245, hinged down-rolling table extension assembly, $75.
32. #70248, 50" table travel extension bar set, $125. ($75 if purchased with saw).
33. #9HT 24218, adjustable dado insert, $6.99.
34. #9HT 32581, dado set, $20.99.
35. #9HT 22282, molding insert, $9.99.
36. #9HT 3222, molding head set, $20.99.
37. #9HT 24168N, same as Model #9 HT 24169N except it has a 1 HP motor, two formed steel extensions (not cast iron), no quick-release fence or hold down clamp, $489.99.
38. See Sears Power and Hand Tools catalog for options and accessories.
39. #R1201, leg stand, no price available.
40. #34-430, same as Model #34-429 except it has a 1.5 HP, 230/460V, TEFC motor, 24V pushbutton station, magnetic starter, transformer and 3-leg overload protection, weight 346 lbs., $1,379.

41. #31-208, same as Model #31-205 except it includes a steel stand, weight 60 lbs. w/stand, $231.
42. #34-765, same as Model #34-764 except it has a 200V motor.
43. #34-761, same as Model #34-764 except it has a 1.5 HP, single phase, pushbutton switch w/overload, TEFC, 115/120V motor, weight 455 lbs., $1,569.
44. See Powermatic catalog for various equipment and electrical options.
45. #716, steel stand, no price available.
46. #2013, comb jointer, no price available.
47. #2107, sawing carriage, no price available.
48. #2105, fence for short workpieces, no price available.
49. #2169, repeat cut stop, no price available.
50. #2158, set of table extensions, no price available.
51. #80090, tool stand, $58.34.
52. #80053, molding head kit, $34.88; uses #80070 insert, $8.00.
53. #80072, sanding disc, $10.59; uses #80051 insert, $8.00.
54. Machine is priced without motor or controls. Single phase motors available from ¼ HP to 5 HP in 110V and 220V; the 3 HP and 5 HP single phase motors are available in 220V only. Three phase motors available from ½ HP to 5 HP - specify voltage.
55. #350-3, dado insert, $35.22.
56. #1950-1, stop rods for mitre gauge, $21.70.
57. #350-6, motor cover, $86.31.
58. #350-8, extension tables and supports, $182.73.
59. #350-17, 72" guide bars, $124.85.
60. #F42R50L12, T-square fence, $332.

SHAPERS

Woodworking shapers are simple but versatile machines. They are most often used to cut edge moldings but can also perform hundreds of other cutting and forming operations.

Many furniture and cabinet makers consider the shaper to be an indispensable machine. Hobbyists, however, may not be able to justify the addition of this machine. The beginning woodworker or hobbyist must ask this question. Do I really need a shaper, or would a good portable router be sufficient? Shapers and routers can both be used to produce a wide variety of edge moldings. The shaper, however, can produce almost an infinite number of large moldings which are not possible with routers. If your molding needs are small and somewhat infrequent, a router may be best. If you foresee a frequent need for large moldings, a shaper should be considered. Shapers will usually allow for a faster production output since heavier cuts can be taken. Rabbets and tongue and groove joints can be formed with both machines, but the router, when properly equipped, can be used to cut multiple dovetail joints. Shapers cannot produce this type of joint. Shapers can be used to produce coped cabinet joints or sticker joints and raise panels. These operations are not commonly done on a router. Some of the very small direct drive shapers sold today are really nothing more than a router motor with a table.

Shapers range in size from small, single spindle bench models to large, double spindle machines used in industry. Double spindle shapers are heavy machines with large tables and two identical spindles. The spindles on these machines will frequently be fitted with identical cutters but will rotate in opposite directions. This will allow the

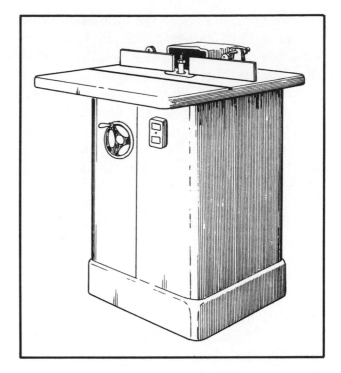

operator to switch from one spindle to the other during a cut to be sure the cut direction will minimize tear out. Most small shops use single spindle machines. The basic parts of a single spindle shaper include the following: table, spindle, fence, spindle raising adjustment, spindle lock, guards, motor, and base.

SIZE AND SPINDLE DESIGN

Important shaper size specifications include the following: the diameter of the spindle, the size of the table, and the size of the motor. Smaller units will generally have ½″ diameter spindles, relatively small tables, and motors of approximately 1 HP. Larger machines will have ¾″ to 1¼″ spindles, large tables, and motors up to 7½ HP.

The diameter of the spindle determines how much heavy work can be performed on the unit. Smaller spindles are weaker, more easily bent and are not suitable for heavy production work. Shapers with ½″ spindles should not be purchased with production use in mind, but they may be just fine for the average shop.

Better shapers will have interchangeable spindles. This feature makes it possible to have two or more spindle sizes available on the same machine, adding versatility. Many woodworkers find, however, that they will actually seldom change spindles once they have tooled up to fit one diameter. If you are planning to do relatively heavy shaping and panel raising, a ¾" spindle should be the smallest size to consider.

The accuracy of the spindle is critical. Spindles should turn perfectly true. Shaper spindles are subjected to a considerable amount of side thrust, and it is very possible that they can be bent during use. Bent or inaccurate spindles cause excessive vibration and are dangerous. The accuracy of a spindle really should be checked with a dial indicator. You should expect the spindle on a new machine to be straight with no "run-out." Bent spindles are relatively common on used machines. "Run-out" will show up higher up on the spindle. Check it near the bearing and near the end of the shaft. Bent spindles can usually be replaced, but it is an added expense and trouble.

Spindles are usually supported by two ball bearings. You can check the condition of the bearings by removing the belt and slowly turning the spindle through by hand. On a new machine you should feel no roughness nor notice any side or end play. Old machines may have poor bearings. The bearings used in most shapers are generally available through bearing supply companies and may not be too hard to replace.

Shaper spindles generally turn at higher speeds than many machines. Speeds range from 2,800 to 18,000 RPM, with the 7,000 to 10,000 RPM being most common. Slower spindle speeds are necessary for some large cutters, and some of the larger shapers have this low speed option. It is certainly important to know the RPM of your shaper since some cutters are dangerous to operate at high speeds.

The shaper should be equipped with a number of spindle collars which are used when mounting the cutter and in collar shaping. When cutters are mounted on the spindle, they should have at least one collar below and one or more above the cutter. Manufacturers usually supply a basic collar set with a new machine. Be sure that this is the case, because you should not use the machine without them. You may later want to purchase additional collar sizes which are offered as options by many manufacturers.

CUTTERS

Unlike saws and planing machines, new shapers are usually sold without a single cutter. A shaper without cutters is absolutely useless, so you will need to purchase a few basic shapes at the time you purchase the machine. You will soon discover that there are many to choose from.

Cutters are either carbide tipped or made from high speed steel.

Carbide tipped tools are most expensive but will provide the longest lasting cutting edges. Solid three wing cutters (three cutting faces) are the most common today. It is best when tooling up a shaper to first purchase cutters which will give the greatest versatility. Simply look at the cutters available and decide which ones you could use most. You might consider buying a set of cutters, but beware, many people who have done this find that they only use a few from the set. You can actually do quite a bit of shaper work with a few carefully selected cutters.

Molding heads, similar to those sometimes used on table saws, can be purchased for a shaper. These cutters are not as safe as a solid tool, but they enable molding knives used on a table saw to be used on a shaper.

Loose knives are the most dangerous type of shaper cutter. These cutters use two knives which are held between two grooved collars. OSHA regulations forced this cutter design to be modified, and the new improved models are safer. Even with the improved design, loose knife cutters should be used with caution. With loose knives, you can purchase high speed steel cutter blanks and grind your own shapes. Some industries use this cutter type today because it is possible to easily modify the molding shape to fit customer specifications.

FENCE

The shaper should be equipped with a fence for use when running straight edges. Quality fences should be fully adjustable. It should be possible to move the fence forward and back on the table, and the infeed and outfeed surfaces should have adjusting features which allow you to move the two halves independently.

Shaper fence problems include the following: awkward or inaccurate adjustment features, fences which do not lock positively in position, infeed and outfeed surfaces which are not straight, and fence surfaces which are not perpendicular to the table.

Better fences will be made from cast iron and will have replaceable wooden face board. Provisions should be in the fence for mounting various types of hold down accessories.

TABLE

The best shaper tables are made from cast iron and have smooth, solid surfaces. You should inspect the casting carefully for cracks and accuracy. Some tables will have a convenient milled slot for a miter gauge or other sliding jigs. Small machines sometimes have tables with a number of fairly large "grill-like" openings in the surface. This table design bothers some woodworkers, especially those accustomed to solid table surfaces on most other machinery. The actual reason for making these "filigree" tables is not clear. Maybe it is an inexpensive way to increase the size of the working surface. The weight of the machine is reduced considerably with this design, and this fact alone is thought to be a disadvantage in machine design by many.

The best machines are provided with a table insert around the spindle. Inserts can be changed to allow for large cutter diameters, and they are sometimes equipped with rubbing collars of different diameters for collar or pattern shaping.

The table or the table insert is sometimes drilled and tapped to accommodate starting pins. This feature is used when starting a cut while doing shaper work without a fence.

The size of the table is an important consideration. You will find most of the time it is easier to use machines with larger tables. Machines in the low price range will have the smallest tables. Optional table extensions are occasionally available for some machines to increase the overall working surface. Since most shaper tables are solidly secured to the machine's base and will not tilt, wooden table extensions are not very difficult to make and install. Woodworkers sometimes add extensions like this to the infeed and outfeed sides of the machine.

GUARDS

Spindle cutter guards are essential for safe shaper operation. A guard system of some type should be included with the machine. Spindle guards range from weak, poorly designed plastic units to sturdy, steel rings supported by spring steel bars. The guards provided with some of the cheaper machines are made almost entirely of injection molded plastic and will have a very short life expectancy. Ring guards with spring steel supports can be used as a hold down aid as well as providing cutter protection. Circular plastic guards with ball bearings are available as an optional guard for shapers. These units are mounted on the shaper spindle, above the cutter, and offer good cutter protection but do not provide hold down pressure.

DELTA
43-122

DELTA
43-371

EMCO
TF-65

CONCORD
T5020

WILKE
MACHINERY
T-50

KITY USA
7229

GRIZZLY
G1024

WILKE
MACHINERY
TC-50

JET
JWS-18

JET
WSS-3

KITY USA
623

SHAPER

BRAND *No photo Available	Model	Motor**	Special Features***	Options****	Table Size	Spindle Diameter	Spindle Travel	Spindle Speed (RPM)	Insert Opening Diameter	Table Height	Table Construction	Shipping Weight	Suggested Retail Price
*CRAFTSMAN	9 HT 23939N	.5 HP 3-12	2-46	35	27×19	–	⅞"	9,000	–	–	CI	141 Net	$449.99
DELTA	43-122	1 HP 1-12	1-2-3-4 58	1 thru 9	15½×18	½"	⅞"	9,000	3" and 1⅜"	34"	CI	163 Net	680
DELTA	43-371	2 HP 1-5-10-13	1-59 5 thru 10	1-3-4-5-6-7 9 thru 13	20×27	½" and ¾"	3"	7,000 and 10,000	6¾"-3½" 3"-1⅜"	34"	CI	423	2111
*ELEKTRA BECKUM	TF-100	3 HP 4	2-22-28 29	26 thru 30	20½×16½	¾"	4"	4,800 7,200, 9,900	6" max.	33½"	–	108 Net	985
EMCO	TF-65	2.5 HP 3	26-27	1-21-22 23-24-25	25½×17	–	2½"	5,400 7,200 9,900	–	–	–	–	595
GRIZZLY	G1024	.75 HP 1-12	2-36-37 38-39	33	–	½"	⅝"	–	–	–	CI	150	245
*HAMMER MACHINE	101	3 HP 2	25	18-19-20	25¾×35⅝	1" or ¾"	–	7,000 and 8,000	–	–	CI	–	2820
J. PHILIP HUMFREY (MFG-CONCORD)	T5020	3 HP 1-12-18	1-2-13-36 55-56	43	28×40	1¼"	7"	4,250 8,500	–	–	CI	1040	3311.40
JET	JWS-18 708515	1 HP 1-7	2-40-41 61	34	15½×18	½"	⅞"	9,000	3" and 1⅜"	34½"	CI	125 Net	408
JET	WSS-3 708517	3 HP 1-7-8-13	2-22-37 42-43-44-45	–	29¼×21½	½", ¾", & 1"	3"	7,000 and 10,000	–	34"	–	396 Net	1699
KITY USA	623	2 HP 1 or 2 11-16-17-19	2-14-18-19 20-21-22-23	16-17	18×23½	¾"	–	4,800 6,400 8,700	–	–	–	–	1205.15
KITY USA	7229	1.5 HP 2	2-14-14 22-24	17	16×22	¾"	2"	6,200	–	–	–	–	933.90
*POWERMATIC	Model 26 1260010	2 HP 1-7-9-10	2-21-22-60 30 thru 35	31-32	28×29½	½" and ¾"	3"	7,000 and 10,000	5½"-4" 2¾"-1⅜"	34"	–	450	2215
*SUNHILL (MFG-REXON)	RXW-S22	1 HP 1-3-20	2-40 46-47	–	15½×18	½"	–	7,500	–	–	–	230 Net	399

SHAPER

BRAND *No photo Available	Model	Motor**	Special Features***	Options****	Table Size	Spindle Diameter	Spindle Travel	Spindle Speed (RPM)	Insert Opening Diameter	Table Height	Table Construction	Shipping Weight	Suggested Retail Price
*SUNHILL (MFG-CHAMP FOND)	SP-100	1 HP 1-6-12-20	2-48-49	—	16×20	½"	—	10,000	—	—	CI	198 Net	$650
*SUNHILL (MFG-CHAMP FOND)	SP-101	2 HP 1-4-10-12	2	36-37-38	27½×40	1"	3"	7,500 and 10,000	—	—	CI	485 Net	1600
*SUNHILL (MFG-CHAMP FOND)	MP-200PRO	2 HP 1-10-12	2-50-51	36-39	—	¾" and 1"	3"	7,000 10,000 14,000	—	—	CI	660 Net	2135
*SUNHILL (MFG-CHAMP FOND)	MP-210	2 HP 1-10-12	2-33-41 52-53	36-40	37½×37½	¾" and 1"	3"	7,000 10,000 14,000	—	—	CI	880 Net	3170
*SUNHILL (MFG-CHAMP FOND)	MP-230	3 HP 1-10-12-20-21	2-50 53-54-62	41-42	37½×40	¾" and 1"	3"	5,000 7,000 10,000 14,000	—		CI	1200 Net	3895
WILKE MACHINERY (MFG-BRIDGEWOOD)	T-50	5 HP 2-4-9-14-15	11 thru 17	14-15	36×36	1½"	8"	3,000 4,500 6,000 9,000	—	—	CI	1190	2695

(PRICES INCLUDE FREIGHT TO THE NEAREST TERMINAL OF OUR HOUSE CARRIER [SUNHILL])

MOTOR

1. Single phase
2. Three phase
3. 115V
4. 220V
5. 230V
6. 110/220V
7. 115/230V
8. Prewired to 230V
9. 3600 RPM
10. TEFC
11. Thermal overload protection
12. Reversing switch
13. 24V pushbutton station, magnetic starter, transformer, and overload protection (LVC)
14. Visual ampere motor
15. Two speed motor
16. Fan-cooled with integrated thermal sensor
17. Electrical breaking
18. Magnetic starter and low voltage overload protection
19. Dust proof, sealed industrial motor
20. Sealed bearings
21. Motor protected by full magnetic switching

***SPECIAL FEATURES

1. Interchangeable spindles.
2. Adjustable split fence; each half independently adjustable.
3. Belt guard completely covers motor and belt.
4. Lubricated for life ball bearing spindle.
5. Table size with extra extension, 28″ × 27″; with two extra extensions, 36″ × 27″.
6. Overall width with two extra extensions is 36″.
7. Unitized drive mechanism.
8. The spindle, housing, motor, raising and lowering mechanism are a single self-contained unit, securely assembled to the underside of the table.
9. Precision ground ribbed table.
10. Fence guard assembly is heavy cast iron; has access opening for hook-up to dust collection system.
11. Spindle has keyed slot and double jam nuts.
12. Special high precision spindle bearings.
13. Supplied with two roller type hold down bars.
14. All machines are run in and tested before shipment.
15. Spindle has a foot brake to stop rotation.
16. Screw-type work hold downs.
17. Adjustable fence.
18. Maximum tool diameter is 7″.
19. Two removable inserts.
20. Control box stationed above work table with a lockable off/on switch, start/stop buttons, fuses and indicator lights.
21. Dust collector.
22. Spring hold downs.
23. Speed change is activated by a simple lever.
24. Die cast ribbed aluminum alloy table.
25. O.D. distance between bearings of spindle is 8½″; spindle quill is 3″ O.D.
26. Cutting stop height is 4⅓″.
27. Maximum tool diameter is 5¼″.
28. Tabletop made from die cast aluminum, precision milled.
29. Spindle rides in three extra heavy duty roller bearings.
30. One extension wing, 8″.
31. Largest table opening is 7″.
32. Safety ring guard.
33. Cast iron ribbed table.
34. Base is heavy gauge steel; cabinet with clean-out door.
35. Spindle is mounted in heavy duty precision ball bearings.
36. Ball bearing construction.
37. Includes mitre gauge; guard.
38. Maximum diameter of cutters is 3″.
39. Maximum height of cutter is 1⅛″.
40. Precision ground table.
41. Guard included.
42. Spindle assembly is mounted to bottom of table for perfect alignment and rigidity.
43. Spindles are raised and lowered by means of a rack and scroll gear.
44. Spindles are alloy steel mounted on coupled bearings.
45. Base is one piece, heavy welded steel.
46. Includes steel stand.
47. Adjustable ring spindle guard.
48. Precision safety fence.
49. High speed bearings.
50. Three table insert rings: 6″, 7″, and 8″.
51. Machine accepts router bits with optional collets.
52. Tilting arbor.
53. Five collet sizes: ¼″, ⁵/₁₆″, ⅜″, ½″, ⅝″.
54. Tilt, 0° to 45°.
55. Cast iron and steel construction.
56. Removable table rings.
57. Safety guard.
58. Spindle capacity under the nut: ½″ spindle - 2⅜″.
59. Spindle capacity under the nut: 1″ spindle - 4″; ¾″ spindle - 3¾″; ¾″ extra long spindle - 4⅜″; ½″ spindle - 2½″.
60. Spindle capacity under the nut: 1″ spindle - 4⅞″; ¾″ spindle - 3″; ½″ spindle - 2¼″; ⁵/₁₆″ spindle - 1⅛″.
61. Spindle capacity under the nut: ½″ spindle - 2⅜″.
62. Tilting spindle.

****OPTIONS

1. High-speed steel, three-lip shaper cutters, see Delta catalog for sizes and prices.
2. #43-817, ring guard, $43.10.
3. #34-895, mitre gauge, $44.15.
4. #43-983, spring hold downs, $39.10.
5. #34-568, clamp attachment for mitre gauge, $34.40.
6. #43-186, sliding shaper jig, $147.75.
7. #43-170, tenoner, $164.80.
8. #43-198, table insert, $40.25.
9. #43-824, spindle accessory accepts ¼" and ½" shank router bits, no price available.
10. #43-822, spindle carriage assembly, $229.30.
11. #43-821, extra-long ¾" spindle carriage assembly, $229.30.
12. #43-372, same as #43-371, except has three phase, 3 HP motor, 230/460V, $2,173.
13. #43-373, same as #43-372, except has 200V motor, $2,173.
14. Single phase machines available.
15. #TC-50, same as #T-50, except has 6 HP, 220V, three phase motor, 3600 RPM; sliding table insert is made of cast iron and rides on sealed roller bearings, $3,195.
16. Tenoning carriage with advanced, sliding mechanism.
17. See catalog for options available.
18. Choice of ¾" or 1" spindle.
19. Also available with: single phase motor, $2,930; single phase 5 HP motor, $3,300; three phase, 5 HP motor, $2,963; magnetic starter, $2,995; 208V, $2,880.
20. #527, shaper fence, $544.
21. #663.140, hold down attachment, $49.95.
22. #663.150, ring and guide for curved workpieces, $32.
23. #664.230, attachment for dust extractor, $11.
24. #663.200, sliding table for supporting wide workpieces, $139.95.
25. #664.070, grooving attachment with carbide tipped circular saw blade, $225.
26. Spindle shaft, 1", with mounted bearings, $199.
27. Spindle shaft, 1¼", with mounted bearings, $199.
28. Sliding carriage, 9½" × 13", $195.
29. Table extension, 40" × 8", $138.
30. Bearing ring with safety guard, $62.50.
31. Motors and controls are available for any voltage, single or three phase. Consult catalog for description and prices.
32. Optional accessories, including different size spindles and attachments are also available. Consult catalog for description and prices.
33. Carbide-tipped three wing cutters, ¾" and ½" bore, $25. Various cutters available.
34. Mitre gauge, no price available.
35. Options are hold down clamps, mitre gauge, various cutterheads and knives. See catalog for description and prices.
36. Also available with three phase, 3 HP motor, same price.
37. Spindle options: ½", ¾", 1¼", $90 each.
38. Collets for use with router bits, $75 each.
39. 1¼" spindle available; no price available.
40. 1¼" spindle available; $120.
41. Also available with three phase, 5 HP motor, same price.
42. Additional spindles are $120 each.
43. Also available with 4 HP, three phase motor, $3,404.50.
44. #T50EX, exhaust hood, $174.55.
45. #T50RB, router bit spindle, ½" collet, $208.26.
46. Spindle c/w make-up collars and locking nuts available in ¾", 1", 1⅛", 1¼", 1⅜", $208.26 each.
47. #T50ST, sliding table, available on request.

RADIAL ARM SAW

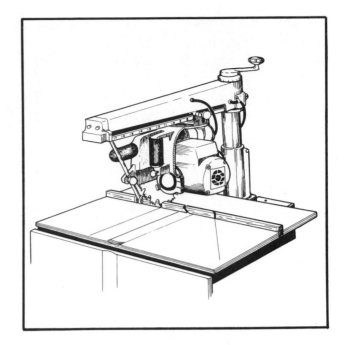

Radial arm saws are versatile machines. They are used most often for crosscutting and mitering operations but can also be utilized for ripping and a host of other operations when equipped with the appropriate attachments.

TABLE SAW OR RADIAL ARM SAW?

Which saw should I purchase, a radial arm saw or a table saw? You will probably get different preferences from every woodworker you talk with. Since the two machines can be used to perform many of the same operations, it is important to carefully consider the advantages and disadvantages of each machine before making a choice.

A radial arm saw has one distinct advantage over a table saw in that it requires less floor space. You need space only at each end of this machine. A table saw requires space on all sides, or at least, on three sides. For this reason a radial arm saw might be the best tool to opt for if space is at a premium.

Crosscutting operations, including mitering and bevel cuts, can be done on both machines. This is the type of operation which radial arm machines do best. It is possible to crosscut long pieces of stock easily on a radial arm saw, and this is one reason the machine is preferred as a construction or carpenter's saw. Much of the work in carpentry involves cutting stock (many times long boards) to length, and this is awkward to do on a table saw. It is possible to adjust a radial arm saw to produce accurate work, but a common complaint

aimed at this machine has to do with the fact that accuracy seems hard to maintain. This is possibly due to the complex design of the head system, but because of this problem, some woodworkers use the machine primarily as a rough cut-off machine and rely on a table saw for accuracy.

Ripping is possible on a radial arm saw, but it is a very precarious operation. It is much easier and safer to rip stock on a table saw.

Some radial arm saws have a power take-off on the right end of the motor which will accept drill chucks and sanding accessories. With the drill chuck attachment, the machine can be converted into an overhead router with radial movement capabilities.

Dado and molding heads, which are used on a table saw, can also be used on a radial arm saw. Shaper spindle attachments are available for some radial arm machines which use conventional shaper cutters. Shaper spindle attachments cannot be used on a table saw.

If your shop space is limited, or if your woodworking interests center around general repair and carpentry with occasional furniture projects, a good radial arm saw would be a wise choice. If your interests are chiefly in furniture making and involve frequent, accurate ripping and crosscutting, a good table saw is probably best. You will find that many serious woodworkers and small cabinet shops will have both machines. If your budget will allow, this would actually be best.

Radial arm saws are sized by the maximum diameter of blade they will swing. Sizes range from 10″ through 18″ with 10″ through 14″ being most common. The basic parts of a radial arm saw include the following: table, fence, column, over arm, arm track, elevating crank, motor, yoke, blade, motor controls, and guards.

OVER ARM DESIGN

All radial arm saws function in a similar manner, but you will actually find three separate designs used on the over arm: sliding arm, single fixed arm, and double or "turret" arm.

With a sliding arm saw, the entire arm slides through a bearing assembly in the column. The operator must pull and push both the cutterhead and the over arm during an operation. A machine of this type cannot be placed against a wall since space must be allowed at the rear of the machine equal to the total arm travel. This design does, however, eliminate the permanently extended over arm which can be annoying at times. Sliding arm saws are rare today, however, you may find some large, older machines of this type.

Single and double fixed arm machines are most common. With both of these machines, the over arm is always extended over the work, and the motor slides on a track under the arm. The single fixed arm has fewer adjustments and is easier for most operators to "fine tune" than a double arm machine. Many of the smaller radial arm saws are of the single fixed arm design. The double arm has an additional "turret like" feature on the

arm which allows for some operational advantages. This added feature, however, brings another assembly into play which must be adjusted for accuracy.

TABLES

Radial arm saw tables are usually made from plywood or particle board. As you can imagine, it is not possible to achieve and maintain a high degree of accuracy with a wooden table. This type of table is satisfactory, however, since most radial arm saw work doesn't require extreme accuracy.

The machine should have some type of leveling system so the table can be adjusted to a parallel position. You can check the table accuracy by raising the blade about $\frac{1}{16}$″ above the table and swinging the arm over the table in several random positions while moving the head in and out. The table should be approximately the same distance from the blade at all points.

BLADES

The quality of work from a radial arm saw is dependent upon the quality of the blade. Most new machines will come with a conventional chisel tooth combination blade. It is a good idea to consider purchasing a quality carbide tipped combination blade as soon as your budget allows. There are some saw blades especially designed for use on radial arm machines. It would be good to take a close look at these designs.

MOTORS

Radial arm saws are typically direct drive, single speed machines, with 3450 RPM being a common speed. This speed is excellent for sawing operations but is relatively slow for shaper and router set-ups. Motor horse power ranges from 2 HP to 7½ HP with 2 to 3 HP units being common for 10″ machines.

DeWALT 10"
7739

DeWALT 10"
7770-10

DeWALT 12"
7790

CRAFTSMAN 10"
ELECTRONIC
9HT 19065N

DELTA 12"
33-890

DELTA 10"
DELUXE
33-990

RYOBI 10"
RA-2500

RADIAL ARM SAW

Brand *No Photo Available	Model	Size	Motor**	Special Features***	Options****	Table Size	Maximum Depth of Cut W/Guard	Maximum Depth of Cut At 45° Bevel W/Guard	Bevel Positive Stops	Mitre Positive Stops	RIP Capacity	Crosscut Capacity	Arbor Diameter	Table Height	Shipping Weight	Suggested Retail Price
BLACK & DECKER (MFG-DEWALT)	7739	10"	2 HP 11-14-17-24	1-2-11-12	—	26⅜×36	3"	2⅛"	—	—	24¹¹/₁₆"	13½"	—	—	140	$489
*BLACK & DECKER (MFG-DEWALT)	7749 Deluxe	10"	2.5 HP 4-11-13-16-17-24	1-2-11-12-13	—	26⅜×36	3"	2⅛"	—	—	24¹¹/₁₆"	14½"	⅝"	—	142	554
*BLACK & DECKER (MFG-DEWALT)	7779 Contractor	10"	2.25 HP 1-8-11-13-16-17-20-24	1-2-11-12-13	—	26⅜×36	3"	2⅛"	—	—	24¹¹/₁₆"	14½"	—	—	155	639
BLACK & DECKER (MFG-DEWALT)	7770-10 Contractor	10"	3 HP 13-20	1-2-13-14	—	26¾×36	3"	2⅛"	—	—	25⅛"	14½"	—	35⅛"	145	729
BLACK & DECKER (MFG-DEWALT)	7790 Contractor	12"	3.5 HP 8-11 13-16-17-20	2-12-13	—	29⅜×38½	4"	2¾"	—	—	27"	16"	⅝"	—	242	979
*BLACK & DECKER (MFG-DEWALT)	3436	12"	5 HP 2-9-13-19	2-14-15	—	29⅜×38½	4"	2¾"	—	—	27"	16"	—	—	226 Net	1482
*CRAFTSMAN	9HT19927N	10"	2.5 HP 13-17-22	1-2-21-22 23-24-25	13	27½×40	3"	2¼"	0°-45°-90°	90°-45°R&L	26"	15½"	⅝"	—	193 Net	539⁹⁹
*CRAFTSMAN	9HT19941N	10"	2 HP 4-14-22	1-2-21-23 24-25	14	27½×40	3"	2¼"	0°-45°-90°	90°-45°R&L	26"	15½"	⅝"	—	152 Net	454⁹⁸
*CRAFTSMAN	9HT1993N	12"	3.5 HP 8-13-17-22	1-2-21-23 24-25	15	27½×40	3"	2¼"	0°-45°-90°	90°-45°R&L	26"	15½"	⅝"	—	159 Net	602²⁸
*CRAFTSMAN	9HT1989N	12"	3.5 HP 6-13-17-22	1-2-21-23 24-25	16	27½×44	4"	2¹¹/₁₆"	0°-45°-90°	90°-45°R&L	26"	15½"	⅝"	—	171 Net	649⁹⁹ w/o stand
*CRAFTSMAN	T9HT2318N Industrial	12"	3.5 HP 8-13-17-22	1-2-13-25	17	29⅜×38½	4"	2¾"	0°-45°-90°	90°-45°R&L	27"	16"	⅝"	—	235 Net	949⁹⁹
CRAFTSMAN	9HT19065N	10"	2.5 HP 4	2-21-26	—	27½×40	3"	2¼"	—	—	—	—	—	—	195 Net	689⁹⁹
DELTA	33-890	12"	1.5 HP 1-7 10-11-15-17	1-2-3	1-2-3-10	25½×30	3¾"	1¼"	0°-45°-90°	90°-45°R&L	24¼"	14⅜"	⅝"L.H.	—	300 Net	1367

RADIAL ARM SAW

BRAND *No Photo Available	Model	Size	Motor**	Special Features***	Options****	Table Size	Maximum Depth of Cut W/Guard	Maximum Depth of Cut At 45° Bevel W/Guard	Bevel Positive Stops	Mitre Positive Stops	RIP Capacity	Crosscut Capacity	Arbor Diameter	Table Height	Shipping Weight	Suggested Retail Price
DELTA	33-990 Deluxe	10″	1.5 HP 11-15-16-18	2-3-4-5 6-7-8-9	—	24¾ × 42	3″	2¼″	0°-45°-90°	0°-45°R&L	24″	12¾″	⅝″L.H.	—	198 Net	$654.80
*DELTA	33-081	14″	3 HP 1-5 11-15-23	2-3-5 7-8-9-10	4-5-10	26 × 42	3⅜″	¾″	0°-45°-90°	90°-45°R&L	30¾″	17¾″	1″	32″	600	3413
*DELTA	33-071	16″	3 HP 1-5 11-15-23	2-3-5 7-8-9-10	6-7-10	32 × 42	4¾″	2¼″	0°-45°-90°	90°-45°R&L	37″	23″	1″	32″	610	4228
*DELTA	33-061	18″	5 HP 1-5 11-15-23	2-3-5 7-8-9-10	8-9-10	29 × 44	4⅝″	3 9/16″	0°-45°-90°	90°-45°R&L	37¾″	23¼″	1″	32″	810	4872
RYOBI	RA-2500	10″	2.25 HP 3-12-21	1-2-16 17-18-19	10	25 × 40	3″	2¼″	0°-45°-90°	—	24¼″	14½″	⅝″	—	—	577
STARMARK	Maximizer	12″	1.5 HP 1-7-11-16-19	2-20	11	25 × 31½	—	2¾″	0°-45°-90°	90°-45°R&L	25″	17¾″	⅝″	31½″	145 Net	1258
STARMARK	Maximizer	14″	3 HP 1-7-11	2-20	12	35 × 47	—	3¼″	0°-45°-90°	90°-45°R&L	33¾″	26⅜″	1″	31½″	320 Net	2108

****MOTOR**

1. Single phase
2. Three phase
3. 115V
4. 120V
5. 230V
6. 240V
7. 115/230V
8. 120/208/240V
9. 208/240/480V
10. Wired for 230V
11. 3,450 RPM
12. 4,500 RPM
13. Automatic brake
14. Manual brake
15. Automatic electromagnetic brake
16. Capacitor start
17. Overload protection
18. 1.5 HP; develops 2.5 HP
19. Magnetic-type, low-voltage start
20. Induction motor, totally enclosed
21. Ball bearing motor
22. Induction motor
23. 24V pushbutton station, magnetic starter, transformer, and overload protection (LVC), TEFC
24. 100% ball bearing, industrial type, induction motor

SPECIAL FEATURES

1. Off/on key lock switch.
2. Blade guard w/anti-kickback attachment; retractable leaf guard.
3. "Turret arm" permits saw blade to rotate a full 360° above work table; gives full capacity for left and right hand motors.
4. Rear arbor shaft, ½"-20 R.H.
5. Cast iron track and column support.
6. Four ball bearing roller head.
7. Split column base with adjustable gibs.
8. Solid steel column.
9. Heavy, deep channel box-type constructed frame.
10. Track is replaceable, hardened, nickel-alloy rods.
11. Cast iron construction.
12. Rollerhead track-precision, machined from cast iron.
13. Cast iron arm and column base construction.
14. Extra heavy duty rollerhead design.
15. Heavier deep "beam" arm is super-rigid.
16. Accessory spindle RPM, 15,800; for routing and shaping operations.
17. All steel arm.
18. Motor rotates full 360° for bevel cutting.
19. Carriage slides on six ball bearings.
20. Automatic head return.
21. Aluminum construction.
22. Quick connect terminals allow 120V or 240V.
23. Carriage glides on replaceable steel tracks.
24. Double end shaft, ½"-20 thread end.
25. Anti-kickback pawls.
26. Electronic; lets you program automatic elevation adjustments with use of a computerized control panel. LED display shows elevation; bevel movement to ½°.

****OPTIONS

1. #33-891, same as #33-890 except w/24V at on/off key lock switch; magnetic starter, transformer, and overload protection, $1,556.
2. #33-892, same as #33-891 except has three phase operation, wired for 230V, 1.5 HP, develops 3.5 HP, $1,667.
3. #33-893, same as #33-892 except with 200V, $1,667.
4. #33-082, same as #33-081 except has three phase, 5 HP, 230/460V, $3,413.
5. #33-083, same as #33-082 except with 200V, $3,433.
6. #33-072, same as #33-071, except has three phase, 5 HP, 230/460V, $4,333.
7. #33-073, same as #33-072, except with 200V, $4,373.
8. #33-062, same as #33-061, except has three phase, 7.5 HP, 230/460V, $4,805.
9. #33-063, same as #33-062, except with 200V, 5 HP, $4,861.
10. See catalog for accessories.
11. Also available with 2 HP, three phase, 230/460V motor, $1,258.
12. Also available with 5 HP, three phase, 230/460V motor, $2,108.
13. #9 HT 19937N, same as #9 HT 19927N except includes cabinet with locking front panel, three drawers, and casters, 256 lbs., $599.99.
14. #9 HT 19936N, same as #9 HT 19941N except includes cabinet with locking front panel, three drawers, and casters, 252 lbs., $549.99.
15. #9 HT 19938N, same as #9 HT 1993N, except includes cabinet with locking front panel, three drawers, and casters, 255 lbs., $702.28.
16. #9 HT 19939N, same as #9 HT 1989N, except includes cabinet with locking front panel, three drawers, and casters, 271 lbs., $749.99.
17. #T9 HT 2319N, same as #T9 HT 2318N with three phase, 5 HP motor, 242 lbs., $1,199.99.
18. #T9 HT 23189, tool guard for molding, dadoing, $44.99.

WOOD LATHE

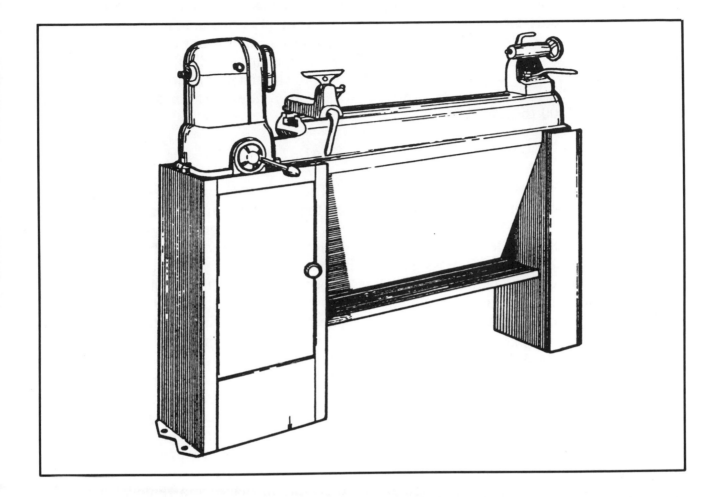

Wood turning has been practiced for hundreds of years. Today the hand wood lathe is basically a hobby tool and has very limited use in production situations. With a properly equipped lathe, woodworkers are able to turn a rough wooden blank into a finished product without the need for other machines. Some hobbyists actually center all of their woodworking around the lathe, while others never have a use for the machine. Hand wood turning is a fascinating craft, and a lathe can offer many hours of enjoyment. If your woodworking interests involve projects with turned parts, a lathe is a must.

Basically wood turnings can be divided into two groups, spindle and faceplate turnings. Spindle turnings are objects which are turned while being supported by the two centers of the lathe. Table legs and other similar objects are produced this way. Faceplate turnings are produced by turning stock which is fastened to a lathe faceplate. Bowls are typical examples of faceplate work.

The size and type of wood turning you plan to do will determine the type of lathe to consider. For example, if your interests are chiefly in the area of model making or miniature furniture, a small light weight machine will perform well. If you are interested in large spindle turnings, like table legs or even bed posts, you should consider heavier machines. If your interest is faceplate turning only, it may be well for you to investigate bowl lathes or machines which are designed for only faceplate work.

The basic parts of a typical wood lathe include bed, headstock, tailstock, lathe centers, faceplate, tool rest, tool rest support, motor and base. Lathes range in price from less than $100 through $3000.

SIZE

The size of a lathe is designated in several ways. The largest diameter that can be turned is referred to as the "swing". The swing is twice the distance from the center of the spindle to the bed. A common swing is 12 inches. Some lathes are made with special "gap" beds which increase the maximum swing just in front of the headstock for large faceplate turnings. A gap-bed lathe may have a 12 inch swing over the bed but a 16 inch swing over the gap. While the swing over the bed is important for faceplate turning, the swing over the tool rest support is more critical for spindle turning. The swing over the tool rest support can be as much as 4″ less than the swing over the bed.

Overall machine length and the length of the bed are other size designations. These are important but actually the maximum capacity between centers is more important to the wood turner. A common center to center capacity is approximately 36″.

LATHE BED DESIGN

Wood, plastic, steel, and cast iron are the materials most commonly used to make lathe beds. Cast iron is still considered the standard, and lathes in the higher price range will have cast iron beds. Single and twin tubular rails are used for beds on some machines. Tubular beds perform satisfactorily but generally do not offer the rigidity possible with a well designed cast iron bed.

The primary purpose of a lathe bed is to provide firm support for the headstock, tailstock and tool rest. The more rigidity a lathe bed has the smoother the machine will perform. The actual mass of the bed becomes an important consideration. Beds which appear to be light weight will usually not offer sufficient rigidity for large turnings. They may, however, perform well on small projects.

HEADSTOCK

The lathe headstock is the "business end" of the machine. It houses the headstock spindle, spindle bearings, and the drive system. The quality of the headstock design determines, to a large extent, the life expectancy of a lathe. Bearings should be heavy enough to withstand the vibration and lateral thrust associated with turning. Some of the better machines use double row ball bearings or tapered roller bearings in the headstock.

Centers are mounted to the headstock in the following three ways: Morse tapers, set screws or thread-on. Morse tapers (Morse #1, #2, or #3) are probably best since tapered accessories can be interchanged, they stay in place, and removal is simple. Centers with set screws can slip but perform well if they are properly installed and checked occasionally.

Faceplates are either threaded on to the spindle or secured with set screws. Threaded faceplates are generally preferred.

Almost all wood lathes today are belt driven, usually with a single v-belt. The headstock may be equipped with a step cone pulley to allow for speed changes. Some of the more expensive machines will have a more sophisticated variable speed system which uses expandable pulleys. Most importantly a lathe must have some system for changing spindle speed. Check to see how easy or difficult it is to change speeds. On some machines speed changing is a minor hassle, on others it is very easy.

The spindles on some lathes extend all the way through the headstock and are threaded on both ends. This feature makes it possible to mount both inboard and outboard faceplates on the machine.

Some lathes offer an indexing feature on the headstock spindle. This makes it possible to divide the turning into equal parts for reeding or fluting operations. It also serves as a handy spindle locking device for holding

---

Some lathes offer an indexing feature on the headstock spindle.

---

the turning for joint making or carving. This is also a good way to lock the spindle while removing faceplates and other thread-on accessories.

The lathe should be equipped with a headstock center, usually called a spur or live center, and a tailstock center or dead center. The best spur centers have three or four spurs which are driven into the end of the stock. Dead, tailstock centers used for wood are usually cup shaped. This design minimizes the tendency of the center to split the stock. Ball bearing tailstock centers are available as options for many lathes. This type of center is well worth the investment. Once you use one, you won't go back to the conventional cup center.

TAILSTOCK

The tailstock is movable and can be positioned anywhere along the bed. The parts of the tailstock include spindle, spindle lock, hand wheel, center, housing and tailstock locking device.

Lathe tailstocks can have as many as three adjustments. First, they can be moved along the bed and clamped in any position. The locking device used to secure the tailstock to the bed must provide a positive locking

system. Some machines require the use of a separate wrench to lock the tailstock while others have a built-in handle. Both systems work well but the separate wrench system is more inconvenient.

Secondly, the tailstock spindle can be advanced forward or retracted inside the housing by adjusting the handwheel. It should be possible to lock the spindle in position with some type of spindle locking handle.

Thirdly, metal lathes and some wood lathes have tailstocks which can be moved within small limits across the bed. This adjustment makes it possible to align the centers exactly or to off-set them for special operations. This feature is seldom found on new wood lathes, but you may find it on some older used equipment.

TOOL REST

The tool rest and tool rest assembly are probably the most often adjusted lathe parts, and they should have simple but secure locking systems. Some lathes require the use of wrenches to make tool rest changes, but better machines will have convenient handles for adjustment.

The tool rest and tool rest assembly are probably the most often adjusted lathe parts

---

Better lathes will be equipped with two tool rests (one long and one short) as standard equipment. You will find, if you have only one size tool rest, it will be inconvenient for turning some items.

Some of the best tool rests are made from cast iron and have straight, smoothly finished top surfaces. The front surface of the rest should also be smoothly finished since the lathe operator will slide one hand along the front while using a tool.

BASE

The base of a lathe, the part that actually supports the bed and contacts the floor, must be well designed. You may actually need to supply this part yourself since many lathes are sold without floor stands. The lathe base should be heavy, the heavier the better.

The lathe base should be heavy, the heavier the better.

Lathes should not be considered portable machines. You will find that the best vibration free performance comes from machines which are securely anchored to a heavy base which is in-turn anchored to the floor.

CHISELS AND OTHER TOOLS

Lathes are usually sold without chisels, and the machine is essentially useless without them. You will need to invest in a basic set of four or five chisels at the time you purchase a new machine. Seldom will woodworkers agree totally as to which chisels are best to start with. You will find that you can actually do quite a bit of turning with relatively few tools. A basic set might include a ⅛" parting tool, a ¾" gouge, a ¾" or 1" skew, a ½" round nose, and a ¼" round nose.

Wood turning chisels are made from high carbon tool steel, high speed steel, or carbide tipped. High carbon steel chisels are most common and will usually perform well for most turning operations. One of the most annoying things associated with wood turning is trying to use tools which do not hold a good edge. It is impossible to determine whether a tool will hold a good edge by just looking at it. You actually need to use it to find out. It is a good idea to talk to others who have purchased the brand of chisels you are considering about cutting edge life. Avoid tools which seem to have a reputation of poor edge quality.

High speed steel chisels will tend to hold an edge longer than carbon steel, but these tools are usually much more expensive.

Carbide tipped chisels can be used for hand turning plastics, soft metals and hard woods. Chisels of this design are special purpose tools and are something you may want to consider in the future as your turning interests expand.

Measuring in wood turning is done with inside and outside calipers. You will need to purchase a good set of calipers. A six inch size is usually adequate.

ACCESSORIES

Better lathes will offer a fairly large assortment of accessories. These will include long tool rests, right angle tool rests, screw centers, sanding drums and discs, steady rests, ball bearing tailstock centers, drill chucks, 3 and 4 jaw chucks, copy attachments, guards and others.

You can get started in wood turning without any of these items, but you will probably want to add accessories to your machine as you gain experience. It is important to determine what accessories are available for the machine you are considering. Usually the more options available the better. This will give you more versatility in the future.

LIGHTING

When you locate a lathe in your shop be sure to consider lighting. Good lighting and quality wood turning go hand-in-hand. Natural back light from a window is nice when possible. Some woodworkers prefer adjustable incandescent lamps over fluorescent lights. If you use fluorescent lighting use double tube units since single tube lights sometimes play tricks on your eyes.

HEGNER   shown with
HDB 175   LQ400 Duplicator

HEGNER   shown with
HDB 200   LKH950 Duplicator

CONOVER 16"
CL16-010

DELTA 11"
46-140

EMCO
DB-6

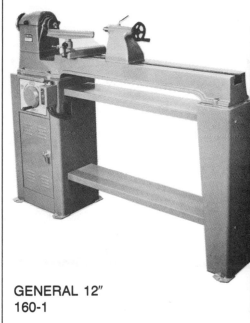

GENERAL 12"
160-1

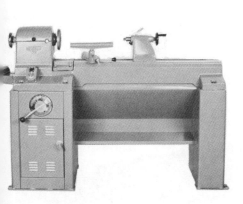

GENERAL 12"
260

KITY USA
6644

KITY USA
2660 Copy Set

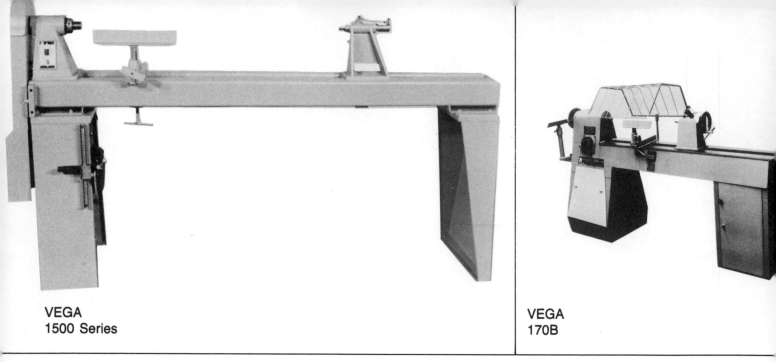

VEGA
1500 Series

VEGA
170B

VEGA
With Extended Bed

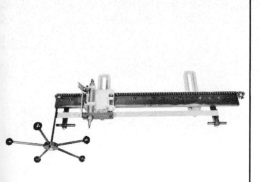

VEGA
Lathe Duplicator

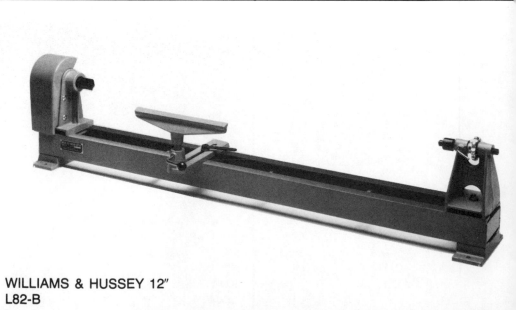

WILLIAMS & HUSSEY 12″
L82-B

WOOD LATHE

BRAND *No Photo Available	Model	Size	Motor**	Special Features***	Options****	Overall Dimensions	Speed (RPM)	Swing Over Bed	Spindle Nose-Inboard	Spindle Nose-Outboard	Headstock & Tailstock Tapers	Distance Between Centers	Height Centerline of Spindle to Floor	Ram Travel	Shipping Weight	Suggested Retail Price
AMI, LTD. (MFG-HEGNER)	HDB 175	—	.5 HP 3-13	4-24 30-31	23-24-25 26-27	—	—	13¾"	M16	M33 DIN800	—	36"	—	—	110 Net	$995
AMI, LTD. (MFG-HEGNER)	HDB 200	—	3-12-13-14	4-12 31-32	27-28	—	800, 1400, 2400, 2800	15¾"	M16	M33 DIN800	—	39⅜"	42"	—	240 Net	1795
CONOVER	CL16-010	16"	See Options 20 & 21	5 19 thru 26	22	—	600 to 2300	16"	1½"-8tpi	—	NO. 3 M.T.	Unlimited	—	4"	114	895 w/o motor
*CONOVER	ML05-10	5"	1/5 HP 20	2-22 27-28	—	—	900 to 2300	5"	½"-20 tpi	—	NO. 00 M.T.	7"	—	—	15	175
*CRAFTSMAN	9HT 22816N	12"	—	30-36-55 56-57	44-45	54½×11×19	875, 1350, 2250, 3450	12"	—	—	—	37"	—	—	88	339⁹⁹
DELTA	46-140	11"	.5 HP 4-8-9-10	1-2-3-4-5	1-2	60×28¼×43½	800, 1350, 2200, 3700	11"	⅞"-14R.H.	¾"-16 L.H.	NO. 1 M.T.	36"	40¼"	1¼"	125	551
*DELTA	46-621	12"	1 HP 1-6-11	6-7-8-9-10 11-12-13	2-3-4	63×22×46½	340 to 3200	12"	1"-8 R.H.	1"-8 L.H.	NO. 2 M.T.	38"	42¾"	2¼"	581	3098
*DELTA	46-221	12"	.75 HP 1-6-11	6-7-8-12 13-14-15	2-5-6-7 8-9-10	60×16½×45¼	915, 1380, 2150, 3260	12"	1"-8 R.H.	1"-8 L.H.	NO. 2 M.T.	39"	41¾"	2¼"	305	2349
*ELEKTRA BECKUM	HDM 1000	—	3 HP 3	3-33-34	29-30	—×—×46	960, 1560, 2160, 3000	15"	—	—	—	40"	—	—	125 Net	695
*ELEKTRA BECKUM	HDM 800	—	.5 HP 10	3-33-34	30	—×—×46	960, 1560, 2160, 3000	15"	—	—	—	32"	—	—	88 Net	615
EMCO USA	DB-6	—	1.36 HP 4	48-49	35-36	—	660, 1100, 1800, 3000	15.8"	—	M33 DIN800	—	39.4"	41"	—	110	729
*GRIZZLY	G1025	15"	.5 HP 3	30-46-47	36	—	850, 1250, 1750, 2510	15"	1"-8 R.H.	—	—	40"	—	—	100	139⁹⁵
J. PHILIP HUMFREY (MFG-GENERAL)	160-1	12"	See Option II	3-5-10 13-16-7	12	58½×16×44½	850, 1375, 2160, 3500	12"	1"-8 R.H.	1"-8 L.H.	NO. 2 M.T.	38"	41"	2"	290	915⁷⁰ w/o motor
J. PHILIP HUMFREY (MFG-GENERAL)	260	12"	See Option II	5-8-10 13-17	13-14-15-16 17-18-19	63×23×45	375 to 3300	12"	1¼"-8 R.H.	1⅛"-8 L.H.	NO. 2 M.T.	38"	41"	—	610	2010²⁰ w/o motor

WOOD LATHE

BRAND *No Photo Available	Model	Size	Motor**	Special Features***	Options****	Overall Dimensions	Speed (RPM)	Swing Over Bed	Spindle Nose-Inboard	Spindle Nose-Outboard	Headstock & Tailstock Tapers	Distance Between Centers	Height Centerline of Spindle to Floor	Ram Travel	Shipping Weight	Suggested Retail Price
*JET	JWL1240	12″	.5 HP 1-5-11-15	35-36-37	—	57½ × 19 × __	875, 1350 2250, 3450	12″	—	—	—	40″	—	2⅜″	110	$284
KITY USA	6644	—	1 HP 1-7	3-31	36-40	61 × __ × __	600 to 3200	15¼″	—	M33 DIN800	NO. 2 M.T.	39″	—	—	165 Net	1282^{65}
*MINI MAX	T90	14″	.5 HP	3-46	36-37	60 × 16 × __	600 & 1200	14″	—	—	—	35.4″	—	—	198 Net	595
*MINI MAX	T100	—	1 HP	3-46	36-38	65.7 × 17.7 × __	500, 900, 1600	17.2″	—	—	—	39.3″	—	—	246 Net	650
*MINI MAX	T120	—	1 HP	3-46	36-39	73.6 × 17.7 × __	500, 900, 1600	17.2″	—	—	—	47.2″	—	—	253 Net	700
*POWERMATIC	Model 45 1450300	12″	.75 HP 1-4-19	12 58 thru 63	36 46 thru 54	63 × __ × __	330 to 2100	12″	1″-8 R.H.	1″-8 R.H.	NO. 2 M.T.	39″	36″	3¾″	439	2254
VEGA	1553S-2	15″	1 HP 2-11-16	12-38-39	31-33-34-36	—	320 to 3400	15″	1¼″-12 R.H.	1¼″-12 L.H.	NO. 2 M.T.	53″	39½″	2½″	285 Net	1435
VEGA	170B	15″	1 HP 1 or 2 11-17-18	12 40 thru 45	32-33-34-36	72½ × 21 × 42	See Special Feature 40	15″	1⅛″-8R.H.	1″-8 L.H.	—	48″	39½″	4″	—	1800
WILLIAMS & HUSSEY	L82-B	12″	.5 HP 8	2-4-29-30	—	57 × 7½ × 13⅝	800, 1200, 2500, 3750	12″	¾″	—	—	46″	—	—	95	309^{95}
*WOODCRAFT SUPPLY (MFG-MYFORD)	ML8B	16″	.5 HP 1-8-9-10-11	30-50-51 52-53-54	41-42-43	—	700, 1140, 1780, 2850	16″	1″-12 R.H.	⅞″-12 L.H.	NO. 1 M.T.	36″	—	—	—	884

****MOTOR**

1. Single phase
2. Three phase
3. 110V
4. 115V
5. 110/220V
6. 115/230V
7. 1500 RPM
8. 1725 RPM
9. Ball bearing
10. Capacitor start
11. TEFC
12. .55 kw
13. Magnetic safety switch
14. Induction motor
15. Prewired to 110V
16. Specify voltage
17. Magnetic relay
18. Fusetron overload protection
19. Magnetic control
20. Foot pedal control

***SPECIAL FEATURES

1. Expandable two-piece bed can be enlarged to increase the distance between centers.
2. Cast iron construction.
3. Includes open steel stand.
4. Lifetime lubricated ball bearing drive.
5. Completely guarded headstock.
6. Maximum thrust headstock spindle.
7. Double row pre-loaded sealed for life ball bearings on the infeed.
8. Floating ball bearing construction on the outboard end allows for expansion as spindle warms up.
9. Gap filler block.
10. Spindle has 48 index stops.
11. Includes deluxe cabinet.
12. Includes safety shield.
13. Fine grain cast iron bed.
14. Includes steel cabinet.
15. Indexing mechanism in headstock.
16. Recommended motor: .5 HP to 1 HP.
17. Spindle made from alloy steel mounted on large sealed for life ball bearings.
18. Welded steel reinforced cabinet stand.
19. The spindle rides in timken tapered roller bearings.
20. Spindle has 12 index stops.
21. Instructions are given for the user to build his own timber bed.
22. Grade 30 gray iron construction.

23. Yellow poplar bed, 45" between centers.
24. Has outboard turning.
25. Cast iron hand wheels and key washers allow for quick, easy adjustment of parts.
26. Nut for adjusting pre-load in spindle.
27. Pre-loaded miniature ball bearings.
28. Cantilever bed design.
29. Ground steel way bed construction.
30. Benchtop model.
31. Closed steel box beam bed construction.
32. Welded steel legs.
33. Torsion-free galvanized steel tubing bed.
34. Die-cast aluminum footstock and spindle-stock.
35. Cast iron head and tail stock.
36. Singular steel tube bed for rigidity and quick tool rest positioning.
37. Headstock spindle size is $3/4 \times 16$.
38. Spindle rides in timken $1\frac{1}{4}$" tapered bearings.
39. Lathe bed is made from two $3/16$" $\times$ 3" $\times$ 4" precision cold rolled steel tubing. Holes are provided to allow the user to fill the tubing with concrete.
40. Variable speed drive: high range is 630-3450 RPM, low range is 350-1930 RPM.
41. Outboard capacity is 28".
42. Includes closed stand.
43. All steel face plates.

44. Lathe spindle is mounted on precision roller bearings.
45. Steel, ground after fabrication, bed construction.
46. Square tubing lathe bed.
47. All ball bearing spindle.
48. Swing between centers is 13".
49. Quill adjustment is 2.75".
50. Includes rear outboard turning attachment.
51. Heavy gauge seamless drawn steel tube bed.
52. Headstock and tailstock are one piece castings.
53. Headstock spindle runs in precision bearings.
54. Spindle has 24 index stops.
55. Spindle has 36 index stops.
56. Cast iron head.
57. See Craftsman Power and Hand Tools catalog for accessories.
58. One piece cast iron bed.
59. Reinforced steel cabinet base.
60. Choice of straight or gap bed.
61. Spindle runs in lubricated for life ball bearings.
62. Spindle has 60 index stops.
63. Slow-start motor standard on variable speed models.

****OPTIONS

1. Also available with #62-138, .5 HP, sleeve bearing, split phase motor, 1725 RPM, 115V, deduct $43.
2. See Delta Machinery catalog for accessories.
3. #46-622, same as #46-621 except has 24V pushbutton station, magnetic starter, transformer and overload protection (LVC), $3,337.
4. #46-623, same as #46-622 except has three phase motor, 3 HP, 230/460V, $3,337.
5. #46-222, same as #46-221 except has 24V pushbutton station, magnetic starter, transformer and overload protection (LVC), $2,561.
6. #46-223, same as #46-222 except has three phase motor, 3 HP, 230/460V, $2,561.
7. #46-541, same as #46-221 except has variable speed of 340-3200 RPM, $2,529.
8. #46-542, same as #46-222 except has variable speed of 340-3200 RPM, $2,750.
9. #46-543, same as #46-223 except has variable speed of 340-3200 RPM, $2,750.
10. #46-840, wood turning duplicator, $273.40.
11. Machine is priced without motor or controls. Single phase motors available from .25 HP to 5 HP in 110V and 220V; the 3 HP and 5 HP single phase motors are available in 200V only. Three phase motors available from .5 HP to 5 HP—specify voltage.
12. #160-2, same as #160-1 except has variable speeds from 500-3000 RPM, $1,126.40.
13. #2610, outboard turning bracket with tool rest base, $190.31.
14. #2645, gap filler block, $73.68.

15. #2655, safety face shield, $317.54.
16. #260B, bed extension, 60" with floor stand, $953.68.
17. #2610A, outboard bracket with extended tool rest base, $211.52.
18. #2614, extended tool rest base, $116.09.
19. #2648T, spinning tool rest, $79.
20. #CL16-424, Westinghouse, industrial quality ball bearing motor, thermal protection, 1725 RPM, includes switch and cord line, .75 HP, $123.
21. #CL16-425, same as #CL16-424 except is 1 HP, $160.
22. See Conover Woodcraft Specialities catalog for accessories.
23. #LQ400, universal duplicator, $695.
24. Safety shield, $95.
25. Outboard tool rest, $85.
26. Base, $175.
27. See AMI, Ltd. catalog for accessories.
28. #LKH950, duplicating attachment, $1,145.
29. Also available with 220V motor, deduct $25.
30. See Elektra Beckum catalog for accessories.
31. Available in four different lengths between centers: 96"—$1,585, 53"—$1,435, 31"—$1,405, 19"—$1,385. Motors available for each in both .75 HP and 1 HP, single and three phase.
32. Motor available in .75 HP and 1 HP, single or three phase.
33. #36, lathe duplicator, maximum diameter of 12", maximum travel of 36", $450.

34. #48, lathe duplicator, maximum diameter of 12", maximum travel of 48", $550.
35. #641.461, copy attachment, $368.
36. See catalog for accessories.
37. Lathe duplicator, $575.
38. Lathe duplicator, $595.
39. Lathe duplicator, $610.
40. #2660, lathe duplicator, $609.96.
41. Available in three bed lengths.
42. #17M41-D, .75 HP heavy duty motor, available in place of .5 HP, same specifications as .5 HP, add $30.
43. #ML8C, same as #ML8B except is 42" between centers, $960.
44. Lathe duplicator, $110.
45. #9 HT 24922, sanding table, $59.99.
46. #6470716, .75 HP, single phase motor, 1800 RPM, $157.
47. #6470707, .75 HP, three phase motor, 1800 RPM, 230/460V, $141.
48. #6470712, .75 HP, three phase motor, 1800 RPM, 200V, $171.
49. #2398114, switch, single phase, 115/230V, $67.
50. #2398115, switch, three phase, 200/230/460/575V, $87.
51. #2398144, magnetic controls, single phase, 115/230V, $254.
52. #2398150, magnetic controls, single phase, 200/230/460/575V w/24V transformer, $341.
53. #2398151, magnetic controls, three phase, 200/230/460/575V, $275.
54. #2398152, magnetic controls, single phase, 115/230V w/24V transformer, $319.

DRILL PRESS

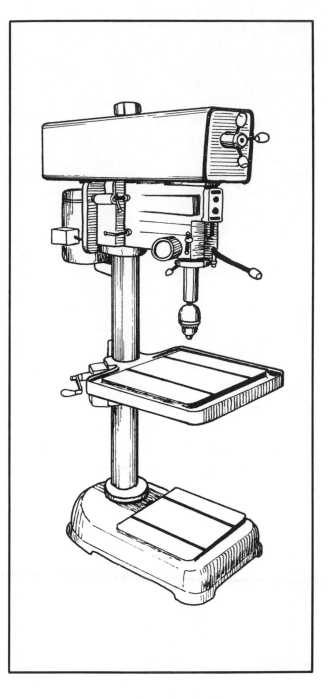

The drill press is one of the most versatile machines made and is found in almost all woodworking and metalworking shops. Woodworkers use the drill press for drilling, counter boring, countersinking, plug cutting, mortising, router work, shaper work, drum sanding, and even surfacing. Many

---

The drill press is one of the most versatile machines made and is found in almost all woodworking and metalworking shops.

---

people consider the drill press to be *one* of the first, if not *the* first, machine to purchase when setting up a home shop.

Drill presses are either bench or floor models. Their size is determined by twice the distance from the center of the chuck to the column. For example, a 15″ drill press will have a 7½″ distance from the chuck center to the column. The basic parts of a typical drill press include base, column, table, head, quill, quill lock, quill return spring, spindle, chuck, feed lever, guard, and motor.

CHUCK

Most woodworking drill presses will have a key type geared chuck. The most common size chuck is one with a 0 to ½″ capacity. A chuck of this size will hold the smallest numbered twist drills and bits with shanks up to ½″ diameter. This capacity range is sufficient for most woodworking needs.

BASE/COLUMN/TABLE

The drill press base, sometimes called the lower table, should be made from cast iron and sufficiently large to provide a firm foundation for the machine. These machines are naturally top heavy and the base must be securely anchored to the floor or bench. On better machines the top surface of the base will be milled flat and have T-slots to form another working surface.

The diameter of the steel column has a lot to do with the overall stability of the machine. Small columns do not offer enough rigidity, especially for heavy drilling and mortising operations. A 15" floor model machine should have a 2¾" to 3" diameter column, generally the larger the better.

Many woodworkers prefer the tilting table design since it makes angle drilling so much easier.

Column diameters should increase as the size of the machine increases.

Drill press tables should be made from cast iron and have a smoothly finished top surface. Tables are available in several different styles including tilting tables, non-tilting tables, and production tables (with or without T-slots). The common standard table for a low or medium priced drill press is a relatively small, non-tilting table. Tilting tables will tilt to 90 degrees, left and right, and are usually offered as an option on new machines. Many woodworkers prefer the tilting table design since it makes angle drilling so much easier. Production tables are usually larger and heavier than other types. Because of their size and weight, they are harder to lift by hand; therefore, you will find table lifting options available, especially on larger machines. Production tables will

usually have an oil trough and T-slots. The T-slots are handy for some woodworking operations, but the oil trough isn't needed for oil, but it does serve as a chip collector. Being able to push chips into these table recesses helps keep the work surface clean, but thorough drill press clean-up is a bit more difficult.

A safety hazard associated with drill press tables has to do with the possibility of dropping the table while attempting to raise or lower it. The table can slide down the column and crush a foot or hand between the base and the upper table. Safety collars or rings can be installed around the column which will catch the table before it gets to the base. Some bases are designed with a collar built in the casting which will serve as a safety collar. If your drill press is designed so the upper table and the lower table contact would create a safety hazard, you should install a collar. You can make a simple one from strap iron or even wood. It may prevent a painful injury.

HEAD ASSEMBLY

The head of a drill press includes chuck, spindle, quill, quill lock, quill spring, feed lever, depth stop, motor, guards, belt, drive system, switch, and motor. The head assembly is clamped near the top of the column and should have a safety collar under it. This collar will keep the head from sliding down the column when it is being adjusted from side to side.

Speed changing is essential on a drill press, and it is accomplished in one of two ways, step cone pulleys or expanding pulleys. Expanding pulleys give a much wider range of speeds but are most expensive. Improvements in V-belt design, especially the use of new smaller belts have made it possible to make cone pulleys which are capable of many more speeds than older designs. It is somewhat disconcerting, however, to look at the small belts on these machines. They don't look like much more than a heavy rubber band. They will, however, wear and perform well. With step cone pulleys, it takes longer to change speed and the speed range is not infinitely variable. Most woodworkers can live with these features, and step cone pulley machines are most common in small shops.

The speed range of the drill press is an important consideration in machine selection. Some manufacturers sell these ma-

The speed range of the drill press is an important consideration in machine selection.

chines as high speed or slow speed models. Higher speed models are generally needed in woodworking and slow speed in metalworking. If you plan to use your drill press as an occasional router or shaper, you need a maximum speed of approximately 5000 RPM or more for the smoothest work. Most drilling can be done at speeds from 500 to 3000 RPM.

A quality drill press will be a smooth running machine even at higher speeds. When checking the machine be sure to run it in all available speeds. Balancing and vibration problems will sometimes show up at higher speeds.

ACCESSORIES

When considering a new drill press be sure to find out exactly what accessories are available for the machine. Some, for example, do not have a mortising attachment available, however, many of the other accessories used on drill presses are interchangeable.

The most common accessories needed are bits for drilling. These will include twist drills, machine spur bits, multi-spur bits, spade bits, and Forstner bits. When tooling

up a drill press it is best to purchase the most versatile bits first. High speed steel twist

When considering a new drill press be sure to find out exactly what accessories are available for the machine.

drills used for metalworking can be used for wood and other materials and are the most versatile. A good set of twist drills is an excellent first item. Machine spur bits are wood boring tools that look like a cross between a twist drill and an auger bit. They have a brad point that helps keep the bit from drifting off center, but because of their design they are for wood only. Machine spur bits will produce very accurate holes in wood and are preferred over twist drills by most woodworkers. Multi-spur and Forstner bits

A good drill press vise is a useful accessory.

are special purpose tools used primarily to produce holes of large diameters.

A good drill press vise is a useful accessory. Tilting vises are most versatile since they can be used horizontally or adjusted to angular positions. If you are only going to have one drilling vise, this type is probably best.

Some drill presses offer an optional foot feed accessory. This idea sounds like it may be convenient, but many people who have tried to use these items are not happy with their performance. Be sure to check this item out carefully before you add it to your machine.

Mortising attachments, sanding drums, hole saws, fly cutters, router bits and planing head are examples of other possible accessories.

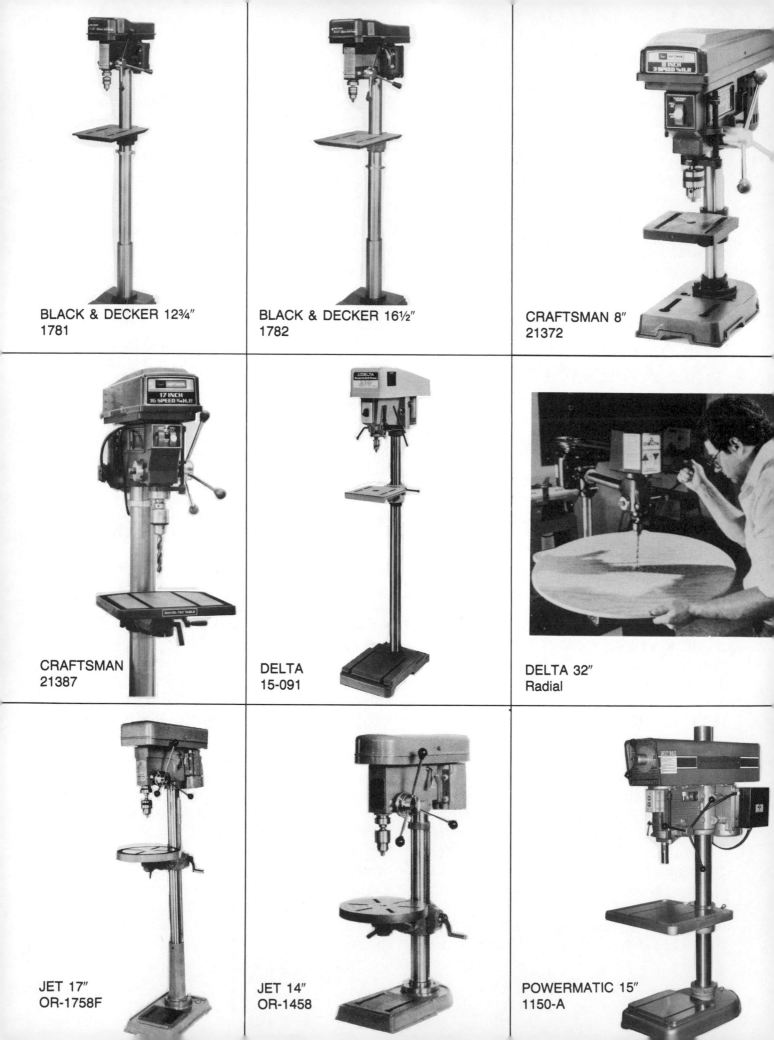

BLACK & DECKER 12¾″
1781

BLACK & DECKER 16½″
1782

CRAFTSMAN 8″
21372

CRAFTSMAN
21387

DELTA
15-091

DELTA 32″
Radial

JET 17″
OR-1758F

JET 14″
OR-1458

POWERMATIC 15″
1150-A

DRILL PRESS

BRAND *No Photo Available	Model	Size	Motor**	Special Features***	Options****	Table Size	Chuck Capacity	Spindle Travel	Quill Diameter	Column Diameter	Spindle Speed (RPM)	Overall Dimensions W×D×H	Shipping Weight	Suggested Retail Price
BLACK & DECKER	1781	12¾″	⅓ HP	24-25	—	10×14½	½″	3 5/16″	—	2⅞″	500-3100 5 Speed	—	145	$299
BLACK & DECKER	1782	16½″	.5 HP	24-25	—	12×18¼	⅝″	4 21/32″	—	3 5/32″	250-3000 12 Speed	—	190	379
CRAFTSMAN	21372	8″	1/6 HP	17	19	6¼×6¼	⅜″	2⅛″	1 21/32″	—	700/1500/3000 3 Speed	7×12×23½	44	145
*CRAFTSMAN	21385	15″	.5 HP	12-18-19-20	19	12×12	⅝″	—	—	—	300-4600 12 Speed	—	167	400
CRAFTSMAN	21387	17″	3 HP	12-19-20 26-27	19	14×14	—	—	—	—	240-4800 16 Speed	—	—	550
DELTA	15-091	15″	.5 HP	1-2-3 4-5-6	1-3-4 5-6-7	10×10½	5/64″ to ½″	4 5/16″	2″	2¾″	470 780 1300 1950	—	145	486
DELTA	Radial	32″	.5 HP	7-8-9-10	2-3-4 5-7-8	8½×9	0″ to ½″	3⅜″	1¾″	1⅞″	700 1250 2400 4700	24×30×63¼	120	470
*FINE TOOL SHOP (MFG-KING FENG FU)	204-0017	8 3/16″	.25 HP	12-17-18	—	—	½″	1 5/16″	—	—	700-3000 5 Speed	—	52	149^{95}
*FINE TOOL SHOP (MFG-KING FENG FU)	204-0019	13″	.5 HP	12-18-19	—	—	⅝″	3 5/16″	—	—	340-2800 12 Speed	—	161	249^{95}
*FINE TOOL SHOP (MFG-KING FENG FU)	204-0021	17″	.75 HP	12-18-19	—	—	⅝″	3 5/16″	—	—	240-3800 16 Speed	—	177	299^{95}
*GRIZZLY	G-1119	14″	.5 HP	17-18-20 21-22-23	—	12″ dia.	⅝″	—	—	—	250-3100 12 Speed	_×_×40	160	165
*GRIZZLY	G-1200	14″	.5 HP	18-20 21-22-23	—	12″ dia.	⅝″	—	—	—	250-3100 12 Speed	_×_×66	210	189
*GRIZZLY	G-1201	18″	.75 HP	18-20 21-22-23	—	15″ dia.	—	5″	—	—	180-2430 8 Speed	_×_×68	300	349^{95}
*J. PHILIP HUMFREY (MFG-GENERAL)	34-01	15″	.5 HP	2-3-5-12	14-15-16-17-18	10×11	0″ to ½″	4½″	2″	2¾″	460-4910 6 Speed	10×12×66½	227	626^{50}

DRILL PRESS

BRAND *No Photo Available	Model	Size	Motor**	Special Features***	Options****	Table Size	Chuck Capacity	Spindle Travel	Quill Diameter	Column Diameter	Spindle Speed (RPM)	Overall Dimensions W×D×H	Shipping Weight	Suggested Retail Price
*JET	OR-1412F	14"	.5 HP	12-13-14-15-16	—	12" dia.	½"	3⅜"	—	2⅞"	460-2420 5 Speed	12½×19¾×66	186	$239
*JET	OR-1458F	14"	.75 HP	12-13-14-15-16	—	12" dia.	⅝"	3¼"	—	3⅛"	260-3650 12 Speed	12×20×66	223	279
JET	OR-1758F	17"	.75 HP	12-13-14-15-16	—	12" dia.	⅝"	4⅜"	—	3⅛"	260-3650 12 Speed	12×20×66	229	299
*JET	OR-2501F	20½"	1 HP	3-12-13 14-15-16	—	18⅜×16⅛	¾"	4⅝"	—	3⅜"	1800-4200 12 Speed	14×22×66	331	499
*JET	OR-1012F	10"	⅓ HP	12-13-14 15-16-17	—	7½×7½	½"	2½"	—	2½"	540-3600 5 Speed	8×14×29	75	137
*JET	OR-1412	14"	.5 HP	12-13-14 15-16-17	—	12¼" dia.	½"	3⅜"	—	2⅞"	460-2420 5 Speed	10×16×40	154	168
JET	OR-1458	14"	.5 HP	12-13-14 15-16-17	—	12¼" dia.	⅝"	3¼"	—	2⅞"	260-3650 12 Speed	10×16×40	159	215
*JET	OR-1758	17"	.5 HP	12-13-14 15-16-17	—	13¾" dia.	⅝"	4⅜"	—	3⅛"	260-3650 12 Speed	11×18×42	187	239
POWERMATIC	1150A 1152826	15"	.75 HP	11-23	9-10-11-12-13	10×14	0" to ½"	6"	2³⁄₁₆"	3"	400/840/1580 2800/5300	_×_×63	—	1055
*SUNHILL (MFG-REXON)	RDM-150F	14"	.5 HP	—	—	—	—	3½"	—	—	200-3630 16 Speed	—	170	315
SUNHILL (MFG-REXON)	RDM-250F	17¾"	1 HP	—	—	—	—	5"	—	—	150-2470 9 Speed	—	280	450

(ALL PRICES INCLUDE FREIGHT TO THE NEAREST TERMINAL OF OUR HOUSE CARRIER—[SUNHILL])

**MOTOR

1. Single phase
2. Three phase
3. Split phase
4. 110V
5. 115V
6. 120V
7. 1725 RPM
8. 1750 RPM
9. TEFC
10. Ball Bearing
11. Sleeve Bearing
12. Capacitor start
13. Industrial, induction motor
14. Four pole
15. Induction motor

*** SPECIAL FEATURES

1. Lubricated for life ball bearings.
2. Full belt guard.
3. Pivoting motor mount plate permits quick belt tension release, fast speed changes.
4. Floating spindle drive.
5. Adjustable positive locking depth stop.
6. Threaded spindle collar accomodates six interchangeable spindle adapters.
7. Includes open steel stand.
8. Head swivels 360° around column and tilts 90° right and left.
9. Will drill to the center of a 32" circle.
10. Can be turned to do horizontal drilling.
11. Snap-open spring-loaded guard.
12. Table tilts 45° right and left.
13. Rotating, tilting crank-operated work table with quick release clamp.
14. Quick adjustment depth gauge and stop.
15. Slotted work table and base.
16. Adjustable spindle return spring.
17. Bench top model.
18. Table swivels 360°.
19. Rack and pinion table elevation.
20. Built in light.
21. Rack-up table mechanism.
22. Variable depth stop with fast setting.
23. Table tilts 90° right and left.
24. All ball bearing construction.
25. Spring-loaded for quick change of belts.
26. Adjustable feed tension.
27. Table has parallel T-slots.

****OPTIONS

1. #15-091, bench model, $486.
2. #62-142, .5 HP, ball bearing motor, capacitor start, 1725 RPM, 115V, add $43.
3. #25-858, lamp, $26.65.
4. #24-902, Universal vice, $302.15.
5. #20-620, drill press vice, $185.15.
6. #15-840, mortising attachment, $80.60.
7. Various sanding drums, spindle adapters and bits available. See catalog.
8. #11-976, mortising attachment, $106.80.
9. #1152825, same as #1152826, except has variable speed of 475-4800 RPM, $1,177.
10. #2028013, mortise attachment, $102.
11. #6856003, tilting vice, $75.
12. #6856005, straight vice, $56.
13. See Powermatic catalog for other options and accessories.
14. #34-04, mortising attachment, $95.95.
15. #34-26, Albrecht keyless chuck, $1/32$" to $1/2$", $159.59.
16. #24-18, table raising attachment, $133.66.
17. #34-06, foot feed attachment, $182.73.
18. #34-17, slow speed attachment, range of speeds 130-6150 RPM, $153.81.
19. See Craftsman Power and Hand Tools catalog for accessories.

STATIONARY SANDERS

Almost all stationary sanding machines fall into one of three broad groups: belt, disc, and drum. Belt sanding machines include vertical and horizontal belts, edge sanders, stroke sanders, and wide belt sanders. Drum or spindle sanders are either vertical or horizontal, and disc sanders are sold as separate machines or combined with small belt sanders.

The two most common abrasives used on wood sanding machines are garnet and aluminum oxide. Woodworkers do not agree on which is best. Both will perform well, and the cost of each is almost equal. Aluminum oxide abrasives may tend to have a longer life since the abrasives' particles are harder than garnet. Garnet, on the other hand, fractures as it wears, creating new cutting edges. Garnet particles become smaller as the abrasive is used, and aluminum particles become dull. Aluminum oxide is the most widely used abrasive at the present time.

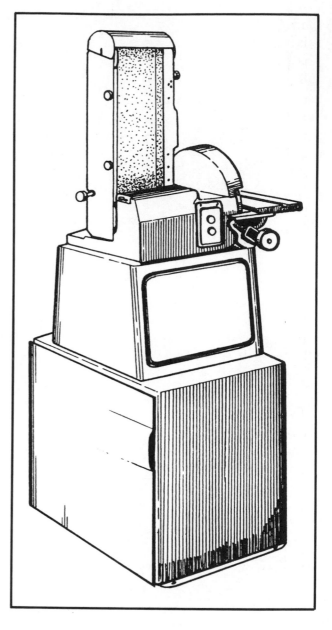

BELT SANDERS

Probably the most common sanding machines in small shops are small belt or belt/disc combinations. These sanders are useful for many smoothing and shaping operations. The size of a belt sander is usually referred to in terms of the size (width and length) of the belt used. Sizes generally range from 4″ to 6″ width with a 48″ length being common. It is important when selecting a sander to consider the availability of replacement belts. Purchase a machine with a common belt size. Six inch by 48″ is probably the most common size, and belts this size are available in small quantities from a number of suppliers. Odd belt sizes are sometimes hard to obtain and must be ordered from the machine's manufacturer or specially prepared. If you have belts specially prepared, you will find that you are faced with a large minimum order. Most companies will not make up fewer than 20 belts at a time.

The parts of a typical belt sander include pulleys, platen, tracking/tension mechanism, table, base, and motor. All belt

58

sanders will have one drive pulley which is in a fixed position and is driven by the motor or a belt system to the motor. The second wheel will be adjustable for belt tension and tracking. The most frequent adjustment on a belt sander has to do with the belt tension/tracking mechanism. It is important that this mechanism have some type of locking system to use to secure the pulley in position when proper tension/tracking is achieved. The lock should keep the pulley from vibrating out of adjustment while the machine is being used. The tracking/tension adjustments should be easy to get to and convenient to use. Wrenches should not be required.

Quality sanders will have a cast iron table with a smoothly milled surface. A milled slot will usually be provided for a miter gauge of other sliding jigs. The table will usually tilt up to 45 degrees.

Typical 6″ by 48″ or 4″ by 48″ belt sanders will be designed to be used in either a vertical or horizontal position. Woodworkers frequently use the machine in one of these two positions and seldom change, but it is nice to know that it can be used both ways if the need arises.

The machine's platen is a smooth, flat, cast iron or steel surface which supports the belt. The belt runs over this surface and the accuracy of the machine is dependent upon the platen and table accuracy.

Belt sanders must be provided with adequate guarding to cover possible "pinch points" between the belt and pulleys. The guard on the upper idler or tracking/tension pulley is frequently removable so the round surface of this pulley can be used in some contour sanding operations.

It is nice to have more than one speed on belt sanders and some machines have step cone pulleys which provide two or three speed options, however, most machines are single speed units. Most small belt sanders are belt driven with relatively small motors, ½ HP to 1 HP being common.

DISC SANDERS

Disc sanders are sold as separate machines or may be combined with a belt sander. Sizes range from 6″ to 24″ with 10″ and 12″ being the most common. Disc sanders are not quite as versatile as belt sanders, but they are used to perform some accurate sanding operations. Since the abrasive disc is cemented firmly to a flat disc, you can produce square, flat surfaces. The abrasive area is smaller on this machine, and discs will obviously not last as long as a belt.

When purchasing a disc sander look carefully at the disc accuracy. Roll the disc through slowly by hand and look for wobble or "run-out" on the face. The front of the disc should be wobble free and disc spindle should have no end or side play. Turn the machine on and check it for smoothness. Quality machines will have balanced discs which produce a smooth, almost vibration free, machine. A good disc sander should pass the nickel test.

Sanding tables on these machines should be similar in quality to the ones found on belt sanders. The best ones are cast iron with smooth, flat surfaces. The table should tilt to 45 degrees and have a slot for a miter gauge

---

When purchasing a disc sander look carefully at the disc accuracy.

---

or sliding jigs. One model has a tilting disc rather than a tilting table. This feature makes the machine much more comfortable to use during angle sanding.

Pressure sensitive adhesive backed discs are available now which take much of the work out of changing discs. Conventional discs must be cemented in place using stick disc adhesives or special rubber cements. Some woodworkers have had good luck using common office grade rubber cement.

It is relatively inexpensive and is easily removed with rubber cement thinner.

Disc sanders are either direct or belt driven. With belt driven machines it will be possible to have step cone pulleys and speed options. Some people prefer this added

---

Pressure sensitive adhesive backed discs are available now which take much of the work out of changing discs.

---

speed change versatility. Often the machine will be direct drive with the disc being mounted directly to the motor shaft. It is possible in fact, to buy metal sanding discs and make your own sander using your own motor. If the sander is direct drive, the motor bearings should be designed to take a certain amount of end thrust. Just any old motor won't hold up very long under disc sanding loads.

Motors are usually relatively small with ½ HP to 1 HP being common. Large disc sanders, 18″ to 24″ and belt disc combination machines will be 1½ HP to 2 HP units.

EDGE BELT SANDERS

Edge belt sanders are relatively common machines in woodworking industries. The belt on these machines is oriented "on edge" or in a position to sand edges of stock. Edge sanders will typically have large working tables which completely surround the belt, making it possible to use either side of the machine. The size of an edge sander is determined by the belt width/length and the size of the platen's working surface. Belt widths generally range from 4″ to 8″ with lengths depending upon platen size.

Some of the more sophisticated edge sanders have an oscillating mechanism which moves the belt up and down as the machine is running. This feature will prolong the belt life considerably.

Edge sanders are expensive machines with prices ranging from approximately $1000 to over $3000. Because of this they are not usually found in home shops.

WIDE BELT SANDERS

During the past fifteen years wide belt sanders have become the preferred industrial machine for sanding wide surfaces. These machines range in size from 13″ to over 48″. Abrasive planers are specially designed, heavy duty, wide belt sanders used to sand stock to thickness rather than using a conventional knife planer. Wide belt sanders and abrasive planers are expensive machines ranging from $3,000 to over $15,000, and they are virtually non-existent in home shops. If you are in the furniture making business, a wide belt sander is certainly worth investigating.

STROKE SANDERS

Stroke sanders are large belt sanding machines used to sand flat surfaces. This type of sander has been used in industry for many years but has been replaced in many companies by drum and wide belt sanders. It is seen by some woodworkers as the least expensive way to get into wide surface sanding, therefore, stroke sanders are still manufactured and used. Stroke sanders typically use long belts approximately 6″ wide. The belt will run over two, three, or four pulleys. The work to be sanded will be placed on a movable table under the belt. The machine operator will place a pad or block against the belt as it passes over the work piece, manipulating the work piece back and forth with the moving table. Accurate surface sanding with a stroke sander requires quite a bit of skill, and sander operators must be carefully trained.

DRUM AND SPINDLE SANDERS

Drum and spindle sanders are available in several different types including pneumatic drums, horizontal surface sanding drums, and vertical spindle sanders.

Pneumatic drum sanders are machines with inflatable drums used primarily to sand contoured edges and surfaces. The machine resembles a buffing machine having a single or double end arbor which is usually belt

---

Pneumatic drum sanders are machines with inflatable drums used primarily to sand contoured edges and surfaces.

---

driven. These machines are fabulous for sanding contours such as those on a cabriole leg, but if your woodworking doesn't involve frequent contour sanding, a pneumatic sanding drum probably won't be very useful.

Surface drum sanders are machines which resemble and operate similar to a planer, except the surface of the work piece is sanded rather than being cut with knives. These machines are sized by the maximum width of stock they will sand with sizes ranging from 12″ to 48″. Large expensive industrial drum sanders will have two or three oscillating heads and are designed for heavy production use. Drum sanders for small cabinet shops are available with prices ranging from approximately $700 to over $3,000. These smaller sanders range in size from 12″ to 36″ and will have one or two non-oscillating heads. These machines really are not intended to be used for heavy thickness planing, but will, of course, sand stock to thickness. They typically have rubber infeed and outfeed rollers and no rollers in the bed. The bed of the machine must be very smooth since the work piece must slide over it with as little friction as possible.

Guitar and violin makers have used shop built machines similar to these for years to sand thin wood to thickness. Before buying a drum sander, be sure to have clearly in mind the way you plan to use the machine. If you are interested in using the machine to sand thin wood, be sure that it will handle thin materials, some units will not. The minimum thickness will be determined by the design of the feed system.

Spindle sanders are machines which resemble wood shapers, having a single vertical spindle which extends through the center of a table. These machines are available as tilting table or tilting spindle models, and usually have oscillating spindles. Most machines will come with an assortment of spindle sizes ranging from ¼″ to 4″ in diameter. This type of machine is used for curved edge sanding. If you only have an occasional need for spindle sanding you may find that a spindle sanding attachment for the drill press will suffice, however, if you are in a production situation with large quantities of curved edge sanding, a spindle sander is a must.

DUST COLLECTION

Sanders produce more hazardous dust than any other woodworking machine. When purchasing any type of sander, you should consider buying a suitable dust

---

Sanders produce more hazardous dust than any other woodworking machine.

---

collector. Some sanders, especially surface drum and wide belt sanders, will not function well if the dust isn't pulled away from the sanding head as fast as it is generated. Small portable collectors, even large shop vacuums, will provide adequate pick up for most smaller sanders.

BLACK & DECKER
1763

BLACK & DECKER
9418

CRAFTSMAN
22642C

DELTA
Belt & Disc

DELTA
6″ Belt

DELTA
12″ Disc

DELTA
Sander/Grinder

GRIZZLY
G1183

GENERAL
100-5

JET
JSG-96

JET
JSG-1

JET
JSG-6

POWERMATIC
33-B

POWERMATIC
35-B

POWERMATIC
30-B

STARMARK
Max Five-in-One

STARMARK
Handy Max

SAND-RITE
DD-63

VEGA
304

VEGA
148

BRIDGEWOOD
80

WOODMASTER
1200

STATIONARY SANDERS

BRAND *No photo Available	Model	Motor**	Special Features***	Options ****	Type *****	Table Size	Table Tilt	Platen Size	Belt Size	Belt Speed (SPM)	Disc Diameter	Disc Speed (RPM)	Shipping Weight	Suggested Retail Price
BLACK & DECKER	1763	.5 HP 10-14-15	1-3-11-12	—	3	6 × 13½	45°	6 × 16	6 × 48	—	10″	—	—	$349
BLACK & DECKER	9418	5	12-13-14 15-16-17	—	5	—	—	—	3 × 24	1450	—	—	9	74^{95}
CRAFTSMAN	22642C	⅓ HP	1-30-39	—	3	8⅞ × 6¼	45°	—	4 × 36	2000	6″	3200	67	144^{95}
*CRAFTSMAN	22594N	.75 HP 13-14	1-18-31-33	—	3	6¼ × 12	—	—	6 × 48	2100	9″	2700	128	399^{99}
*CRAFTSMAN	22612C	⅓ HP	28-30-40	—	7	7 × 9	60° Forward	—	1 × 42	3000	8″	—	54	199^{99}
*CRAFTSMAN	2476	—	—	—	7	—	—	—	1 × 30	2700	5″	4400	11	99^{99}
DELTA	—	1.5 HP 1-8-9	1-2	1-2-5-6-7	3	7⅜ × 14¾	45° out 20° in	6¼ × 14¾	6 × 48	3030	—	—	283	1384
COMBINATION	—	—	—	—	(Disc: 9¾ × 16¼)		45° out 20° in	—	—	—	12″	2100	—	—
DELTA	—	1.5 HP 1-8-9	1-2-3-4 5-6-7-8	1-2-5-6-7	1	7⅜ × 14¾	45° out 20° in	6¼ × 14¾	6 × 48	3450	—	—	233	1269
DELTA	—	1 HP 1-8-9	9	3-4-7	2	9¾ × 16¼	45° out 20° in	—	—	—	12″	2100	162	1077^{75}
DELTA	31-352	.5 HP 11-13	3-10	—	4	7 × 8	90° out 10° in	—	⅛-1 × 42	4600	—	—	55	257
*FINE TOOL SHOP (MFG-CHANGIRON)	204-0005	1 HP 6-17	1-11-12	—	3	9 × 13½	45°	—	6 × 60	—	12″	—	242	599
*FINE TOOL SHOP (MFG-KING FENG FU)	204-0025	.5 HP 5	1-12-18 33-34	—	3	—	—	—	6 × 48	2100	9″	—	135	249^{95}
GRIZZLY	G1183	1 HP 1-3-12	1-3-12-24 27-28-29-30	—	3	7⅜ × 14½	—	—	6 × 48	—	—	—	160	330
COMBINATION	—	—	—	—	(Disc: 7 × 16½)		—	—	—	—	12″	—	—	—

STATIONARY SANDERS

BRAND *No photo Available	Model	Motor**	Special Features***	Options****	Type*****	Table Size	Table Tilt	Platen Size	Belt Size	Belt Speed (SPM)	Disc Diameter	Disc Speed (RPM)	Shipping Weight	Suggested Retail Price
*GRIZZLY	G1014	3 HP / 1	3-11-18-28-31	—	3	—	45°	—	6×48	—	9"	—	140	$195
*GRIZZLY	G1013	.5 HP / 3-14	24	—	7	—	—	—	1×42	—	8"	—	PPD	110
J. PHILIP HUMFREY (MFG-GENERAL)	100-5	1.5 HP / 1-9-13-14-18	1-4-12-24 35-36-37	—	3	6⅝×17⅞	—	—	6×60	3770	—	—	650	2030[73]
*J. PHILIP HUMFREY (MFG-GENERAL)	100-1	1.5 HP / 1-9-13-14-18	—	—	2	9½×25	45° down 12° up	—	—	—	16"	1800	625	1634[73]
*J. PHILIP HUMFREY (MFG-GENERAL)	100-3	1.5 HP / 1-9-13-14-18	—	—	1	6⅝×17⅞	—	—	6×60	3770	—	—	625	1931[73]
JET	JSG-96	.75 HP / 1-8	1-18-*9-27 28-30-38	—	3	—	45°	—	6×48	—	9"	—	137	279
JET	JSG-1	.5 HP / 1-8	27	—	7	—	—	—	1×48	—	8"	—	57	139[95]
JET	JSG-6	.5 HP / 1-8	1-27-30	—	3	—	45°	—	—	—	12"	—	160	524
POWERMATIC	33B	1.5 HP / 1-4	1-3-*2-21	24	1	7×17¼	45° down 15° up	—	6×48	2850	—	—	224	1308
POWERMATIC	35B	1 HP / 4-9	21-27-72	24	2	7×17¼	45° down 15° up	—	—	—	12"	1800	—	844
POWERMATIC	30B	1.5 HP / 1-4	1-3-12 21-31-33	24	3	7×17¼	45° down 15° up	6½×14½	6×48	2850	12"	2400	242	1500
STARMARK	Max 5 in 1	1.5 HP / 1-8-17-18-20	63-64-65-66	21	10	9½×20	—	—	6×90	4000	9"	3000	195	1370
STARMARK	Handy max	1.5 HP / 1-8	30	—	11	—	—	—	6×90	4000	—	—	85	897
SAND-RITE	DD-63	.75 HP / 1-10-13-14	66-67-68 69-70-71	22-23	12	—	—	—	—	—	—	—	—	641

STATIONARY SANDERS

BRAND *No photo Available	Model	Motor**	Special Features***	Options****	Type*****	Table Size	Table Tilt	Platen Size	Belt Size	Belt Speed (SPM)	Disc Diameter	Disc Speed (RPM)	Shipping Weight	Suggested Retail Price
VEGA	304	1 HP 2-9	12-33-53 54-55-56-57	1-12-13-14-15	3	7⅜×14¾		7¼×14	-	-	-	-	315	$1395
COMBINATION	-	-	-	-		(Disc: 10⅝×16⅝) in	45° out 15° in	-	-	-	12"	-	-	-
*VEGA	307	.75 HP 1-9	12-33-53 54-55-56-57	1-12-13-16-17	1	7⅜×14¾	-	7¼×14	6×48	-	-	-	-	1125
*VEGA	313	.75 HP 1-9	12-33-53-54 65-56-57-58	1-12-13-18-19	9	7⅜×14¾	-	7¼×14	6×48	-	5"	-	-	1455
VEGA	148	.75 HP 1-8-9-18	59-60-61-62	12-20	2	9½×20¾	-	-	-	-	14"	1750	230	995
WILKE MACHINERY (MFG-BRIDGEWOOD)	80	1.5 HP 16	1-12-18	-	6	-		-	6×89	3900	-	-	233	499
*WILKE MACHINERY (MFG-KALAMAZOO)	DS10	.5 HP 1-4	19	-	2	6×11	45° down	-	-	-	10"	-	48	225
*WILKE MACHINERY (MFG-KALAMAZOO)	DS12	3 HP	19		2	6×11	45° down	-	-	-	12"	-	60	439
*WILKE MACHINERY (MFG-KALAMAZOO)	S6MS	3 HP 1 or 2-9	1-11-18-20-21	-	1	-	-	-	6×48	-	-	-	125	735
*WILKE MACHINERY (MFG-KALAMAZOO)	S45	1 HP 1-9-11	1-21-22	-	1	-	-	-	4×36	-	-	-	80	369⁵⁰
*WILKE MACHINERY (MFG-KALAMAZOO)	1SM	.25 HP 1	23	-	1	-	-	-	1×42	-	-	-	40	125
*WILKE MACHINERY (MFG-KALAMAZOO)	2FSM	.5 HP 1	24-25-26	-	1	-	-	-	2×48	-	-	-	75	249⁵⁰
WOODMASTER	1200	1 HP 1-8-11-14	42 thru 52	9-10-11	8	-	-	-	-	-	-	-	205	678

*****TYPE
1. Belt
2. Disc
3. Combination belt and disc
4. Sander/grinder
5. Bench sander
6. Horizontal/Vertical
7. Disc sander/grinder belt and disc
8. Drum
9. Belt and pneumatic drum
10. Combination edge, spindle, belt and disc
11. Combination belt and spindle
12. Pneumatic drum

**MOTOR
1. Single phase
2. Three phase
3. 110V
4. 115V
5. 120V
6. 220V
7. 110/220V
8. 115/230V
9. TEFC
10. 1725 RPM
11. 3450 RPM
12. 3600 RPM
13. Capacitor start
14. Ball bearing
15. Induction motor
16. Two pole
17. Magnetic switch
18. Overload protection
19. Magnetic relay
20. Under voltage

***SPECIAL FEATURES

1. Table can be tilted horizontal and vertical.
2. Has fine thread adjustment for easy belt tracking.
3. Lubricated for life ball bearings.
4. Cast iron platen that won't distort from heat build-up.
5. Adjustable dust deflector and dust spout on lower guard.
6. Completely enclosed drums; guarded sanding belts.
7. Adjustable platen can be removed for free hand finishing of odd shapes.
8. Removeable upper guard for contour finishing on idler drum.
9. Fully machined balanced disc runs vibration free.
10. Wheels are crowned for easy belt tracking.
11. Cast iron construction.
12. Track and tensioning system.
13. Includes die cast mitre gauge.
14. Used for sanding wood, sharpening knives, scissors, etc.
15. Adjustable sharpening angle.
16. Hose connection for vacuum.
17. Includes sharpening guide attachment.
18. Includes heavy duty steel stand.
19. Heavy duty all steel construction.
20. Reversible platen tilt work table.
21. Full safety guard.
22. Easy opening side door for belt change.
23. Removeable rubber wheels.
24. Tilt table.
25. Removeable platen.

26. Fully hinged guard for quick belt change.
27. Cast iron table(s).
28. Includes mitre gauge.
29. Quick change belt tension lever.
30. Table top model.
31. Single cast iron table.
32. Spring-loaded arm keeps tension on belt.
33. Includes backstop.
34. Cast aluminum table.
35. One piece cast bell housing with 2" steel shaft running on sealed bearings.
36. Cabinet stand with hinged, vented door.
37. Cast iron disc sander is perfectly ground and balanced, completely shielded.
38. Sanding belt is complete with a fence.
39. Priced at $124.99 if purchased with one other bench top tool.
40. Steel table.
41. Belt has fixed table, disc has 45° tilting table.
42. Maximum width of stock, 12³/₈".
43. Stock thickness range, ³/₃₂" to 4".
44. Shortest sandable stock not butted, 7".
45. 1½" diameter rubber infeed and outfeed rollers.
46. V-Belt drive.
47. Rate of feed is 11 feet per minute.
48. 3¾" solid machined steel sanding head.
49. 1" sealed self-aligning permanently lubricated ball bearings.
50. Bed is one piece polished steel, 12¾" × 18⅛".

51. Heavy gauge steel hood covers all moving parts.
52. Feed role pressure adjustment uses self-aligning spring tension.
53. Enclosed cabinet; floor model.
54. 1" double sealed bearings.
55. Swing away guards.
56. Graphite coated canvas wear pad to cover the platen.
57. Pre-tested, shipped assembled, ready to run.
58. 3½" wide disc.
59. Only finisher made with tilting disc instead of tilting table, 45° back, 15° forward.
60. Ribbed gray iron table.
61. ⅝" Acme tilt screw.
62. 12 gauge welded steel base.
63. ¾" diameter 5" long spindle.
64. Stopfence and backfence standard on the belt sander.
65. Rotates to make an edge sander.
66. Includes open steel stand.
67. 6" diameter 7" wide pneumatic drum and 3" diameter 7" wide pneumatic drum.
68. Arbor is 1" outside diameter, turns 1200 RPM, mounted on a fabricated steel base within flange ball bearings.
69. Driven by V-Belt.
70. Drums have metal housing covered with a rubber tube, protected by canvas jacket.
71. The size and shape of the drum is controlled by the amount of air that is in the drum.
72. Pedestal style steel stand.

****OPTIONS

1. #52-612, single phase, 115/230V, 1.5 HP motor, 24V pushbutton station, magnetic starter, transformer and overload protection, add $204.
2. #52-613, same as #52-612 except has three phase motor, 230/460V, same price.
3. #31-126, single phase, 115/230V, 1 HP motor, 24V pushbutton station, magnetic starter, transformer and overload protection, add $226.
4. #31-131, same as #31-126 except has three phase motor, 230/460V, add $154.
5. #31-403, backstop, $41.85.
6. #31-014, wood fence, $63.65.
7. #34-895, mitre gauge, $44.15.
8. #22239C, steel stand, $64.99.

9. #1200P, 2 HP, single phase motor, 115/230V, 3450 RPM, ball bearing, add $48.
10. #630M, dust and chip collection system, $197.50.
11. Self-adhesive cloth back sandpaper; see catalog for types and prices.
12. #150311, mitre gauge, $35.75.
13. #156119, fence assembly, $55.
14. Also available with single phase motor, .75 HP, TEFC, $1,395.
15. Also available with built in dust collector, $1,515.
16. Also available with three phase motor, 1 HP, TEFC, $1,125.
17. Also available with built in dust collector, $1,180.

18. Also available with three phase motor, 1 HP, TEFC, $1,455.
19. Also available with built in dust collector, $1,560.
20. Also available with three phase motor, 1 HP, TEFC, $995.
21. Also available with three phase motor, 2 HP, 230/460V, $1,370.
22. A 1 HP, three phase motor available on request.
23. Drums, brush heads, sanding discs, abrasives and replacement parts available.
24. See Powermatic catalog for options and accessories; motors in single and three phase available.

JOINTER

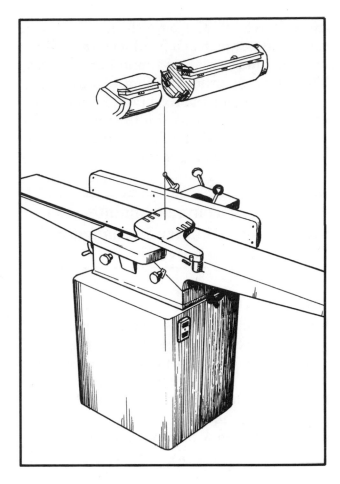

Jointers are planing machines which are used primarily to smooth edges and faces of stock. They evolved from the hand plane and can be used to perform many of the same operations done with a plane. The name jointer comes from the edge butt joint which can be made easily on a properly adjusted machine. The machine can also be used to plane tapers, bevels, and chamfers.

Jointers are not absolutely essential machines. Some woodworkers prefer to use hand planes because a plane will produce a smoother surface than a jointer. Hand planes have a fixed knife or blade and take a continuous shaving. Jointers cut with revolving knives which leave a rippled surface. These jointer knife marks are commonly referred to as "mill marks". A jointer made surface is actually a "trade off" when compared to a hand planed surface. With the jointer you loose smoothness but you certainly gain speed. In furniture and cabinetmaking jointers are almost essential, especially when speed is important.

In furniture and cabinetmaking jointers are almost essential, especially when speed is important.

The basic parts of the jointer include front infeed table, rear outfeed table, fence, cutterhead, cutterhead guard, table adjustment handles, and motor.

SIZE

Jointers are sized by the length of the knives in the cutterhead or the maximum width of stock which can be faced. A 6″ jointer will face a board 6″ wide. Jointer sizes commonly range from 4″ to 16″, with 4″, 6″, and 8″ being most common in small shops. Choose a jointer which will give you adequate cutting width for most of your work. If you are like many woodworkers, you will probably use the jointer most for edging operations. Edging doesn't require much width. Boards are faced to flatten surfaces and sometimes to prepare rough boards for the surfacer or planer. Larger jointers are necessary for wide facing operations.

Table length is another important size consideration. Longer tables generally make it easier to straighten longer boards.

CUTTERHEAD DESIGN

Jointer cutterheads should be made from steel, precision ground and balanced. They will have two or more knives with three knife cutterheads being the most common. The more knives in the cutterhead, the more knife cuts per inch at a fixed feed rate. More cuts per inch produce smoother surfaces. The jointer operator can control the cuts per inch by changing the feed rate. Manufacturers who make two knife jointers will frequently speed up the cutterhead to produce more cuts per inch.

The most common maintenance activity on a jointer is changing the knives.

Woodworkers sometimes use the diameter of the cutterhead as an index of quality, generally avoiding those of small diameter.

The most common maintenance activity on a jointer is changing the knives. When buying be sure to take a good look at the system used to hold the knives in the cutterhead. It may or may not include lifting screws which are really helpful when installing knives. A good jointer should also include well prepared instructions on how to replace the knives.

Jointer knives are usually made from high speed steel. They should be ground so they are the same size and perfectly straight. It is probably best, unless you have a good sharpening rig, to have the knives ground at a sharpening shop. Many woodworkers will buy an extra set of knives at the time they buy the jointer. This extra set serves as a back-up and can be installed in the machine when the other knives need sharpening.

Knives in a new jointer should be sharp and in proper adjustment. Sharp knives should be "shaving sharp". Don't buy a new machine with dull or nicked blades.

A well balanced cutterhead runs smoothly. Check the machine for smoothness with the "nickel test". Balance a nickel on edge on the jointer table while it is running. The coin shouldn't fall over or move if the machine is running smoothly.

TABLE DESIGN

Cast iron is generally considered the best material for jointer tables. The table castings should be inspected carefully for cracks or inaccuracies. Warped or cracked tables, either infeed or outfeed, are serious flaws.

Sometimes, especially on long bed jointers, the tables sag on the ends. It is impossible to produce accurate work on a machine with sagging tables. Sagging can sometimes be eliminated by adjusting the table gibs but not always. Be sure to check the jointer tables for sagging. A new machine certainly should not have this defect.

Less expensive jointers will generally have solid, non-adjustable outfeed tables. Some woodworkers really don't like this feature. With a solid outfeed table you are locked in to only one acceptable cutterhead knife

---

Cast iron is generally considered the best material for jointer tables.

---

projection. There are times when some people prefer a close knife projection to minimize tear-out on certain woods. Knife projection cannot be changed with a solid table. Better jointers will have adjustable outfeed tables.

The knives in the cutterhead must be aligned with the top surface of the outfeed table for proper jointer performance. If the table is too high a taper will be produced. If it is too low the work will be gouged at the end of the cut. This defect is called a "sniped end". If your jointer has an adjustable outfeed table it is much easier to fine tune the knife to cutter relationship than it would be if the knives themselves needed to be moved.

The space between the table and the cutterhead is a safety consideration. If the machine has a fixed outfeed table and small diameter cutterhead, it is likely to be more hazardous. There would be a greater chance

70

of serious injury if somehow the operator got a finger between the cutterhead and the table. On better jointers there is not much space between the cutterhead and table.

The gap between the infeed and outfeed tables actually determines the minimum length of stock which can be safely run over the machine. The larger the gap is the longer the shortest piece should be. A rule of thumb that some people use to determine minimum length is to measure the gap between the tables and add approximately 5″ to each side. For example, if the gap is 2″ between tables the minimum length of stock will be 12″.

The table adjusting handles should be large enough to adjust easily. Better jointers will have table locking knobs which prevent the tables from slipping out of adjustment. A "depth of cut scale" should be installed somewhere on the infeed table.

Wedge shaped dovetail systems are generally used to raise and lower the jointer tables. The better ones are made from cast iron. Tables of this design have proven to be very satisfactory over the years. Adjustable tables should have gib adjustments which can be used to take up any wear in the dovetail ways.

FENCES

Jointer fences should be easy to adjust from side to side and tilt. Fences will usually tilt to at least 45 degrees. Better fences have adjustable stops which can be used to quickly change the fence angle from 90 to 45 degrees.

Cast iron is the best fence material. Be sure to check the fence for straightness. A warped fence can create serious problems. Better fences are designed so that they cover the cutterhead which is behind the fence, serving as a guard when the fence is moved to the left edge of the table. If the jointer you are looking at doesn't have a fence of this design or some other rear guard for the cutterhead, it is unsafe.

GUARD

There are many former woodworkers around with badly damaged hands from using a jointer without a guard. Sometimes people complain that the guard on their machine doesn't work properly, so they take it off. Never use a jointer without a guard. If the guard on your machine is not functioning properly, fix it or get it fixed, but don't use a jointer without it.

Jointer guards should cover the cutterhead completely at all times, fit closely to the table surface, move freely, and have an efficient spring return. Probably one of the most common guard problems has to do with poor spring return. Better machines will generally be equipped with quality guards with adjustable spring systems.

BASE DESIGN

Jointers should have sturdy base designs. If you purchase a machine without a base be sure to anchor it securely to a heavy support system. Floor models should actually be anchored to the floor if possible.

DRIVE MECHANISM AND ELECTRICAL INFORMATION

Most jointers produced today are belt driven, using one or more v-belts to transfer the power from the motor to the cutterhead. Some jointers, usually cheaper models, use direct drive. Jointer cutterhead speeds range from approximately 3600 to over 7000 RPM. The average speed seems to be approximately 5000 RPM. Generally machines with only two knives in the cutterhead will have the higher speeds.

Jointer motors generally range from ¾ to 5 HP. The larger the machine, the larger the motor. Unless you have three phase current, you will be looking for a single phase, 115-220 volt unit. The electrical control features available for jointers are the same as those for other machines.

DELTA 6″
37-223
On Enclosed Stand

DELTA 8″
Long Bed
37-315

DELTA 6″
37-255

GRIZZLY 8″
G1018

GENERAL 6″
1180

JET
JJ-6

WILKE MACHINERY
HJ-12L

MAKITA 8″
2020

VEGA 6″
660A

WILKE MACHINERY
BW-8J

JOINTERS

BRAND *No photo Available	Model	Motor**	Special Features***	Options****	Table Size	Fence Size	Maximum Cutting Width	Maximum Cutting Depth	Rabbeting Capacity	Cutterhead Speed (RPM)	Number of Cutterhead Knives	Adjustable Outfeed Table Yes/No	Table Height	Table Construction	Shipping Weight	Suggested Retail Price
*CRAFTSMAN	9 HT 20694N	.5 HP 11-15	3-6-22 39-40-41	18	—	—	6"	—	—	4,300	3	—	—	CI	173	$499.99
DELTA	37-223	.75 HP 1-8-10-12-20	1-2-3 4-5-6	1-2-3 4-5-6	7×42½	4×36¾	5"	½"	½×6	4,500	3	Yes	35"	CI	208 Net	1177
*DELTA	37-291	.5 HP 1-4-10	1-2-3 4-5-6	1-2-3	5¼×27¼	3¼×21½	4"	¼"	¼×4	4,200	3	Yes	35¼"	CI	110 Net	550
DELTA	37-315	1.5 HP 1-6-12	2-3-4 6-7-8-9	2-7-8 9-10-11	9×66	4×34	8 1/16"	½"	½×8 1/16	5,175	3	Yes	32⅜"	CI	423 Net	1850.70
DELTA	37-255	3 HP 14	3-4-6-7	—	6⅛×35½	3¾×24	6"	⅜"	⅜×6	4,300	3	No	34"	CI	143 Net	495
*GRIZZLY	G1020	1 HP 1-3-15	2-6-19 22-31-32	16	7×45	—	—	½"	—	—	3	Yes	—	CI	260	325
GRIZZLY	G1018	1.5 HP 1-5-19	2-6-16-19 21-32-33-34	17	—	—	8"	½"	½×8	—	3	Yes	40"	CI	500	575
J. PHILIP HUMFREY (MFG-GENERAL)	1180	See Options 40-41	2-3-6-39 46-47-48-49	43-44-45 46-47	7⅛×42	—	6"	½"	½×6	4,200	3	Yes	35"	CI	185	727.90 w/o motor
*J. PHILIP HUMFREY (MFG-GENERAL)	480-1	See Options 41-48	2-36-39 46-47-48-49	46-48-49 50-51-52	9×64	4×34	8"	½"	½×8	4,500	3	Yes	33"	CI	440	1410.80 w/o motor
JET	JJ-6	3 HP 1-8-9	2-3-4-6	—	7×42½	4×28	6"	½"	½×6	4,500	3	Yes	—	—	203	428
MAKITA	2020	—	3-6-35 36-37-38	—	7⅞×59	4¾×31½	8"	⅛"	⅛×8	6,000	—	—	—	—	300	1700
*POWERMATIC	Model 50 1500040	.75 HP 1-4	2-3-6-19-21-23 40-42-43-44-45	19 thru 28 31	7×48	4×34½	6"	½"	½×6	5,000	3	Yes	40"	CI	290	1139
*POWERMATIC	Model 60 1610050	1.5 HP 1-4	2-3-6-19-21 23-40-43-44	19 thru 27 29 thru 39	8½×64	4×34½	8"	½"	½×8	5,000	3	Yes	40"	CI	440	1516
*SUNHILL (MFG-CHIU TING)	CT-60	1 HP 1-7-18	4-6-10 19-22	—	7⅕×42⅕	—×36	6"	—	—	4,500 and 6,500	3	Yes	—	—	—	495

JOINTERS

BRAND *No photo Available	Model	Motor**	Special Features***	Options****	Table Size	Fence Size	Maximum Cutting Width	Maximum Cutting Depth	Rabbeting Capacity	Cutterhead Speed (RPM)	Number of Cutterhead Knives	Adjustable Outfeed Table Yes/No	Table Height	Table Construction	Shipping Weight	Suggested Retail Price
*SUNHILL (MFG-CHIU TING)	CT-60B	1 HP 1-7-18	2-6-19 20-21-22	—	7½×45	4×26⅜	6"	½"	½×6	4,500 and 6,500	3	Yes	—	—	200	$495
*SUNHILL (MFG-CHANG IRON WORKS)	CM-08	2 HP 1-5-18	6-10-16		9×72	—	8"	—	—	6,000	3	Yes	—	CI	700	1650
*SUNHILL (MFG-CHIU TING)	CT-200	2 HP 1-17-18	2-6-21-23 24-25-26-27	—	9×67	4×36	8⅛"	½"	—	4,500	3	Yes	—	—	500	1350
VEGA	660A	.5 HP 1-12-13-16-19	4-6-7 28-29	12-13-14	6×56½	4½×32	6"	½"	½×6	4,300	3	—	33½"	—	285	1125
*VEGA	680A	.75 HP 1-12-13-16-19	4-6-7 28-29-30	12-13-15	8×70½	4½×32	8"	⅜"	⅜×8	4,300	3	—	33¼"	—	345	1595
*WILKE MACHINERY (MFG-BRIDGEWOOD)	FM-250S	2 HP 1 or 2 7-20	6 10 thru 14	—	9⅞×57	—	9.84"	¼"	¼×9.84	4,100	4	Yes	33"	CI	500	1095
WILKE MACHINERY (MFG-BRIDGEWOOD)	HJ-12L	3 HP 1-5-12-21	6-7-11-14 15-16-17-18	—	12×72	—	—	—	—	5,000	—	Yes	—	CI	1056	1995
WILKE MACHINERY (MFG-BRIDGEWOOD)	BW-8J	2 HP 1-7-12-20-22	2-3-4 6-7-14	—	9×66	4×36	8⅛"	½"	½×8⅛	4,500	3	Yes	31½"	S	512	734

(ALL PRICES INCLUDE FREIGHT TO THE NEAREST TERMINAL OF OUR HOUSE CARRIER [SUNHILL])

CI = CAST IRON
S = STEEL

**MOTOR

1. Single phase
2. Three phase
3. 110V
4. 115V
5. 220V
6. 230V
7. 110/220V
8. 115/230V
9. Prewired to 115V
10. 1725 RPM
11. 3450 RPM
12. TEFC
13. Specify voltage
14. Induction motor
15. Ball bearing motor
16. Overload protection
17. Fully magnetic protected
18. Sealed bearings
19. Magnetic starter
20. Heavy duty ball bearing motor
21. Pushbutton switch
22. Fan cooled

***SPECIAL FEATURES

1. Cartridge type cutterhead, precision-ground and balanced, lubricated for life ball bearings.
2. Jointer table has gibbed dovetailed table ways.
3. Fence tilts in and out 45°.
4. Positive stops at 90° and 45°.
5. Includes open steel stand.
6. Adjustable tension guard.
7. Cutterhead runs in sealed, lubricated for life ball bearings.
8. Precision-ground index stop that locks the cutterhead in the correct position for setting cutter knives.
9. Cutterhead has built in springs to hold knives at the proper height when locking them in place.
10. Guide fence tilts 90° to 45°.
11. Dust hood.
12. Sturdy, wide base with wheels.
13. Both tables are adjustable up and down and sideways.
14. All machines are tested before shipping.
15. Center mounted cast iron fence with rack and pinion handwheel adjustment of fence cross travel.
16. Cast iron base.
17. Handle for easy adjustment of fence angle.
18. Fluted table ends near cutterhead reduces noise from rotating cutterhead.
19. Cutterhead runs in fully sealed bearings.
20. Positive stops at 0° and 90°.
21. Fence is center mounted for extra rigidity.
22. Includes steel stand.
23. Chip chute built into base.
24. Precision gib adjustments on ways.
25. Entire cutterhead assembly, including bearings, is removable.
26. Spring-loaded, laminated, HSS knives.
27. Includes enclosed stand.
28. Knife adjustment is by two jacking-screws under each knife.
29. Base is welded, 14 gauge steel.
30. Depth of cut adjustment reads directly and precisely in $1/64''$ increments.
31. Up and down sliding motion on both sides.
32. Table has rabbeting lip.
33. One piece stand has chip chute.
34. Lever operation for raising and lowering tables.
35. Rack and pinion fence adjustment.
36. Electric brake on cutterhead.
37. Key safety switch.
38. Built in dust chute.
39. Cutterhead runs in permanently lubricated ball bearings.
40. Cast iron fence.
41. Removable locking key.
42. Fence can be swiveled to cut material on a skew.
43. Positive fence hold down clamp.
44. Patented control chip cutterhead.
45. Rigid, re-inforced cabinet-type steel base with built-in dust chute.
46. Ribbed gray iron casting base.
47. Three steel knives are held in place by chip breakers and jack screws.
48. Gray iron fence.
49. Enclosed stand with chip chute; heavy gauge steel welded together.

****OPTIONS

11403

1. #49-889, enclosed steel stand with motor and controls, includes 3 HP motor, 115/230V, 3450 RPM, single phase, TEFC, pushbutton switch, motor pulley, V-belt and pulley guard, 86 lbs., $377.

2. #37-815, knife grinding and jointing attachment with motor #37-816, $748.50.

3. #37-811, complete cutterhead assembly, $187.05.

4. #52-892, 24V pushbutton station, magnetic starter, transformer and overload protection (LVC), single phase, $250.

5. #49-900, same as #52-892 except has 230/460V three phase motor, $250.

6. #52-096, same as #49-900 except has 200V, $250.

7. #49-055, 24V pushbutton station, magnetic starter, transformer and overload protection (LVC), single phase, $156.

8. #49-066, same as #49-055, except has 230/460V, three phase motor, $156.

9. #49-067, same as #49-066 except has 200V, $156.

10. #37-308, set of three high speed steel cutter knives, $59.70.

11. #37-342, cutterhead assembly, $364.50.

12. Also available with three phase motor, 1 HP, same price. Specify voltage.

13. #22-0096, blade setting gauge, $75.

14. #26-0062, set of three knives, no price available.

15. #30W400, set of three cutterhead knives, no price available.

16. #G1175, set of three extra high speed steel blades, $14.

17. #G1176, set of three extra high speed steel blades, $18.

18. See Craftsman Power and Hand Tool catalog for accessories.

19. #6470809, .75 HP, three phase motor, 3600 RPM, 200V, TEFC, $108.

20. #6470810, .75 HP, three phase motor, 3600 RPM, 230/460V, TEFC, $123.

21. #2398336, single phase magnetic control, 115/230V, $212.

22. #2398487, single phase magnetic control, 115/230V, 2/24V transformer, $290.

23. #2398118, three phase magnetic control, 200/230/460/575V, $257.

24. #2398230, three phase JIC controls, 200/230/460/575V, $718.

25. #2398371, switch, three phase, 200/230/460/575V, $87.

26. #2398435, three phase magnetic controls, 200/230/460/575V, w/24V transformer, $306.

27. #2230001, quick set knife gauge, $68.

28. #2397076, cutterhead retrofit kit controlled chip, 6 in., $181.

29. Also available with 2 HP, 230V, magnetic control, with knife setting gauge, $1,757.

30. #2397077, cutterhead retrofit kit controlled chip, 8 in., $223.

31. #6470801, .75 HP, single phase, 3600 RPM, 115/230V, $151.

32. #6471100, 1 HP, single phase, 3600 RPM, 115/230V, TEFC, $130.

33. #6471400, 1.5 HP, single phase, 3600 RPM, 115/230V, TEFC, $173.

34. #6471118, 1 HP, three phase, 3600 RPM, 200V, TEFC, $133.

35. #6471119, 1 HP, three phase, 3600 RPM, 230/460V, TEFC, $157.

36. #6471412, 1.5 HP, three phase, 3600 RPM, 200V, TEFC, $148.

37. #6471413, 1.5 HP, three phase, 3600 RPM, 230/460V, TEFC, $148.

38. #2398369, switch, 115/230V, single phase, $61.

39. #6427002, set of three high speed steel knives, $59.

40. Recommended motor: .5 HP to 1 HP.

41. Machine is priced without motor and controls. Single phase motors available from .25 HP to 5 HP in 100V and 220V; the 3 HP and 5 HP single phase motors are available in 200V only. Three phase motors available from .5 HP to 5 HP—specify voltage.

42. #1180-C, three piece carbide tipped knives, $225.

43. #1180-H, three piece HSS knives, $35.55.

44. #11803, three piece HSS throw-away knives, $9.46.

45. #11804, chip breaker for throw-away knives, two required, $16.63.

46. #1533, knife setting gauges, $148.50.

47. #1820, rear guard, $44.83.

48. Recommended motor: 1 HP to 2 HP.

49. #480-C, three piece carbide tipped knives, $266.95.

50. #480-3H, three piece HSS knives, $49.95.

51. #480-4, three piece HSS throw away knives, $11.24.

52. #480-5, chip breaker for throw away knives, two required, $20.73.

BAND SAW

Woodcutting band saws range from large band mills used to saw logs into boards to small bench models. The ones found in most small shops are used for all kinds of curved sawing, resawing, rough crosscutting and ripping.

The band saw is an often used machine in most shops. The downward cutting action of the blade makes it safer to use than a table saw or radial arm saw. The hazard of a kick back isn't present, and stock can be cut safely free hand. Fences and miter gauges can be used on a band saw, but they are not absolutely necessary.

All band saws operate in basically the same way. The blade is a continuous strip of flexible steel with teeth on one edge. This "band like" blade is what the machine is named after. The blade runs on two or more rubber covered wheels.

The basic parts of a band saw include table, blade, blade guides, blade guards, wheels, wheel covers, arm or frame, and base.

SIZE

The size of a two wheel band saw is generally referred to in terms of the diameter of the wheels. A 14″ band saw, for example, will typically have 14″ wheels. The actual width cutting capacity of the machine may be slightly less than 14″ due to the rear blade guard. Two wheel band saws, not including the large ones used to saw logs, range in size from 10″ through 36″, with the 14″ and 20″ sizes being most common in small shops.

Three wheel band saws are also manufactured today. The third wheel is added to increase the width cutting capacity of the machine without enlarging the wheel diameter. The size of a three wheel band saw is

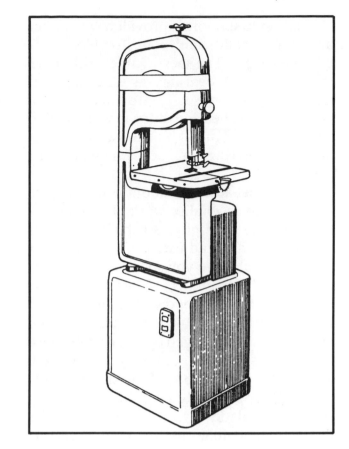

usually referred to in terms of the actual width cutting capacity.

The maximum depth of cut under the upper blade guide is another important size consideration. This capacity can be increased on some machines by adding an optional height attachment to the saw frame. This height option is not available on all machines. If you think that you may want to increase the depth cutting capacity in the future, be sure that it can be done on the machine you are considering.

Quality machines will have well designed blade guards and wheel covers. Be sure that the machine you are considering was designed with safety in mind.

BLADE GUIDES

Blade guides are designed to give the blade side and back support. Machines should have both upper and lower guides (one above and below the table).

Blade side support is provided with either adjustable, solid steel plates or blocks, or ball bearings. The best guides will have adjustable ball bearings as side support. Back support is usually provided with an adjustable ball bearing, but you will also find adjustable solid metal blocks used occasionally. Ball bearings are best for blade back support.

The correct adjustment of the blade guide is important in quality work. Examine the blade guides carefully. All blade supports should be easily adjusted. The operator's manual should give you specific instructions for proper "fine tuning". Most manufacturers suggest that the solid side guides be set so they barely clear the blade on each side. Side clearance can be gauged by using a thin piece of paper as a feeler gauge. The saw teeth should run just in front of the side supports with the support only touching the smooth part of the blade. Ball bearing, side guides can actually contact the blade on each side and offer the best "drift free" support.

Some cheaper guides have blade back supports that are not ball bearings. If this is the case the blade will slowly wear a groove in the surface of the support, and sooner or later, it will be ruined. The blade also "work hardens" faster with this kind of contact, and this will shorten its life.

The guide post is the adjustable bar to which the upper blade guide is attached. The upper guide height is adjusted repeatedly so the convenience and ease of adjusting the guide post is important. The locking knobs or handles used on some guide posts are poorly designed and do not hold up under frequent adjustment. The post itself should be designed so it moves up and down without twisting. Square or hexagonal posts are subject to the least amount of deflection.

WHEELS

Aluminum and cast iron are the materials most often used to make band saw wheels.

Generally larger band saws will have cast iron wheels. Cast iron produces a heavier wheel which, because of its weight, is harder to start and stop. When they are machined and balanced properly, they will run for many years without trouble. The overall life expectancy for aluminum would be less. Many of the smaller saws have die cast aluminum wheels.

You can detect high or low spots in the wheel rim or tire by simply rolling the blade through slowly, by hand, and watching the side movement of the blade between the

---

The wheels could be perfectly true and still be out of balance.

---

guide blocks. Perfectly true wheels will show no side movement. Sometimes the metal wheel can be true, and the rubber tire may have high or low spots in it. These can be dressed out but should not be present on a new machine.

The wheels could be perfectly true and still be out of balance. Wheel balancing can only be checked by operating the machine. Poor wheel balancing will cause excessive vibration. A smooth running band saw should pass the nickel test just like other machines. Place a nickel on its edge on the saw table while the machine is running. The coin should not fall over or move.

Band saw wheels are covered with rubber or plastic rims to protect the blade. These rims are attached by gluing them to the metal surface or by fitting them into a special groove. Glued rims are harder to install but will last just as long and maybe longer than other types. Some woodworkers even prefer to glue the rims on wheels with special mounting grooves.

The lower wheel on two wheel band saws is the non-adjustable wheel and is connected either directly or through belts to the motor. The upper wheel is adjustable. It can be raised and lowered to increase and decrease blade tension, and tilted for blade tracking. The design of the tracking/tension mechanism is an important item. You will need to use these adjustments many times during the life of the machine. Better machines will have a blade tension indicator located on the upper wheel assembly. These gauges are supposed to tell you when you have the correct tension for a blade of a given width. The gauges generally work fairly well on new machines but actually many woodworkers say experience is the best teacher. The wheel tilting (tracking) system should be designed so the wheel can be locked securely in the desired position. A quality band saw will include complete instructions related to blade replacement, tracking, and tension.

The diameter of the wheels influences the frequency of broken blades. Machines with large wheels generally break fewer blades than smaller machines. If you own a 14″ band saw don't compare your blade breaking frequency with a 36″ unit. The 14″ machine will break more.

Large band saws sometimes have brake systems to slow and stop the wheels after the machine is turned off. This feature is not found on smaller machines.

BLADES

Blade replacement is probably the most common band saw maintenance activity. Blades are replaced when they are broken, dull, or when changing to a different width.

Basically there are two types of blades used today for cutting wood, conventional wood blades and skip tooth blades. Conventional blades have teeth which resemble rip saw teeth and the teeth have conventional set. Skip tooth blades have smaller teeth and as the name implies, appear to have a missing tooth between each tooth. These blades will have a set tooth, a straight tooth, and another set tooth. Skip tooth blades can be used to cut wood, plastic, and soft metals. Woodworkers do not agree on

which blade is best. It would probably be best for you to try each and draw your own conclusions.

Usually a new band saw will come with only one blade. It is best to go on and purchase two or three additional blades to have in reserve.

Blade breakage happens on band saws. If you use one very long, you are bound to eventually experience this problem. Blades break when they work harden due to many trips around the wheels and many contact hours with the blade guides. Poor operator techniques can also cause breakage. If you experience frequent blade breakage problems, even with new blades, it may not be the machine's or operator's fault at all. It may be the blade itself or the way it was welded. Band saw blades are butt welded. After welding the joint, the area around it must be annealed (softened) or the blade will be brittle at this point. Always examine broken blades carefully to see where the break occurred. If the break is at or near the weld on a new blade, it is probably an annealing problem. Your blade supplier should be told about the problem.

Broken blades can be welded again and put back into use if they are long enough and sharp enough. It is generally best to purchase the longest blade your saw will take so it could be welded and used again if necessary.

It is possible to sharpen band saw blades, but most people don't. It is so much easier simply to discard dull blades and buy new ones.

TABLE

The best band saw tables are made from cast iron. Tables on quality machines will tilt 45 degrees to the right, 15 degrees to the left, and have a positive stop at 90 degrees. One milled slot is usually provided in the table for a miter gauge. The table will have a cut from the center to the outer edge for blade installation. This cut should be equipped with an alignmenty pin to keep the two table halves aligned.

The table insert around the blade is usually made from aluminum. Some of these inserts have a tendency to turn as you turn work on top. When this happens you will cut up the insert. Better machines should have inserts which are keyed to prevent slipping. Inserts will need to be replaced when the space around the blade becomes excessive. They are usually easy to make.

Some tables have provisions for mounting guide rails for a fence attachment. Usually the guide rails and fence are not standard parts and must be purchased as an option. Fences are convenient for certain kinds of work, and you will find that often a wooden fence, clamped to the table, will work beautifully. Some woodworkers prefer not to use a fence for ripping and use a pivot style ripping guide instead. With this type of device, you can feed stock at the correct angle dictated by the lead of the blade. This is something that is harder to do with a straight fence.

You may find that the miter gauge for your table saw will work satisfactorily on your band saw. Sometimes this is the case, especially if the machines are from the same manufacturer.

If you are considering a new or used machine, inspect the table carefully for cracks. Old machines will frequently have a missing alignment pin. If this is the case you may find that the table has warped. Sometimes the table halves can be realigned by simply installing a new pin.

WORK LAMP

Most band saws do not come with a work lamp as a standard item. You will find that this accessory will be well worth the added cost. Good lighting is essential to good work and the very nature of the upper blade guide makes it even harder to see your work because of shadows. Manufacturers will usually offer a work lamp as an option. If you find that is not the case with the machine you are considering, you might investigate the possibility of installing one. Ask your dealer about light possibilities.

WHEEL COVERS AND BASE

The wheels should be completely covered for safety. The covers should be designed so they can be easily removed for blade replacement and cleaning.

Band saws tend to be somewhat top heavy so their bases and floor stands should be wide enough to eliminate the possibility of the machine tipping over. It is best to securely bolt the machine to the floor or a heavy base.

SPEED AND ELECTRICAL INFORMATION

Small band saws are usually single speed units. Larger machines are sometimes available in variable speed models. The optimum blade speed is theoretically different as different materials are cut. If you intend to be cutting a wide variety of materials, a variable speed model would be best. If you intend to cut mostly wood, a single or two speed model will do. Some woodworkers prefer slower blade speeds for operations such as resawing. If you plan to frequently resaw stock you might want to invest in a two speed model.

High blade speed does not necessarily mean good quality. The theoretical optimum speed and the speed many woodworkers prefer are sometimes different. Blade speed is frequently faster than many prefer.

The motor and control options available on band saws are essentially the same as those found on other machines. Motors range from ½ HP to 3½ HP, with ¾ HP being common for 14″ machines.

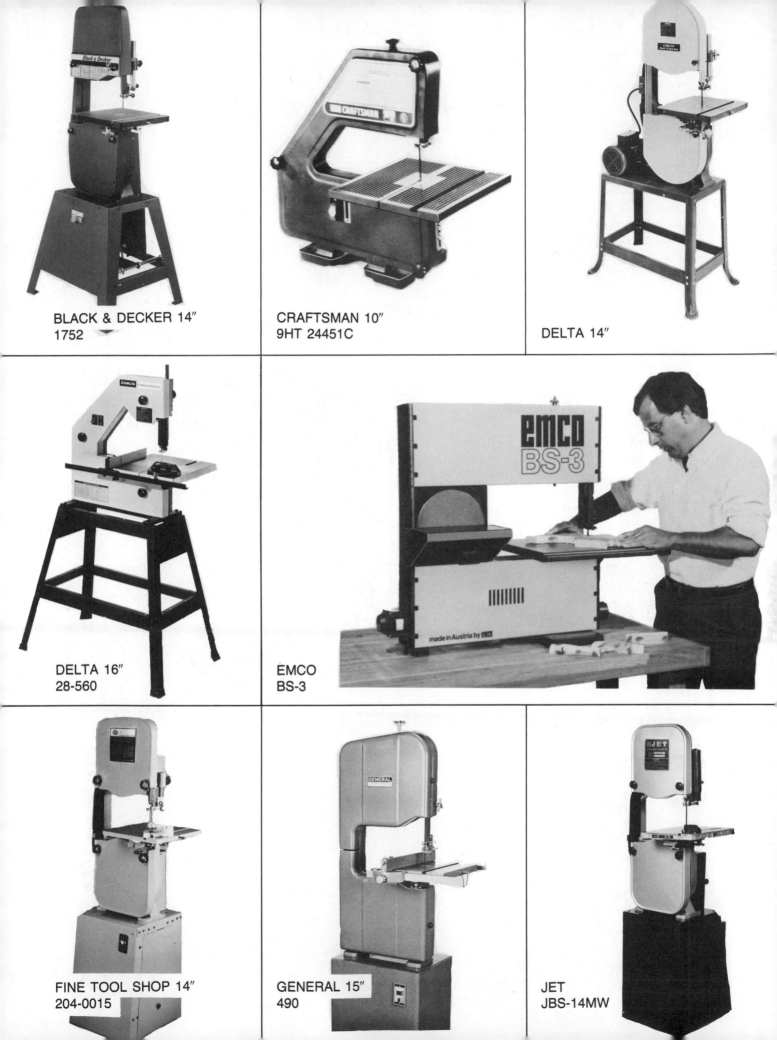

BLACK & DECKER 14"
1752

CRAFTSMAN 10"
9HT 24451C

DELTA 14"

DELTA 16"
28-560

EMCO
BS-3

FINE TOOL SHOP 14"
204-0015

GENERAL 15"
490

JET
JBS-14MW

KITY 12″
613

DUPLI-CARVER
249

PARKS 18″
No. 2

POWERMATIC 14″
141

SKIL 10″
3104

RYOBI 10″
BS-50N

RYOBI 14″
BS-360NR

VEGA 14″
400

BAND SAW

BRAND *No photo Available	Model	Size	Motor**	Special Features***	Options****	Capacity (Blade to Frame)	Capacity (Under Guide and Wheel)	Maximum Blade Width	Maximum Blade Length	Table Tilt Right	Table Tilt Left	Overall Dimensions H×W×D	Cutting Speed (SPM)	Table Construction	Table Height	Table Size	Shipping Weight	Suggested Retail Price
BLACK & DECKER	1752	14″	.5 HP 13-19	1-13-73	—	13¾″	6⁵⁄₁₆″	¾″	92½″	45°	—	—	—	CI	—	14×14½	190	$479
*BLACK & DECKER	9411	12″	.5 HP 11	29-74-80	—	12⅞″	4″	³⁄₁₆″	59½″	45°	—	—	750/1900	—	—	13¾×12¾	22	228^{95}
*BLACK & DECKER	9422	7½″	5	14-29-80	—	7½″	3¾″	¼″	52¾″	45°	—	—	650	—	—	10×10	27	132^{95}
CRAFTSMAN	9 HT 24451C	10″	⅕ HP	12-14-19 41-42-44-80	20-21	10″	3″	—	—	45°	—	23×13½×22	—	CA	—	11½×11½	45	144^{99}
*CRAFTSMAN	9 HT 24331N	12″	.5 HP 5-11	14-43-44 45-46-47	22-23	—	—	—	—	45°	—	—	—	CA	—	14×12½	120	449^{99}
*CRAFTSMAN	9 HT 2444N	10″	⅓ HP	14-42-43 44-45-80	22-23-24	10″	4″	—	—	45°	—	—	—	—	—	14×12½	55	289^{99}
*CRAFTSMAN	9 HT 24391N	9″	.75 HP	21-29 45-48-49	—	—	6¾″	2″	72⅝″	—	—	—	—	—	—	15¾×15¾	135	799^{99}
*CRAFTSMAN	9 HT 2442N	10″	⅝ HP 5	14-29-45-80	—	10″	4″	—	62⅝″	45°	—	—	—	—	—	14×13	38	199^{99}
DELTA	—	14″	.5 HP 1-4-11-12-13	1-2-3-4-5 6-7-8-9-10	1-2-3-4-5 6-7-9	13¾″	6¼″	¾″	94″	45°	10°	65½×25×17½	3000	CI	42¾″	14×14	201 Net	717
DELTA	28-560	16″	.5 HP 1-4	11-12-13	9	16″	8″	⅜″	82″ Standard	45°	3°	60⅝×31×21	450/2400	CI	—	16×16	156 Net	449
*DELTA	—	10″	.5 HP 1-4-11-12-13	6-14-15	8-9	9⁷⁄₁₆″	6″	½″	71¾″ Standard	45°	5°	60×19¼×10¾	2400	CI	41¼″	10×11	120 Net	497
*ELEKTRA BECKUM	BAS450WRN	18″	1.5 HP 6-15-16	2-21-22 23-24-25	10-11-12-13	17¼″	12¼″	1″	133¹⁄₁₆″	45°	—	75½×33¼×26½	260/690 1470/3800	DA	36½″	21½×19¼	280 Net	1360
*ELEKTRA BECKUM	BAS315/4W34	12″	.75 HP 3	2-21 23-24-25	10-12-14	12¼″	6¾″	¾″	82.2″	45°	—	74×24×23	1456/3150	DA	43¼″	14¼×15¾	121 Net	710
EMCO	BS-3	—	⅔ HP 3	48-50	25-26-27-28	15″	6¼″	—	83½″	45°	—	31½×19¼×37⅜	170/863 1380	S	—	16×18	86 Net	395

BAND SAW

BRAND *No photo Available	Model	Size	Motor**	Special Features***	Options****	Capacity (Blade to Frame)	Capacity (Under Guide and Wheel)	Maximum Blade Width	Maximum Blade Length	Table Tilt Right	Table Tilt Left	Overall Dimensions H×W×D	Cutting Speed (SPM)	Table Construc-tion	Table Height	Table Size	Shipping Weight	Suggested Retail Price
FINE TOOL SHOP (MFG-KING FENG FU)	204-0015	14″	.5 HP 5	10-14-29 40-44-54	—	—	—	—	—	45°	—	—	880/3170	DA	—	14×14	198	$399.95
*GRIZZLY	G-1015	—	⅓ HP 1-13	12-15-21-29 30-36-37-38	—	14″	5½″	—	70¼″	—	—	—	120/750 1200	DA	—	14×14	62 Net	135
*GRIZZLY	G-1131 Heavy Duty	18″	2 HP 1	1-8 10-13-39	—	18″	7.88″	1½″	121″	—	—	—	—	CI	—	—	450 Net	595
*GRIZZLY	G-1019	14″	3 HP 1	6-13-19 21-29-40	19	14″	6″	¾″	93½″	45°	—	—	—	CI	—	—	200 Net	275
*HITACHI	CB75F	—	2.7 HP 1-4	4-20-21 29-48-60	39	14½″	11 13/16″	3″	111 3/16″	45°	—	60 11/32 × 36 27/32 × 29 9/64	—	—	—	20 43/64 × 19 19/64	309 Net	2420
*J. PHILIP HUMFREY (MFG-GENERAL)	390	20″	See Options 31-32-33-34	4-14-50-51 53-55-56-57	30-35-36-37	20″	12½″	1″	148″	45°	12°	79¼ × 45¼ × 31½	4500	—	42″	24×24	820 Net	2703.20 w/o motor
J. PHILIP HUMFREY (MFG-GENERAL)	490-1	15″	See Options 31-32-33-34	3-4-10-33 37-48-58	35-36-37-38	14¾″	6¾″	¾″	100″	45′	10°	66½ × 18 × 26¾	3000	RCI	42″	15×15	295 Net	820.40 w/o motor
*JET	DBS-14	—	.5 HP 1-8-9	21-26-27-28 29-30-80	—	—	5″	⅜″	70″	45°	—	28 × 17½ × 28¾	637/3000 4650	—	—	15¾ × 15¾	64	184
JET	JBS-14MW	—	.75 HP 1-8-9	6-10-13 29-31	15	—	6″	¾″	93½″	45°	10°	65 × 24½ × 19¼	735/1470 2350	S	—	14×14	218	385
KITY	613	12″	1 HP 1 or 2-15	1-21-37-47 48-62-63	46-47	12″	8″	¾″	—	20°	—	—	—	CAL	37″	20×20	145 Net	966.65
LASKOWSKI ENT. DUPLI-CARVER	249	—	.5 10-13	1-2-10-37-47 70-71-72	49-50-51 52-53	24½″	9″	¾″	109½″	48°	10°	—	1375/1650 2050	—	—	12×12	—	658.90
*MINI MAX	S45	—	1.5 HP	4-10-37-38-48 50-51-52	—	17.25″	11.8″	¾″	144″	—	—	67.7 × 30.7 × 21.2	3000	CI	—	20×20	330 Net	995
*MINI MAX	PRO-32	—	3 HP 1 or 2	10-37-38-51 52-53-54-80	29	12.4″	6.5″	¾″	85.5″	45°	—	39 × 22.8 × 21.2	3000	CI	—	15×15	147 Net	695
PARKS	No. 2	18″	1 HP 1-7-14	4-6-16-17	—	17″	12″	—	—	45°	—	—	3500	—	39″	18×20	430	1866

BAND SAW

BRAND *No photo Available	Model	Size	Motor**	Special Features***	Options****	Capacity (Blade to Frame)	Capacity (Under Guide and Wheel)	Maximum Blade Width	Maximum Blade Length	Table Tilt Right	Table Tilt Left	Overall Dimensions H×W×D	Cutting Speed (SPM)	Table Construction	Table Height	Table Size	Shipping Weight	Suggested Retail Price
POWERMATIC	141	14″	.75 HP 1-4	4-7-50-75 76-77-78-79	54 thru 66	14″	6½″	¾″	96″	45°	15°	71×25½×13¼	3000	CI	42″	15×15	355	$1324
RYOBI	BS-50N	10″	9	18-19-20-80	—	—	7″	2″	72⁷⁄₁₆″	—	—	34⅝×25¹³⁄₁₆×17¾	—	—	—	15¾×15¾	110 Net	995
RYOBI	BS-360NR	14″	9	18-19	—	—	12³⁄₁₆″	3″	101¾″	—	—	52⅜×34⅝×23⅝	—	—	—	18½×17¾	242 Net	1936
SKIL	3104	10″	⅝ HP	29-45-48-64 65-66-67-68	—	10″	4″	—	62″	45°	—	—	500 to 2000	CA	—	13×14	35 Net	194.99
*SUNHILL (MFG-ELEPHANT CO.)	VBS-14	14″	.75 HP 1-18	1-54-69	—	14″	6″	—	93½″	45°	—	—	—	—	—	14×14	200 Net	399
*SUNHILL (MFG-ELEPHANT CO.)	VBS-143	14″	.75 HP 1-18	1-54-69	48	14″	6″	—	93½″	45°	—	—	735/1470 2350	—	—	14×14	200 Net	420
*SUNHILL (MFG-ELEPHANT CO.)	VBS-18	18″	1.5 HP 1-18	1-29-36	—	17½″	8″	1¼″	121″	—	—	—	—	—	—	20×16	380 Net	1035
(FREIGHT PAID TO NEAREST TERMINAL OF OUR HOUSE CARRIER [SUNHILL])																		
VEGA	400	14″	.5 HP 1-10-15-17	7-8-23-32 33-34-35	16-17-18	13⅞″	8″	¾″	105″	45°	10°	72½×25×28	2000/3000	—	38½″	—	300 Net	995
*WILKE MACHINERY (MFG-BRIDGEWOOD)	KLW-5695	14″	.5 HP 1-4	1-10-37-48	40-41-42	14″	6″	¾″	—	45°	10°	65½×24½×19½	—	CI	—	14×14	210	399.95
*WILKE MACHINERY (MFG-BRIDGEWOOD)	BS-18EB	18″	1.5 HP 1-6-15	4-21-36-61	43-44-45	17.4″	12.25″	1″	132¼″	—	—	76×33×27	204/528 1125/2900	—	36½″	21.7×19.3	310	1295

TABLE CONSTRUCTION
CI —Cast Iron
DA —Die Cast Aluminum
S —Steel
CA —Cast Aluminum
RCI —Ribbed Cast Iron
CAL —Cast Alloy

**MOTOR

1. Single phase
2. Three phase
3. 110V
4. 115V
5. 120V
6. 220V
7. 230V
8. 115/230V
9. Prewired to 115V
10. TEFC
11. 1725 RPM
12. Capacitor start
13. Ball bearing
14. Manual/overload starter
15. Thermal overload protection
16. No-volt release switch
17. Starter system w/magnetic relay and fusetron
18. Sealed bearings
19. Induction motor

SPECIAL FEATURES

1. Open steel stand included.
2. Die cast aluminum wheels with rubber tires.
3. Recessing rim for rubber tires; no cement required.
4. Steel hinged wheel guards.
5. Locked-in table insert that cannot rotate.
6. Upper and lower blade ball bearing support; adjust independently.
7. Exact blade tension scale.
8. Double sealed, lubricated for life ball bearings for upper and lower wheels and blade supports.
9. Chip chute.
10. Adjustable upper and lower blade guides control side movement.
11. Makes cuts to within 1/4" radius when 1/8" blades are used.
12. Three wheel design.
13. Cast iron frame.
14. Blade tensioning and tracking controls.
15. Equipped with accessory sanding attachment.
16. Heavy fabricated steel frame.
17. Fully enclosed welded steel cabinet.
18. Constant blade tension device.
19. Rubber-lined blade wheels.
20. Portable.
21. Includes rip fence.
22. 4" chip/dust ejection hole.
23. Three roller guide blade support.
24. Hand wheel for quick tensioning of saw blade.
25. Quick locking device on both doors.

26. Guard is made of durable plastic.
27. Three step pulley.
28. Blade rides on 3 aluminum wheels with bearings.
29. Includes mitre gauge.
30. Includes circle cutting attachment.
31. Metal and wood bandsaw.
32. Includes 14 gauge steel enclosed cabinet.
33. Main frame made from heavy steel and welded together.
34. Access doors are mounted on continuous hinges with spring-loaded latches.
35. Upper and lower wheels are double pressed steel.
36. Wheels are aluminum and rubber coated.
37. Blade guides at top and bottom; back blade support is ball bearing.
38. Tilting table.
39. Heavy duty adjustable rip fence.
40. Steel stand included.
41. Wheels are 6" in diameter.
42. Direct drive.
43. Both wheels run on permanently lubricated ball bearings.
44. Cast aluminum frame.
45. Locking switch key.
46. Includes steel leg set.
47. Built-in sawdust ejection.
48. Adjustable blade tension.
49. 7" drive and idler wheels in lubricated ball and sleeve bearings.
50. Dust extractor.
51. Wheels are rubber coated cast iron.
52. Adjustable steel fence.

53. Wheel cleaning brush.
54. Steel wheel guards.
55. Foot brake for stopping the drive wheel.
56. Welded, ribbed steel frame.
57. Guides are 45° V-blocks with ball thrust bearings.
58. Ribbed cast iron frame.
59. Tires are reversible for double life.
60. Hand brake.
61. Ball bearing three roller guide.
62. Lateral thrust is supported by hardwood blocks.
63. Cast alloy wheels, rubber coated.
64. Full 10" cut at 45° tilt.
65. Gear drive.
66. Nylon blade guides.
67. Includes sander/grinder conversion kit.
68. Steel frame.
69. Cast drive wheels.
70. Saw frame is constructed of 2 × 4 structural tubing 1/8" wall.
71. Can cut a piece of 4 × 8 plywood in two.
72. Each blade wheel is supported by two sealed ball bearings.
73. Four speed.
74. Variable speed.
75. One piece box type cast iron frame.
76. Heavy duty cast iron wheels and rubber tires.
77. Top saw guide is three ball bearings, lower guide has backup ball bearing and 45° hardened steel side guides.
78. Enclosed steel stand.
79. Includes lamp.
80. Benchtop model.

****OPTIONS

1. Also available with 3 HP motor, add $29.
2. Also available with enclosed steel stand, add $216.
3. #25-858, lamp attachment, $26.65.
4. #28-984, height attachment increases capacity of 14" band saw from 6¼" to 12¼" under the guide, needs 105" blades, $61.10.
5. #28-843, rip fence with 18" guide bars, $57.15.
6. #28-845, rip fence with 32" guide bars, $60.20.
7. #34-895, mitre gauge, $44.15.
8. #62-138, also available with .5 HP, split phase, sleeve bearing motor, 1725 RPM, $43 less.
9. #28-810, sanding attachment on all band saws, $20.65.
10. Circular cutting attachment, $35.95.
11. Belt sanding attachment, $17.40.
12. Crosscut fence with mitre gauge, $28.95.
13. Available with 110V motor for $1,395.
14. Belt sanding attachment, $13.40.
15. #RB-14, riser block kit, $18.
16. Also available with three phase motor, same price.
17. #20W800, rip fence and guide bar, $55.
18. #150311, mitre gauge, $35.75.
19. Cutting height extension block, $39.95.
20. #9 HT 24214, $14.99.
21. #9 HT 22244C, steel stand, $24.99.
22. #9 HT 23433, rip fence, $39.99.
23. #9 HT 29929, mitre gauge, $29.99.

24. #9 HT 22236C, steel stand, $64.99.
25. Drum sanding attachment, $34.
26. Mitre gauge, $24.
27. Attachment for circular and radius cuts, $14.95.
28. Belt sanding attachment, $16.
29. Steel stand, no price available.
30. #390-1, rip fence, $243.32.
31. Machine is priced without motor or controls. Single phase motors available from .25 to 5 HP in 110V and 220V; three phase motors available from .5 to 5 HP—specify voltage. The 3 HP and 5 HP single phase motors are available in 220V only.
32. #C1010MTE, magnetic switch, $77.
33. #C1004, Allen Bradley reversing switch, $63.
34. #C1005, furnace pushbutton switch, $40.
35. #1950, mitre gauge, $72.83.
36. #1950-1, stop rods, $21.70.
37. #1951, work lamp, $47.74.
38. #4949, rip fence, $105.61.
39. Also available with three phase, 220V motor, add $40.
40. #MTG569, mitre gauge, no price available.
41. #RFB569, rip fence, no price available.
42. #RB569, 6" high riser block, no price available.
43. Circle cutting attachment, no price available.
44. Belt sanding attachment, no price available.

45. Crosscut fence attachment, no price available.
46. #2322, mitre gauge, no price available.
47. #4121, table extensions, no price available.
48. #VSB-14, spacer block kit, increases capacity under guide and wheel to 12¼", $45.
49. Particle board scroll table, $15.95.
50. Steel scroll table, $42.
51. Rip fence with extension, $9.95.
52. Table arm extenders, $39.95.
53. Gooseneck work lamp, $16.50.
54. #2028073, circle cutting attachment, $63.
55. #2195015, rip fence, $78.
56. #2250087, guard (retrofit), $2.10.
57. #2471010, mitre gauge, $49.
58. #6470707, .75 HP motor, TEFC, three phase, 230/460V, $141.
59. #6470712, .75 HP motor, TEFC, three phase, 200V, $141.
60. #2398118, magnetic control, three phase, 200/230/460/575V, $257.
61. #2398336, magnetic control, single phase, 115/230V, $212.
62. #2398435, magnetic control, three phase w/24V transformer, 200/230/460/575V, $306.
63. #2398487, magnetic control, single phase w/24V transformer, 115/230V, $290.
64. #2398230, JIC Control, three phase, 200/230/460/575V, $718.
65. #2398114, switch, single phase, 115/230V, $67.
66. #2398115, switch, three phase, 200/230/460/575V, $87.

SCROLL SAW OR JIG SAW

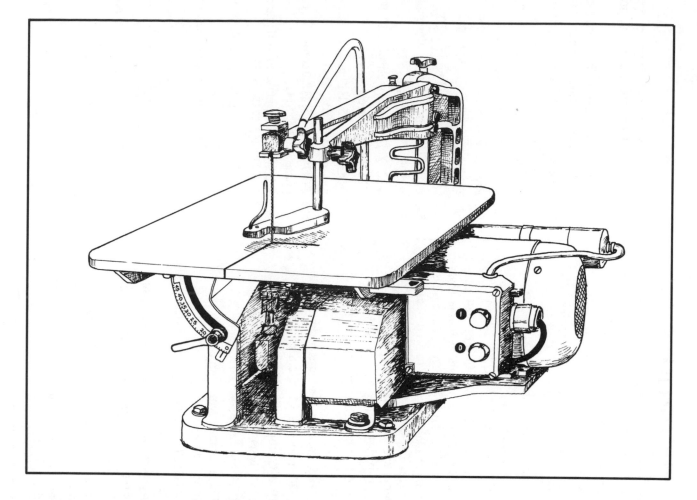

Scroll saws or jig saws are designed for intricate curved sawing or, as the name implies, scroll sawing. This machine can produce extremely small, tight curves and internal sawing. For some woodworkers such as sign makers, toy makers, model makers and marquetry specialists this machine is invaluable. On the other hand, some woodworkers may actually have little use for a scroll saw. It is somewhat like a lathe in the sense that you either need one or you don't.

Conventional scroll saws, which have been on the market for many years, have a rigid arm and a reciprocating blade. The lower end of the blade is clamped into a chuck that is driven by a pitman drive. The upper end of the blade is fastened in a chuck

which is spring loaded and fastened to the rigid saw frame. As the lower chuck moves up and down, the spring loaded upper chuck

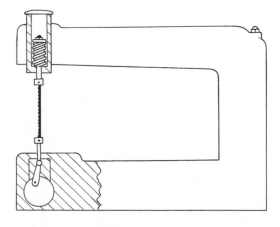

Old Rigid Arm Design

works to keep the blade under tension. Unfortunately, with conventional designs, the blade tension is not always constant throughout the stroke, and blade breakage is common, especially with smaller blades. Several new constant tension scroll saw designs have become available in the past ten years which help overcome this problem. Conventional rigid arm saws are still available, but more and more scroll saw users are going to the new constant tension designs. When you start to compare the new and the old designs, you will see why.

ARM DESIGN

The new constant tension scroll saws are either "C" arm (figure 1) or parallel arm designs (figure 2). In both of these systems the blade is held under constant tension between the ends of the arm and the arm itself rocks or moves up and down. The stroke length ranges from approximately ⅓"

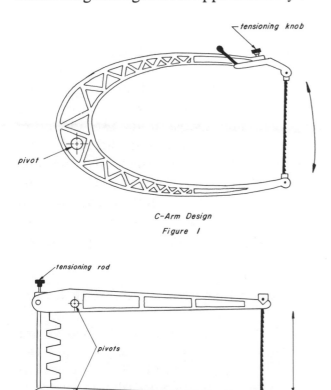

C-Arm Design
Figure 1

Parallel Arm Design
Figure 2

to over one inch, with ¾" to 1" being common. The blade tension on a parallel arm saw is adjusted with a tensioning rod at the rear of the arms. "C" arm machines use a blade tensioning knob and lever which are located at the front of the upper arm.

The blade on all constant tension saws moves back on the up stroke and forward on the down stroke. With this form of blade motion the saw teeth actually act somewhat like a file and smooth the edges of the work being cut. As a result, the typical "wash board"-like saw marks normally associated with work done on band saws and rigid arm scroll saws is eliminated. The sawed surfaces are smooth and most of the tedious sanding usually associated with smoothing scroll cut edges is eliminated. This alone is a very significant advantage of constant tension machines over rigid arm designs.

Most constant tension saws on the market today are parallel arm machines. As the blade on these machines moves up and down it remains perpendicular to the saw's table. On a "C" arm machine, the blade actually moves through an arc or rocks slightly to the rear on the up stroke. Even though the actual blade motion is different between these two machines, the actual difference is slight and performance can be considered essentially the same.

BLADE HOLDING FEATURES

The blade on almost all constant tension scroll saws is attached to the arm with some type of pivoting blade clamp. Blade clamps are either pinned to the ends of the arms or are separate "V" shaped metal blocks which are attached to the ends of the blade and rest in grooves in the arms. Pivoting blade clamps reduce blade breakage since they allow the blade to deflect or bow back as you push wood into the cut. This reduces stress at the ends of the blade and will prolong blade life. If the ends of the blade were solidly locked in a non-pivoting clamp, which is common on rigid arm machines, the blade would be forced to bend at the clamp as work is pushed into the cut. Blades break at or near the chuck for this reason.

TABLES

Scroll saw tables are typically made from cast iron, cast aluminum or steel. Tables are generally small, ranging from 6½" × 12" to approximately 14" × 24" on modern constant tension machines. Since much of the work done on scroll saws is small, small tables do not necessarily present a problem.

Most scroll saw tables tilt, but a few models have fixed tables. Tilting tables range from 45 degrees left side tilt only, to 45 degrees left and right sides, to 30 degrees left side, 45 degrees right and 15 degrees front up and 30 degrees front down. The location on the motor and the design of the drive linkage usually determine the tilting versatility. Many scroll saw users seldom tilt the table and when it is necessary, a 45 degree tilt to one side is often sufficient. Don't necessarily rule out a machine because of the lack of table tilting capabilities.

DUST BLOWERS

The dust generated by a scroll saw will quickly cover layout lines on your work if the machine isn't equipped with some type of dust blowing system. Not all machines come with this as a standard item, but some manufacturers offer blowers as an option. You will certainly enjoy using the machine more if it has a blower and if you are planning to use your scroll saw often, you shouldn't even consider a machine without one.

HOLD DOWNS

An adjustable hold down is needed on a scroll saw to help hold the work firmly against the table through the cut. The best hold down will contact the work on both sides of the blade and fit somewhat closely to the blade. Hold downs of this design are especially good for small work and also perform well on larger jobs.

SPEED

Constant tension scroll saws are available as either single speed or variable speed units. Speed ranges from 40 to 2000 strokes per minute are available on variable speed models, and 1660 to 1725 SPM are common for single speed saws. Variable speed saws utilize belts or electronic control systems to change speed. Electronic systems offer the widest range of speed, a feature which is especially nice when you are sawing harder materials like metal, ivory or bone.

Many scroll saw operators find that they only use one speed most of the time and seldom have a need for a wide speed range.

MOTORS

Scroll saw motors are usually small and are often rated by amperage rather than horsepower. Motors will range from 0.9 amps to 3.6 amps with 1.7 to 2 amps being most common. Most units use induction motors which are totally enclosed and fan cooled (TEFC). This design prevents dust from entering and damaging the motor. Induction motors do not adapt well to electronic speed control systems, so saws with this type of control use special DC motors.

OTHER OVERALL ADVANTAGES

Modern constant tension scroll saws are small machines and can easily fit into the typical home shop. The machines are easy to learn to use and scroll work of high quality is possible with little practice. They are among the quietest of all stationary power tools and don't produce excessive amounts of dust.

HEGNER HOBBYMAX

HEGNER MULTIMAX-2
(SUPPLIED WITH STAND)

HEGNER MULTIMAX-3

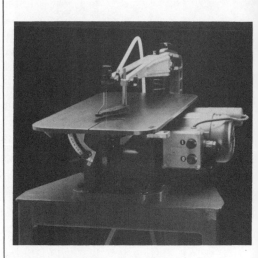

HEGNER POLYMAX-3
(SUPPLIED WITH STAND)

CRAFTSMAN
2076C
SHOWN WITH OPTIONAL STAND

DELTA 40-601
ELECTRONIC

J. PHILIP HUMFREY
EXCALIBUR 24

JET
DSS-15

VEGA
126

WOODMASTER
1600

SCROLL SAW

Brand *No Photo Available	Model	Motor**	Special Features***	Options****	Throat Capacity	Maximum Cutting Depth	Length Cutting Stroke	Cutting Speed (Strokes Per Min.)	Table Size	Arm Style	Overall Dimensions L×W×H	Table Adjustment-Right	Table Adjustment-Left	Drive System	Net Weight	Suggested Retail Price
AMI, LTD (MFG-HEGNER)	Hobbymax	3-12	11-45 33 thru 40	6-7-8 10-11-12	14″	See Special Feature 37	⅓″	1660	6½×12	C-Arm	19×10×9	—	—	Direct	18	$429 w/o stand
AMI, LTD (MFG-HEGNER)	Multimax-2	3-12	1-19-33-34-35 38-41-45	9-10-11-12-13	14.4″	2″	13/16″	1600	7×15	Parallel	19×10×45½	—	—	Direct	50	859
AMI, LTD (MFG-HEGNER)	Multimax-3	3-12	1-19-33-34-35-36 38-39-41-42-45-46	9-10-11 12-13	25″	2″	13/16″ and ⅜″	1200	10×20½	Parallel	31×13×46½	—	—	Direct	92	1499
AMI, LTD (MFG-HEGNER)	Polymax-3	3-12	19-33-34-36-38-39 41-42-44-45-46-47	11-12-13	19.7″	2″	1″ and 9/16″	700, 1100, 1270, 1600	10×19	Parallel	27×15×46½	—	—	Belt	111	1899
CRAFTSMAN	2076C	—	11-44-49 50-51	—	18″	2″	⅞″	1700	9×14⅜	Parallel	28¾×11×12¾	—	—	Direct	29	194^{99}
*CRAFTSMAN	2472C	—	52-53	16	15″	1⅝″	—	3450	8×9½	—	—	45°	45°	Direct	17	99^{99}
*DELTA	40-419	⅓ HP 1-6	8-19-24-59 61-62-64-67-68	19-20 21-22-23	24″	1¾″	1″	610, 910 1255, 1725	14×14	Rigid	36×15×55	45°	15°	Belt	170	1279
DELTA	40-601 Electronic	1-4 13-14-15	1-47 69 thru 75	27	18″	2″	⅞″	40 to 2000	16″ round	C-Arm	30×17¼×47	45°	13°	Direct	132	1074
*FINE TOOL SHOP	204-0001	3	8-54-55-59	—	20″	2″	—	1100	10×10	Rigid	27.2×10×19.2	20°	20°	—	35	299^{95}
*FINE TOOL SHOP	204-0002	3	8-19-47 56-57-58-59	—	20″	2″	1″	1100	12×16	Rigid	28.8×12×23.6	20°	20°	—	101	649^{95}
J. PHILIP HUMFREY (MFG-EXCALIBUR)	Excalibur 24	.25 HP	1 thru 10 15-16	—	24″	2¼″	¾″	0 to 1800	14×24	Parallel	33×20×	20°	45°	Direct	110	1285
*J. PHILIP HUMFREY (MFG-EXCALIBUR)	Excalibur 11	See Options 1-2	11-12-13-14-15	—	19″	1¾″	¾″	See Options 1-2	12×17¼	Double Parallel	37×12×14	45°	45°	Belt	45	495 w/o motor
JET	DSS-15	⅛ HP 1-4	11	—	15″	2″	½″	1725	8×16½	Parallel	18½×9⅞×10¾	45°	45°	Direct	42	179
*POWERMATIC	Model 95 1950100	⅓ HP 1-6	8-19-24 61 thru 67	17-18	24″	1¾″	—	807 to 1653	14×15	Rigid	36×14×54¼	45°	15°	Belt	220	1267
*RBI INDUSTRIES	Hawk	⅛ HP 4	48	14-15	12″	2″	⅝″	1725	11×16	Parallel	—	See Special Feature 48		Direct	48	349

SCROLL SAW

Brand *No Photo Available	Model	Motor**	Special Features***	Options****	Throat Capacity	Maximum Cutting Depth	Length Cutting Stroke	Cutting Speed (Strokes Per Min.)	Table Size	Arm Style	Overall Dimensions L×W×H	Table Adjustment-Right	Table Adjustment-Left	Drive System	Net Weight	Suggested Retail Price
*RBI INDUSTRIES	Hawk 14	⅛ HP 4	—	14-15	14"	2"	$^{13}/_{16}$"	1720	10½×21	Parallel	—	45°	45°	Direct	73	499
*RBI INDUSTRIES	Hawk 20	⅛ HP 4	—	14-15	20"	2"	1⅛"	595 & 1110	14¼×25	Parallel	—	45°	20°	Belt	97	699
*RBI INDUSTRIES	Hawk 26	⅛ HP 4	—	14-15	26"	2½"	$1^{1}/_{16}$"	0 to 1650	14¼×24	Parallel	—	45°	45°	Direct	138	1299
*SUNHILL (MFG-REXON)	SS-15	¹/₁₀ HP 5	34-60	—	15"	2"	¾"	1725	7⅞×17	Parallel	—	—	—	Direct	44	285

(PRICES INCLUDE FREIGHT TO THE NEAREST TERMINAL OF OUR HOUSE CARRIER [SUNHILL])

Brand *No Photo Available	Model	Motor**	Special Features***	Options****	Throat Capacity	Maximum Cutting Depth	Length Cutting Stroke	Cutting Speed (Strokes Per Min.)	Table Size	Arm Style	Overall Dimensions L×W×H	Table Adjustment-Right	Table Adjustment-Left	Drive System	Net Weight	Suggested Retail Price
VEGA	126	⅓ HP 1 or 2 7-10-11	1 22 thru 32	5	26"	2½"	—	430 to 1725	14×14	Rigid	31×21×52½	45°	45°	Belt	235	1200
WOODMASTER	1600	⅛ HP 4-8-9	1-17-18 19-20-21	3-4	16"	2"	$^{15}/_{16}$"	1725	9¾×15⅝	Parallel	23×14½×39½	45°	45°	Direct	65	649

***MOTOR

1. Single phase
2. Three phase
3. 110V
4. 115V
5. 110/220V
6. 115/230V
7. TEFC
8. Totally enclosed
9. Permanently lubricated ball bearings
10. Magnetic relay
11. Fusetron overload protection
12. Oversized induction motor, rated for continuous duty
13. Solid state
14. Electronic
15. Permanent magnet

**SPECIAL FEATURES

1. Includes stand.
2. Frame is one piece casting.
3. Parallel arms move on permanently lubricated adjustable dual ball bearings.
4. Blade is pulled (not pushed) on both the up and down stroke.
5. Upper and lower ball bearing mounted blade chucks.
6. Smooth operation is assured by counter-balanced crankshaft.
7. Blade chucks have hardened tool steel jaws; cannot be thrown from machine if the blade breaks.
8. Air driven blower pump to remove sawdust.
9. Power take-off.
10. Stand has special design which allows rear leg to be weighted with sand.
11. Benchtop model.
12. Three step pulley.
13. Blade tension can be adjusted while saw is running.
14. Double parallel arm system eliminates blade flexing; allows more cutting strokes per minute when using fine blades.
15. Rod saws available for cutting glass and ceramic material.
16. Arm movement is controlled by connecting rod and crankshaft.
17. Table is precision machined from ribbed casting; slotted for quick blade mounting.
18. Blade suspension is by two pivoting blade clamps made of hardened alloy steel.
19. Workpiece hold-down arm.
20. Tensioning rod is fully adjustable.
21. Parallel arms are supported on both sides by heavy castings.
22. Table tilts front and back 45°.
23. Table height from floor is 39½".
24. Entire crank assembly runs in an oil bath

25. for long life.
25. Solid steel drive shaft.
26. Heavy gray iron table and support yoke.
27. Crankshaft runs in two double sealed lubricated for life ball bearings.
28. Blade tension is provided by a tension spring instead of compressed spring.
29. Overarm is formed from structural grade steel tubing.
30. Blade guides have hardened roller sides and back with thumbscrew adjustment.
31. Blades can be changed fast with a single wrench.
32. Pre-loaded cam allows blade change without disturbing spring tension or upper assembly adjustment.
33. Patented blade suspension consisting of two pivoting hardened steel blade clamps supported in "V" grooves.
34. Work table tilts from 0° to 45°.
35. Aluminum work table.
36. Cast iron base and frame.
37. Maximum cutting depth: soft wood—1½", hardwood—1".
38. Parallel arms and C-arms constructed of light metal fatigue-resistant alloys.
39. All drive parts are supported by high quality sealed ball bearings.
40. Features a new frame suspension without bearings to eliminate blade breakage and frame wobble (patent pending).
41. Patented blade suspension and parallel arm design keeps the blade under constant tension and perpendicular to the workpiece throughout the cutting stroke.
42. Sleeve arm support bearing.
43. Cast zinc base and frame.
44. Standard sawdust blower.
45. Bases and frames are ribbed, warp-proofed castings, precision machined.

46. Two stroke setting.
47. Cast iron table.
48. Fixed table; does not tilt.
49. Blade tilts 45° right and left.
50. Die cast aluminum construction.
51. Plastic hold down guard.
52. Steel frame and table.
53. Side mounted accessory power take-off.
54. Hinged arm.
55. Cast aluminum frame and table.
56. Cast aluminum frame.
57. Blade can be adjusted to cut in any direction.
58. Guide roller to keep the blade straight.
59. Blade tensioning adjustment.
60. Arm cover completely encloses rocker arm for safe operation.
61. Table tilts 45° to the front.
62. Height from table to floor is 42¼".
63. Two piece cast iron base and overarm.
64. Overarm removable for use as a saber saw.
65. Choice of variable speed or four speed drive.
66. Blade guide is hardened steel with a back roller assembly.
67. Can be used as a jig saw, saber saw, or filing machine.
68. Universal blade guide and roller support rigidly supports all types of blades.
69. Table tilts 15° up and 30° down.
70. Table rotates 90°.
71. Table height from floor is 42".
72. Cutting strokes per minute digital readout.
73. Electronic controller maintains constant blade speed and torque under all cutting conditions.
74. Ball and roller bearing construction throughout.
75. Pivoting-type blade chucks for extra fast blade changing and tensioning.

****OPTIONS

1. #11804, .25 HP, 1725 RPM, 110/220V motor, three speed 400/800/1400, $119.99.
2. #118VS, .25 HP, variable speed, 0-1800 RPM, 110V only, $399.50.
3. #700, dust blower, $29.95.
4. #W14, gooseneck work lamp, $16.95.
5. #4151, saber blade support, $16.50.
6. Sawdust blower, $24.
7. Hold down arm, $29.
8. Heavy duty 3 legged, welded steel stand, 34½", $75.
9. Electronic speed control, $319.
10. Off/on foot switch, $49.
11. Coolant fluid reservoir with foot pump (used with hard metals), $79.

12. #HLX-3, illuminated magnification system with bulb and bracket, $109.
13. #HLX-2, combination incandescent/fluorescent lamp with bulbs and bracket, $104.
14. #2LK, flexible shaft light, $27.50.
15. #2MK, 2:1 magnifier light, $79.
16. #9 HT 2471, sander accessory and flexible power take-off kit, $35.99.
17. #6470208, ⅓ HP, three phase, 1800 RPM, 200V motor, $104.
18. #6470215, ⅓ HP, three phase, 1800 RPM, 230/460V motor, $114.
19. 40-409, same as 40-419, except has variable speed, $1,352.
20. #40-416, has ⅓ HP, single phase motor,

24V pushbutton magnetic control system with overload protection (LVC), $1,463.
21. #40-406, same as #40-416, except has variable speed, $1,529.
22. #40-417, has ⅓ HP, three phase motor, 24V pushbutton magnetic control system with 3-leg overload protection (LVC), $1,499.
23. #40-407, same as #40-47, except has variable speed, $1,559.
24. #25-858, lamp attachment, $26.65.
25. #40-711, sanding attachment, $30.05.
26. #40-204, lower saber saw blade guides, $12.70.
27. #25-858, gooseneck lamp.

PLANER OR SURFACER

Surfacers or planers are single purpose machines designed to plane wood to uniform thickness. When properly adjusted, these precision machines should be capable of producing work accurate to thousandths of an inch. Single surfacers are most common in small shops. These machines have only one cutterhead and cut on only one surface at a time. Large double surfacers are used in industry and cut on two surfaces with one pass through the machine.

A surfacer gives the woodworker the option of effectively using rough, unsurfaced lumber, which can result in a material cost savings. This machine also makes it possible to produce precise boards of any thickness within the range of the machine. There are many times when special thicknesses are required, and a planer makes this job so easy.

Woodworking without a planer is certainly possible, and many hobbyist do it. They will either purchase wood already surfaced, surface it by hand or with a jointer, surface it through machine sanding, or pay someone to surface it for them.

Planers are relatively expensive machines costing from approximately $800 to over $15,000. Because of this, they are often one of the last major machines a hobbyist will purchase. Prices increase as the size of the machine increases. Planer sizes are usually spoken of in terms of the maximum width of stock which can be surfaced. Width capacities range from 12″ to 52″ with 12″ through 30″ sizes being most common. You will generally find 12″ to 24″ machines in small shops. The maximum thickness of stock which can be surfaced is another size consideration. Thickness capacities will range from 4″ to over 8″.

The basic parts of a single surfacer include infeed table, outfeed table, center table, cutterhead, infeed rollers, chip breaker, outfeed rollers, pressure bar, table adjusting handle, motor, and base.

ROLLERS

The rollers used to feed and support the stock as it passes through the machine vary in design and location from one machine to another. Rollers can be classified in the following ways: infeed rollers and outfeed or delivery rollers, powered rollers and idlers, corrugated rollers and smooth rollers, sectional rollers and solid rollers.

Infeed rollers are the rollers which first grip the stock and feed it into the cutterhead.

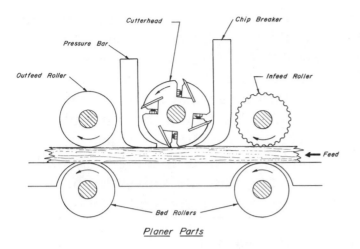

Planer Parts

Surfacers will have one or two infeed rollers. The roller above the table is the one that actually grips the stock and pulls it forward. Upper infeed rollers are designed in several ways. Rubber covered rollers are used on some smaller machines, and this design has one big advantage, it doesn't mar the surface of the board. This gives you the ability to take very light cuts on the planer without worrying about roller marks on the surface. The life expectancy of rubber rollers is considerably less than other designs.

Solid corrugated steel has been a common upper roller design for many years. The corrugations on the roller's surface actually dig into the top of the wood as it is fed into the machine. Shallow indentations are left in the surface of the board as it leaves the feed roller, and the cut must be deep enough to remove these depressions, therefore, very shallow cuts are not possible. Some manufacturers also offer sectional upper infeed rollers. This type of roller is made in spring loaded steel sections which are corrugated on the outer surface. The sections will conform to the surface of uneven stock and feed it through the machine in a straight line. Larger, more expensive machines, will generally have sectional upper infeed rollers.

Planers may also have an infeed roller in the bed or at the end of the infeed table. This steel roller will have a smooth surface and may or may not be powered. On some machines this roller is only an idler, but on more expensive machines, it will be powered and turn with the upper infeed roller. You will find some small planers without the bed rollers. In this case, the stock simply slides across a solid planer bed. With this design the bed must be very smooth to reduce friction. Bed rollers, of course, would reduce friction and make movement through the machine consistently smooth.

Planers have one or two smooth, solid steel or rubber delivery rollers that feed the stock after it has left the infeed rollers. The upper roller will be powered but the lower roller may only be an idler used to reduce friction.

CHIPBREAKER

The chipbreaker, located between the upper infeed roller and the cutterhead, serves two purposes. It helps hold the stock down against the planer table and, as its name implies, helps prevent torn grain. This part can be either solid or made in spring loaded sections. Sectional chipbreakers are found on better machines. They will exert downward pressure on stock even when you are feeding pieces which vary slightly in thickness.

CUTTERHEAD

Cutterheads are cylindrical steel units with two or more knives. Two knife cutterheads have become rather common on some of the newer small surfacers. Two knife machines will usually operate at a higher RPM than machines with 3 or more knives. Large surfacers will generally have 3 to 5 knives.

Planers are famous for being noisy machines. Much of the noise they create is due to the traditional straight knife configuration. Special "quiet design" cutterheads are now available on larger machines which

97

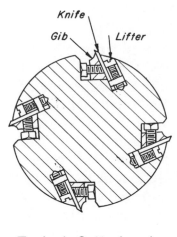

Typical Cutterhead

actually have knives in a helical pattern. This feature is generally expensive, but if your planer is to be used in production situations, the noise reduction may be well worth the investment.

Knife sharpening and changing is a common maintenance activity on a planer. With large machines it may be possible to purchase a knife grinding attachment which mounts on the machine making it possible to grind the knives in the cutterhead. Smaller machines do not usually offer this option and knives must be removed, sharpened, and replaced. The ease of knife adjustment and replacement is an important consideration in surfacer selection. Look over the owners manual carefully and see if you can figure out the knife adjustment procedure.

It is a good idea to purchase an extra set of knives for the cutterhead at the time you buy a new machine. It is certainly nice to have a back-up knife set to install whenever needed. If you use the machine as a production tool the importance of a back-up set increases.

PRESSURE BAR

The pressure bar is an adjustable, solid steel bar which is located just behind the cutterhead and it holds the stock firmly against the bed after the cut is made. A common problem in surfacer operation has to do with an improperly adjusted pressure bar. If the pressure bar is adjusted too high, which is frequently the case, the end of the

---

With large machines it may be possible to purchase a knife grinding attachment which mounts on the machine making it possible to grind the knives in the cutterhead.

---

work will move upward into the cutterhead as soon as it leaves the chipbreaker. The board will have a deeper cut on the last 1½" to 3". This defect is called a "sniped end" and is easy to remedy by simply lowering the pressure bar to a correct setting. Sometimes the pressure bar will vibrate out of adjustment. Better machines will have locking features on the pressure bar to prevent this problem.

DUST COLLECTION

Surfacers rank close to sanders in terms of dust production. You can use this machine without a dust collector but in doing so, you are creating an unhealthy, hazardous environment. Some type of dust collection system should be attached to the surfacer. Small portable collectors are available which function beautifully on small machines. Dust collectors may seem expensive, but when you think about exactly what they are doing for you and your health, they are worth serious consideration.

Be sure that the surfacer you purchase has a convenient means of installing a dust collection fitting. With some machines, a shaving hood is included as a standard item, but with others, it is an optional accessory.

BED DESIGN

Surfacer beds are generally made from cast iron. Be sure to inspect the castings carefully for cracks and straightness. The depth of cut is changed on most machines by raising and lowering the bed. This up and down movement is made possible by heavy screws or sliding wedge shaped castings.

Some small planers have a fixed bed, and the cutterhead assembly is moved up and down to change the cut depth. With this design, it is easy to add infeed and outfeed extensions or rollers to handle long stock.

You will find that some woodworkers prefer the wedge bed planers for accuracy while others prefer a screw lifting system. It is probably best to talk to the owner of one of the planers you are considering and ask about bed adjustment and accuracy problems.

It is important that the raising and lowering mechanism be accurate and rugged enough to hold up under many adjustments since the depth of cut is changed repeatedly.

An adjustable depth-of-cut gauge is usually provided on the infeed side of the bed. If set properly, this gauge will tell you how thick the wood will be after it passes through the machine.

FEED RATE

Many small planers will have a relatively slow, fixed feed rate ranging from approximately 15 to 20 feet per minute. Larger machines have variable feeds ranging from 15 to 100 feet per minute. The feed rate through the machine will determine the cuts per inch on the stock. Slower feeds will produce more cuts per inch and a smoother surface than faster feeds. Production output of the machine, of course, is reduced as the feed rate is decreased. The optimum feed rate for a planer is actually different for each application. Production shops will choose the fastest rate which yields stock of acceptable surface quality. In small shops, where production output isn't important, slower rates are used to produce the smoothest surfaces.

DRIVE SYSTEM

Small surfacers will usually have only one motor. This motor will drive both the cutterhead and the feed rollers. Cutterheads are often belt driven, and the feed rollers are either gear or chain driven. Large machines sometimes have separate motors for the feed system and cutterhead, and in some cases, the cutterhead will be direct drive.

MOTORS

Even with the smallest planers, the cutterhead must have enough power to take a fairly wide cut, therefore, planers generally have large motors. The smallest motors are usually at least 2 HP, and large machines will have motors up to 15 HP. With a planer, you should plan to use 220 single phase or three phase wiring.

USE IDEAS

Planers should be anchored securely to the floor for best performance. Even small, so called "portable" units, need a firm base. Surfacing long heavy boards can cause serious damage to a planer if the work isn't handled carefully, especially on small machines. If long boards are not supported properly, they can exert such a powerful force that they can destroy the entire upper feed system of the machine. Anytime you have long pieces to surface, be sure to carefully support the piece on both the infeed and outfeed side of the machine.

A single surfacer will not straighten a warped board. Boards must be flattened on one side on a jointer before surfacing if warp free pieces are needed.

In addition to machines that are designed to be planers only, there are also multi-purpose models that perform more than one function. Most prevalent of these is the planer/jointer. One comparison chart in this section lists planers by themselves, while another gives the data for the planer/jointer.

DELTA
22-651

GRIZZLY
G1021

HITACHI
P-100F

GENERAL
130

JET
708530

JET
708560

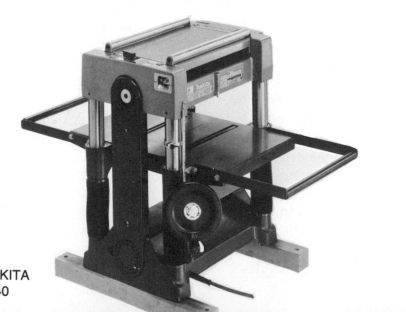

MAKITA
2040

PARKS
97

PARKS
20

POWERMATIC
100

POWERMATIC
Q225

PRO SHOP
SP-20

SHOPSMITH 12"
555082

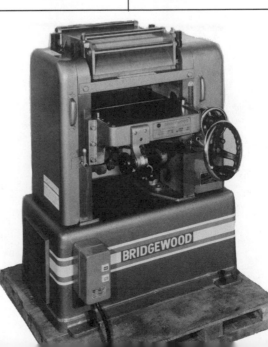

BRIDGEWOOD
SHG-1300AV

BRIDGEWOOD
BWC-508

BRIDGEWOOD
SHG-200A

BRIDGEWOOD
R-500

BRIDGEWOOD
AP-2400

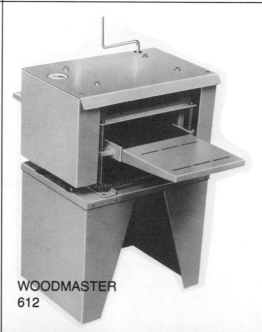

BRIDGEWOOD
SHG-610-AV

BRIDGEWOOD
RE-40

WOODMASTER
612

WILLIAMS & HUSSEY
MODEL W-75

PLANER

Brand *No Photo Available	Model	Motor**	Special Features***	Options****	Capacity W × T	Minimum Length of Stock	Maximum Depth of Cut	Cutterhead Speed (RPM)	Stock Feed (SFPM)	Construction	Overall Dimensions W × D × H	Infeed Rollers	Bed Rollers Quantity/ Type	Cutter-Head Knives	Drive	Shipping Weight	Suggested Retail Price
DELTA	22-651	2 HP 1-4-5-9-10	4-5-6 7-8-9-10	5-6-7 8-9-10	13 × 5.9	10″	⅛″	4500	15½	CI	27 × 27 × 26	Spiral Serrated	2-A	3	B	295	$1729
*DELTA	22-600	7.5 HP 2-4-9-10	4-5-6-7-10 11-12-13-14-15	11	24.8 × 9.45	11″	$\frac{39}{100}$″	5000	25 to 46	CI	35½ × 42½ × 39½	Spiral Serrated	2-A	4	B	1675 Net	6496
*DELTA	22-460	7.5 HP 2-4-9-10	5-7-10-12-13 14-17-18-19-20	12	20 × 9	11″	$\frac{5}{16}$″	5000	25 to 46	CI	36 × 35 × 42	Spiral Serrated	2-A	4	B	1160 Net	4667
*DELTA	22-432	3 HP 1-4-9-10	4-5-7 16-21-22	13-14-15	13 × 6	6″	⅛″	4500	10 to 20	CI	31 × 26 × 39	Spiral Serrated	2-A	3	B	598	4754
GRIZZLY	G1021	2 HP 1-4-5-9-10	1-5-10 20-23-24	18-19-20	15 × 6	—	⅛″	4500	11½	CI-S	Table 15 × 20	Spiral Serrated	2	3	B	530	795
HITACHI	P-100F	2.7 HP 2-3	25-26	21	$12\frac{5}{32}$ × 6⅝	—	⅞″	—	26	—	$25\frac{2}{5} \times 28\frac{7}{8} \times 29\frac{1}{10}$	—	2	—	—	256	1605
J. PHILIP HUMFREY (MFG-GENERAL)	130	See Option #92	1-4 74-75-81	92-93-94 95-96-97-98	14 × 6	7″	⅛″	4500	15	CI	24½ × 30 × 43½	Corregated	2	3	B	520	2526 w/o motor
*J. PHILIP HUMFREY (MFG-GENERAL)	330	See Option #92	69-74-76 77-78-79-80	93-98-99 100-101-102	20 × 8	10¾″	⅜″	4000	20 to 55	CI-S	47 × 40 × 44	Corregated solid or Sectional	—	4	—	2040	5623^{70} w/o motor
JET	708530	2 HP 1-3 or 4	9-23-27	—	15⅝ × 7⅝	—	—	6500	29.5	CI	22½ × 40⅜ × 28⅛	Neoprene	2	2	B	265	1185
JET	708560	5 HP 2-4	10-20-28	—	20 × 7	8″	¼″	5600	26.3	CI	41 × 34 × 50	—	2	3	B	1058	2599
MAKITA	2040	2 HP 3	9-23-27-29	22	15⅝ × 7⅝	—	—	6500	29.5	—	22½ × 28⅛ × 40⅜	Neoprene	2	2	B	353	1780
PARKS	97	2 HP 1-4-10	30-31-32	23-24	12 × 4	6″	⅛″	4000	16	CI	22 × 14 × 22	Fluted Steel	2	3	B	—	1622
PARKS	20	5 HP 2-4-9	28-30	25	20 × 6	—	⅜″	3600	20-40 40-80	SS	36 × 41 × 47	Fluted Steel	2	4	B	1425	4471
POWERMATIC	100	See Options 27 thru 32	1-4-30-33 34-35-36	33 thru 45	12 × 5	7½″	¼″	5300	18	CI	Bed 12 × 24	Corregated Steel	2	3	B	410	2567 w/o motor

PLANER

Brand *No Photo Available	Model	Motor**	Special Features***	Options****	Capacity W × T	Minimum Length of Stock	Maximum Depth of Cut	Cutterhead Speed (RPM)	Stock Feed (SFPM)	Construction	Overall Dimensions W × D × H	Infeed Rollers	Bed Rollers Quantity/Type	Cutter-Head Knives	Drive	Shipping Weight	Suggested Retail Price
*POWERMATIC	180	See Options 28-31-32 46 thru 50	1-37	38-41-42 51 thru 60	18×6	4"	½"	4800	15 to 37	CI	Bed 18×32	Sectional	2-A	3	B	1225 Net	$4309 w/o motor
*POWERMATIC	Q180	Same as Model 180	1-38-39	38-41-42 51 thru 55 58 thru 65	18×6	4"	½"	3600 (FPM)	15 to 37	CI	Bed 18×32	Sectional	2-A	27	B	1255 Net	6216 w/o motor
*POWERMATIC	225	See Option 47 thru 50 68 thru 72	1-36-37-40 41-42-76	41-42-67 73 thru 78	24×8	4"	½"	See Option #66	20 to 100	CI	Bed 24×48	Corrugated Steel-Sectional	2-A	4	—	2885	10,720
POWERMATIC	Q225	Same as Model 225	1-35-37-40 41-42-43-76	41-42-65-67 73-74-75 78 thru 82	24×8	4"	½"	See Option #66	20 to 100	CI	Bed 24×48	Corrugated Steel-Sectional	2-A	36	—	2885	11,640
PRO SHOP	SP20	3 HP 2-3 or 4	27-44 45-46-47	—	20×6	8"	¼"	5600	25	CI	Table 27×21½	Serrated Steel	2-A	3	B	924	2295
*PRO SHOP	SP24	5 HP 2-3 or 4	27-44 45-46-47	—	24×6	8"	¼"	5600	25	CI	Table 30×25½	Serrated Steel	2-A	3	B	1012	3295
SHOPSMITH	555082	1.5 HP 3	71-72	—	12×4	—	⅛"	5750	7 to 20	CI	—	—	—	3	—	151 Net	999
*SUNHILL (MFG-CHIU TING)	CT-38B	3 HP 1-4-6	44	83	15×6	—	¼"	—	13 and 20	CI-S	Table 19×15	—	2	3	—	480	1650
*SUNHILL (MFG-CHANG IRON)	CM-20	3 HP 1-6	28-44	—	20×7	—	¼"	5600	26	CI	—	—	2	3	—	815 Net	3500
*SUNHILL (MFG-CHANG IRON)	CM-510	See Option #84	44-48	—	20×9	—	5/16"	5200	18 to 36	CI	—	Segmented	2	3	—	1188 Net	4650
*SUNHILL (MFG-WOODPECKER)	CM-36	7.5 HP 2	48	—	26×5½	—	—	5500	20	—	—	—	—	3	—	1800	6250
*SUNHILL (MFG-CHENG KUANG)	SP-24	5 HP 2-6	—	—	24×6	—	—	6000	25	—	—	—	—	3	—	1200	4500
*TOTAL SHOP	TS15-6	2 HP 3 or 4	4-49-50-51	85	15×6	—	⅛"	4500	16½	CI	—	Serrated Steel	2	3	B	368	1295

(FREIGHT PAID TO NEAREST TERMINAL OF OUR HOUSE CARRIER [SUNHILL])

PLANER

Brand *No Photo Available	Model	Motor**	Special Features***	Options****	Capacity W × T	Minimum Length of Stock	Maximum Depth of Cut	Cutterhead Speed (RPM)	Stock Feed (SFPM)	Construction	Overall Dimensions W × D × H	Infeed Rollers	Bed Rollers Quantity/ Type	Cutter-Head Knives	Drive	Shipping Weight	Suggested Retail Price
WILKE MACHINERY (MFG-BRIDGEWOOD)	SHG-1300	3 HP 1-4	27-52 53-54-55	86	13×6	—	⅛″	5300	26	CI	26×25×40	Segmented and Serrated	2	3	B	800	$1895
WILKE MACHINERY (MFG-BRIDGEWOOD)	BWC-508	5 HP 1-2-4-5	20-27-30 52 thru 58	87	20×9	9″	5/16″	5200	12 to 25	CI	Bed 31¾×21⅝	Segmented and Serrated	2-A	3	B	1276	3895
WILKE MACHINERY (MFG-BRIDGEWOOD)	SHG-200A	5 HP 1-2-4-5	20-27-30-58 52 thru 56	—	20×6	—	—	5000	26¼	CI	Bed 27×21½	Segmented and Serrated	2-A	3	B	1000	2995
WILKE MACHINERY (MFG-BRIDGEWOOD)	R-500	See Special Feature #59	52-59 60-61-62	—	19.75×19.2	—	—	4500	16 and 52	CI	—	—	—	4	B	1176	4195
WILKE MACHINERY (MFG-BRIDGEWOOD)	AP-2400	5 HP 1-2	27-52-56	—	24×__	—	—	5000	26	CI	Table 28×25	Segmented	—	3	B	990	3995
WILKE MACHINERY (MFG-BRIDGEWOOD)	SHG-610-AV	See Special Feature #65	20-27-63 64-66-67	88-90	24×8	—	—	—	15 to 45	CI	—	See Special Feature #64	2-A	4	B	1870	5995
WILKE MACHINERY (MFG-BRIDGEWOOD)	RE-40	3 HP 1 or 2-4	60-68-69-70	91	15.75×8	—	¼″	4500	16 and 42	CI	34×33×43	Serrated	—	4	B	650 Net	2595
THE FOLLOWING ARE COMBINATION MOLDER-PLANERS:																	
*CRAFTSMAN	9HT 23365N	5 HP 4-5-7-8-9-10	1-2-3	1-2-3-4	12×6	—	3/16″	4500	12	CI-S	—	Rubber	—	3	B	356	1399.99
*WOODMASTER	408	1 HP 3-5	88	117-118-119 120-121-126	8¼×4	10″	3/32″	4200	22	—	—	Molded Rubber	—	3	B	155	784
WOODMASTER	612	3 HP 1-4	48-88	117-119-122-123 124-125-126	12⅜×6	10″	3/16″	4200	11 and 32	—	—	Molded Rubber	—	3	B	280	1190
WILLIAMS & HUSSEY	W-75	See Options #113-114-115	48-83 84-85-86-87	105 thru 112 103-104-116	See Special Feature #82	6″	¼″	7000	15	CI	14⅞×14×17¼	—	—	2	B	80	740 w/o motor

****MOTOR**
1. Single phase
2. Three phase
3. 110V; 115V
4. 220V; 230V
5. Ballbearing
6. Sealed bearing
7. Totally enclosed
8. Permanently lubricated
9. Starter
10. Overload protection

CONSTRUCTION
CI —Cast Iron
S —Steel Stand
SS —Semi-Steel

DRIVE
B—Belt
A—Adjustable

***SPECIAL FEATURES**

1. Ball bearing cutterhead.
2. Cuts moulding up to ¾" deep.
3. Automatic motor shut-off when hood is raised.
4. Instantaneous disengagement of feed.
5. Oil-bath lubricated feed/gear box—chain drive.
6. Feed pressure adjustment.
7. Includes knife setting gauge.
8. Stationary table—cutterhead and feed group adjust for material thickness allowing use of table extensions.
9. Portable.
10. Anti-kickback fingers for added safety.
11. Grouped controls include inch/metric scale.
12. Feed rate decreases proportionately with slow down of cutterhead speed when the machine is under a heavy load.
13. Cutterhead assembly and feed groups are mounted in a modular fashion, permitting easy disassembly for maintenance.
14. Table raises and lowers on four precision self-locking screws. Alignment is achieved by steel gibs. Screws are protected by rubber boots.
15. Includes one extra set of knives.
16. 24 voltage control.
17. Power operated table.
18. Lumber gauge on the front edge of table allows the operator to measure stock before planing.
19. Adjustable rear pressure bar and double outfeed rolls.
20. Includes dust chute.
21. Cartridge-type cutterhead; knives are replaced by removing entire assembly. Spacers can be purchased as options.

22. Sealed, lubricated ball bearings.
23. Table is raised and lowered on two adjusting screws. Built in table gibs compensate for wear. Infeed and outfeed roller table extensions are included.
24. Supported by four columns.
25. Two height setting gauges, one tool box, one driver, one wrench, one box wrench, one blade are included.
26. Spring system method allows simple adjustment of edge height.
27. Rollers on top of machine for returning stock.
28. Gear driven.
29. Ball and needle bearing construction.
30. Ball bearing construction.
31. Individual micro blade adjustment.
32. Open end base for easy cleaning and motor adjusting.
33. Cutterhead unit may be lifted free by removing feed drive, pulley, and two locking screws from flange mounting.
34. Bed size extra large (12" × 24").
35. Jackscrew system to speed accurate knife setting.
36. Bed raised by Acme-thread screws which operate in ball thrust bearings.
37. "Kuik-set" feature offers lever controlled table roll height adjustment from 0 to .040.
38. Cutterhead contains 27 high speed steel knife segments, stagger mounted to create a spiral cutting concept.
39. Curtains of acoustical material at entrance and exit areas.
40. Power feed control is driven by 1½ HP motor, totally enclosed, mounted in machine base; included in basic price of

machine. Cutterhead is driven by separate motor. Motor and controls are options.
41. Sectional infeed roll, corregated cast iron sections mounted on milled alloy steel spline shaft. Reversible without damage.
42. Machine standard equipped with magnetic controls protecting *both* feed and drive motor. With this safety feature *both* motors shut off instantly in the event of overload, low voltage and power failure. Motors will not restart until activated by operator.
43. Cutterhead contains 36 high speed steel knife segments, stagger mounted to create a spiral cutting concept.
44. Prices include delivery in the continental U.S.
45. Chipbreaker flips back, exposing blades and rollers for easy adjustment.
46. Feed rollers have both height and spring tension adjustment.
47. Chain drive to feed rollers.
48. Sealed bearings are used throughout machine.
49. Bed rollers positioned under feed rollers to aid stock movement.
50. Feed roller is spring loaded and adjustable.
51. Oil bath lubricated feed/gear box.
52. All machines are run-in and tested before shipment.
53. Automatic stock feed—chain drive.
54. Double jackscrew height adjustment.
55. Knife setting device.
56. Pushbutton switch, magnetic control.
57. Cutterhead has 5 HP motor, feed has 1 HP motor.
58. Easy adjustment on all feed and bed rollers.
59. Choice of three phase 5.5 HP or single

***SPECIAL FEATURES (CON'T)

phase 5 HP motor; feed motor is 1 HP.
60. Anti kick-back pawls.
61. Two powered advance rollers allowing thickness planing of short parts.
62. Balanced and counterweighted cutterhead.
63. Smooth powered outfeed roll.
64. Dual powered infeed rolls, segmented and serrated cast iron, spring loaded.
65. Choice of single phase 5 HP cutterhead motor and 1 HP feed motor or three phase 7.5 HP cutterhead motor and 1 HP feed motor.
66. Magnetic started with pushbutton control panel.
67. Electric ammeter.
68. Feed motor is .75 HP, 220V, 1725 RPM, single or three phase.

69. Cutterhead and infeed rollers ride in pre-lubricated sealed bearings.
70. All rollers are height and pressure adjustable.
71. Cast iron table with portable casters.
72. Feed motor is 1/20 HP.
73. Shopsmith also manufactures two planers which mount on the Shopsmith Mark V.
74. The table travels on column ways with adjustable gibs.
75. Raised or lowered through helical gears.
76. All feed rolls, top and bottom, are power driven.
77. Motor recommended: 5 HP to 7.5 HP.
78. Table is heavy, ribbed one piece casting.
79. Elevating screws are mounted on thrust bearings.

80. The knives are held in place by chipbreaker and jackscrews.
81. Recommended motor: .5 HP to 3 HP.
82. Capacity of molder may be any width. Open side machine permits processing stock regardless of width. Maximum thickness is 8¼". Capacity for the planer is 7" × 8¼".
83. Maximum molding cut is ¾".
84. Rubber covered infeed rollers.
85. Takes two minutes to change from molder to planer, or vice versa.
86. Produces more than 98% of all types of molding and pattern materials used today.
87. Power infeed and outfeed rolls.
88. Bed is one piece cast iron.

****OPTIONS

1. Same as #9 HT 23365N, except has 2 HP motor, 303 lbs., $1,249.99.
2. Smaller version of #9 HT 23365N, $649.99.
3. Knife setting gauge, $14.95.
4. Replacement knives, set of three, $34.99.
5. Same as #22-651, except includes a 3 HP, 220V, three phase motor. Manual start, no overload protection, wired ready to run, $1,775.
6. Planer without motor, $1,445.
7. #22-658, shaving hood, mounts to planer to be connected to a dust system, $44.05.
8. #50-315, steel stand, $72.80.
9. #49-364, retractable casters, $61.60.
10. #50-651, new steel stand, includes #50-315 stand with two 24" × 14½" folding type tables with high pressure laminate coating and two industrial quality wheels for portability, $276.
11. #22-604, dust chute, $77.80.
12. #22-461, same as #22-460, except with 5 HP, 230V, single phase motor, same price.
13. #22-435, 3 HP, three phase motor, 230/460V, $4,632.

14. #22-436, 5 HP, three phase motor, 230/460V, $4,632.
15. #22-420, ball bearing, 3 knife cutterhead; includes set of three HSS knives, knife adjusting screw, bearings and bearing housing, $548.15.
16. #22-426, knife grinding and jointing attachment, complete with grinding wheel and motor. Allows for grinding without removing knives from the cutterhead, $761.90.
17. #22-422, shaving hood, for use with a dust system, $122.20.
18. #G1196, three HSS blades, $49.95 PPD.
19. #G1037, three carbide tipped blades, $270.
20. #G1197, stand, $49.95 PPD.
21. #948957, blade sharpening holder; #216001, carbide blade; #949002, grinding stone; no prices available.
22. Speed reducing kit available for extra smooth cutting.
23. Direct drive model available.
24. Available with 3 HP motor.
25. Available with 10 HP motor.
26. Knife grinding attachment, $1,076.
27. #6471707, 2 HP, single phase motor, 115/230V, $194.
28. #6472013, 3 HP, single phase motor, 115/230V, $388.
29. #6471706, 2 HP, three phase motor, 230/460V, $190.
30. #6471717, 2 HP, three phase motor, 200V, $179.
31. #6472026, 3 HP, three phase motor, 230/460V, $308.
32. #6472027, 3 HP, three phase motor, 200V, $258.
33. #2398383, single phase switch, 115/230V, $115.
34. #2398385, single phase, magnetic controls, 115/230V, $259.
35. #2398486, single phase, magentic controls, 115/230V with 24V transformer, $329.
36. #2398185, three phase magnetic controls, 200/230/460/575V, $280.
37. #2398204, three phase switch, 200/230/460/575V, $101.
38. #2398230, three phase JIC controls, 200/230/460/575V, $718.
39. #2398481, three phase magnetic controls, 200/230/460/575V with 24V transformer, $352.
40. 3 HP motors require minimum of magnetic controls.
41. #2230002, bed and feed roll gauge, $89.
42. #2230007, cutterhead gauge, $87.
43. #2258010, grinding attachment with indexing mechanism, $747.
44. #2292018, shaving hood, $61.
45. #6427003, set of three replacement knives, $83.
46. #6472328, 5 HP, single phase motor, 115/230V, $509.
47. #6472319, 5 HP, three phase motor, 230/460V, $343.
48. #6472320, 5 HP, three phase motor, 200V, $343.
49. #6472507, 7.5 HP, three phase motor, 230/460V, $477.
50. #6472512, 7.5 HP, three phase motor, 200V, $477.
51. #2398189, single phase magnetic control, 115/230V, $292.
52. #2398494, single phase magnetic control, 115/230V with 24V transformer, $436.
53. #2398186, three phase magnetic control, 200/230/460/575V, $288.
54. #2398498, three phase magnetic control, 200/230/460/575V with 24V transformer, $356.
55. #2258005, heavy duty knife grinding attachment with indexing mechanism, $747.
56. #3292005, shaving hood, $26.
57. #2393005, extra set of three HHS, heat treated knives, $146.
58. #2397062, conversion kit, sectional chip-breaker and infeed roller, $595.
59. #3250015, belt guard for motor, $16.
60. #3717026, two groove B-section motor pulley, $113.
61. #2393012, extra set of 27 HHS knives, $230.
62. #2393017, extra set of 27 carbide tipped knives $718.
63. #2397041, shaving hood and sound insulation kit, $267.
64. #9100008, carbide knives in leiu of HSS knives, $602.
65. #6900031, diamond grinding wheel for carbide knives, $463.
66. Cutterhead speed, belt drive, 4,800 RPM; cutterhead speed, direct drive, 3,600 RPM.
67. #2258007, knife grinding attachment, $886.

***OPTIONS (CON'T)

68. #6472604, 10 HP, three phase motor, 230/460V, $570.
69. #6472606, 10 HP, three phase motor, 200V, $485.
70. #6472702, 15 HP, three phase motor, 200V, $757.
71. #6472703, 15 HP, three phase motor, 230/460V, $810.
72. 15 HP motor available on belt drive only.
73. #2398195, three phase magnetic control, 200/230/460/575V, $549.
74. #2398501, three phase magnetic control, 200/230/460/575V with 24V transformer, $1,049.
75. #2068001, cutterhead break, $56.
76. #2292022, shaving hood, $68.
77. #2393008, set of four HHS, heat treated knives, $279.
78. #3250064, belt guard, $29.
79. #2393014, set of 36 HSS knives, $337.
80. #2393019, set of 36 carbide tipped knives, $957.
81. #2397043, shaving hood and insulation kit, $378.
82. #9100010, carbide knives in leiu of HHS knives, $766.
83. Extra set of three 15" HSS knives, $105.
84. Choice of 3 HP, single phase or 5 HP, three phase.
85. Metal legs, sawdust chute, set of three replacement blades, 5 HP motor, 220V only—must be ordered with initial purchase.
86. #SHG-1300AV, deluxe model, variable speed rate, auto bed roll height adjuster,

dust hood, magnetic starter, feed rate of 15-35 FPM, $2,395.
87. #BWC-508G, same as #508 with addition of knife grinder, $4,395.
88. #BCG-200, planer cutterhead knife setting gauge, $69.95.
89. #BFG-300, feed roll gauge, $89.95.
90. Combination of the two above, $129.95.
91. Variable stock feed rate on Model RE-40V is 15 to 35 FPM.
92. Machine is priced without motor or controls. Single phase motors available from .25 HP to 5 HP in 110V and 220V; the 3 HP and 5 HP single phase motors are available in 220V only. Three phase motors available from .5 HP to 5 HP—specify voltage.
93. #1302-C, three piece carbide knives, $472.50.
94. #1302-H, three piece HSS knives, $82.80.
95. #1303, three piece HHS throw away knives, $17.55.
96. #1305, chip breaker for throw away knives, $23.86 ea.
97. #1304, shaving hood, 5" diameter, $95.90.
98. #1533, knife setting gauge, $148.50.
99. #330-C, four piece carbide knives, $891.
100. #330-H, four piece HSS knives, $191.25.
101. #3304, shaving hood, 6" diameter, $148.
102. #3310, knife grinder with jointing attachment, $635.61.
103. Many different styles of standard molding knives available.
104. Custom molding knives can be supplied from customer specifications.
105. #W-7, molder/planer, hand-fed, $470.

106. #W-7PF, power infeed roll only, $645.
107. Motor mount, $15.95.
108. Bench roller, $12.95.
109. Adjustable telescopic roller support stand, $39.35.
110. Set of two HSS planing knives, $54.75.
111. Belt and pulley assembly for 3,450 RPM motor, 5/8" standard bore, $20.35.
112. Belt and pulley assembly for 1,750 RPM motor, 5/8" standard bore, $34.10.
113. 1 HP ball bearing 3,450 RPM motor, 110/220V, $126.
114. 1.5 HP ball bearing 3,450 RPM motor, 110/220V, $155.
115. 2 HP ball bearing, 3,450 RPM motor, 110/220V, $189.
116. Adjustable table guides, $18.25.
117. #532, jointer attachment; jointer attaches in seconds, w/o interfering with the planer function, 42 lbs., $212.
118. #400A, molding attachment, complete, $99.
119. #KSG, knife setting gauge, $15.
120. #408-S, drum sander attachment, power fed, $139.
121. 2 HP motor, 115/230V, 3,450 RPM, ball bearing, add $48.
122. #600A, molding attachment, complete, $141.
123. #612-S, drum sander attachment, power fed, $219.
124. #612-P, 5 HP motor, 220V, single phase 3,450 RPM, ball bearing, add $106.
125. #314, adjustable extension roller and stand, $32.
126. Various molding cutter bits available.

DE WALT
3590

ELEKTRA BECKUM
HC260M

EMCO
REX 2000

HITACHI
F1000A

KITY
636

MAKITA
2030

MAKITA
2030N

RYOBI
AH-115

JOINTER/PLANER

Brand *No Photo Available	Model	Motor**	Special Features***	Options****	Capacity W × T	Maximum Depth of Cut-Planer	Maximum Depth of Cut-Jointer	Maximum Width of Cut-Jointer	Cutterhead Speed (RPM)	Stock Feed (SFPM)	Overall Dimensions W × D × H	Bed Rollers Quantity/Type	Knives-Planer	Knives-Jointer	Net Weight	Suggested Retail Price
BLACK & DECKER (MFG-DEWALT)	3590	2 HP 6-12	19-20	—	10 × 4¼	3/16″	3/16″	—	—	2 speed	—	—	—	—	135	$1217
*ELEKTRA BECKUM	HC 260ESH	2-4 HP 6-13-14	23-25 31-32-33-34	—	10¼ × 6⅜	3/16″	⅛″	—	7,200	19	—	—	—	—	125	1250
ELEKTRA BECKUM	HC 260M	3 HP 3-13-14-15	23-25 31-32-33	—	10¼ × 6⅜	3/16″	⅛″	—	6,000	16.5	—	—	—	—	110	1295
*ELEKTRA BECKUM	HC 260K	4.2 HP 6-8	14-31-32	—	10¼ × 6⅜	3/16″	⅛″	—	10,200	27	—	—	—	—	190	1375
EMCO	REX 2000	2.5 HP-1 or 2.8 HP-2	27-28-29-30	4	9¾ × 6	⅛″	⅛″	—	6,000	16.5	—	—	2	2	157	995
HITACHI	F1000A	4	4-5-6	—	12 5/32 × 6⅝	⅛″	⅛″	6 9/32″	10,400	26	—	2	—	—	319.4	2100
KITY	636	1.5 HP 7-9-10	22-23 24-25-26	—	10¼ × 6	—	—	—	7,000	19 and 24	—	0	—	—	—	1392
MAKITA	2030	2 HP	1-5-9-10-11	3	12 × 6¼	⅛″	⅛″	6⅛″	7,000	28	27½ × 59 × 28½	2	2	2	275	1980
MAKITA	2030N	—	6-11-12-13 14-15-16-17-18	—	12½ × 7¼	See Special Features 9-10	⅛″	6⅛″	7,000	17 and 26	30¾ × 59 × 30½	—	2	2	330	2160
RYOBI	AH-115	3	1-2-3	1-2	12½ × __	⅛″	3/16″	6 5/16″	7,000	19.7 and 29.5	32 5/16 × 60¼ × 29¾	2	—	—	319	2195

****MOTOR**

1. Single phase
2. Three phase
3. 110V
4. 115V
5. 120V
6. 220V
7. 110/120V
8. 3360 RPM
9. 3450 RPM
10. TEFC
11. Ball and needle bearing
12. Ball bearing
13. Magnetic relay
14. Overload protection
15. Belt drive

***SPECIAL FEATURES

1. Over the top return rollers.
2. Includes blade adjustment gauge.
3. Cast iron construction.
4. Jointer table is $6\frac{3}{8}$" W × $63\frac{1}{32}$" L.
5. Planer table is $12\frac{3}{4}$" W × $24\frac{1}{32}$" L.
6. Four column construction.
7. Planer table is 12" W × $23\frac{1}{2}$" L.
8. Jointer table is $6\frac{1}{8}$" W × 59" L.
9. Maximum depth of cut at 26 SFPM is $\frac{5}{64}$".
10. Maximum depth of cut at 17 SFPM is $\frac{1}{8}$".
11. Planer table is $12\frac{1}{2}$" W × $23\frac{5}{8}$" L.
12. Jointer table is $6\frac{1}{8}$" W × 59" L.
13. Adjustable chip deflector.
14. 0-45° adjustable jointer fence.
15. Simple cutting depth adjustment.
16. Lock-off switch button.
17. Electric brake.
18. Two position drumlock for easy blade change.
19. Makes 1,360 cuts per minute.
20. Exhaust hood for easy chip removal.
21. Micro-adjusting table.
22. Jointer table is $10\frac{5}{8}$" W × $39\frac{1}{2}$" L.
23. One pair of knives is used by both the jointer and the planer.
24. Cutterhead runs in ball bearings.
25. Adjustable tilting fence.
26. Choice of wood or metal stand.
27. Jointer table is $33\frac{1}{2}$" long.
28. Planer table is $17\frac{3}{4}$" long.
29. Chip guard.
30. Guard for jointer knives.
31. Jointer table is 40" long.
32. Planer table is $15\frac{3}{4}$" long.
33. Constructed of toriton free pressure die cast aluminum alloy.
34. Safety cutter guard.

****OPTIONS

1. #X2256, planer blades, $23.
2. #X2257, jointer blades, $7.
3. Speed reducing kit available for extra smooth cut.
4. See catalog for options and accessories.

MITER SAWS

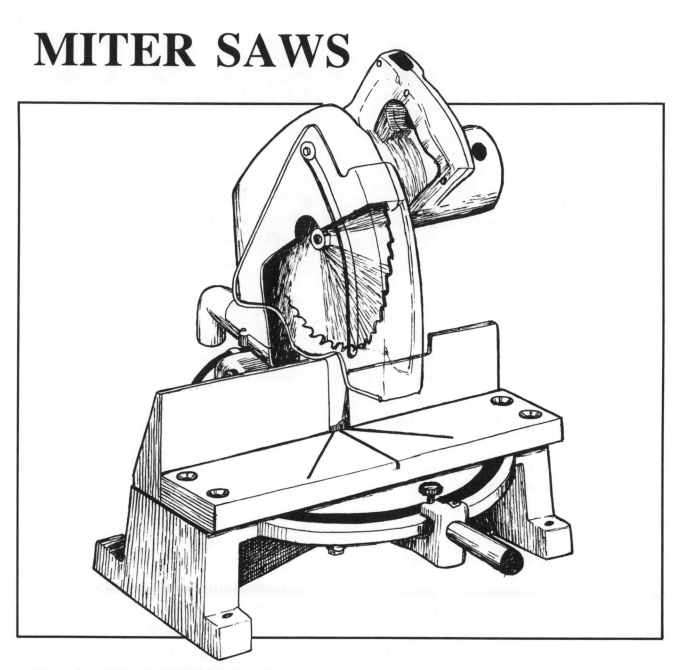

Electric miter saws have essentially replaced the traditional hand miter box as a finish carpenter's tool. These machines are small enough to be easily moved to construction sites and are excellent for cutting wood trim. Woodworkers involved in picture frame work also find them to be invaluable.

A miter saw is a simple tool consisting of a small circular saw mounted on a hinged arm, which allows the tool to cut with a chopping action. The arm will be attached to a base and a small table and fence are provided.

SIZES

The size of a miter saw is usually referred to in terms of the maximum blade diameter, and sizes generally range from 8¼" to 15", with 10" being most common. Most woodworkers will seldom need anything larger than 9" or 10" for trim work.

The overall size of a miter saw increases with blade capacity. Smaller units have the added advantage of being easily moved from place to place.

BLADE

The quality of the blade on a circular saw is directly related to the quality of work it will produce—the better the blade the better the work. Miter saws are cut-off machines which simply means that they are designed to cut wood across the grain, therefore, it is possible to equip the tool with a blade that is designed specifically to crosscut only. Unfortunately some new miter saws are supplied with a conventional "rough cut" (RC) combination blade. If you buy one of these machines it would be best to purchase a high quality, carbide tipped, cut-off blade and replace the RC blade before you ever turn it

---

Electric miter saws have essentially replaced the traditional hand miter box as a finish carpenter's tool.

---

on. One manufacturer has recognized this advantage and is equipping their new saws with Freud LU85M, carbide tipped blades—a definite plus.

TABLE & ANGLE SETTING FEATURES

Miter saws are available with either stationary or pivoting tables. The saw arm on a pivoting table design is actually attached to a circular table insert and the insert moves with the blade as different angle settings are made. The blade is in the same relationship with the table at all angles and a single permanent blade slot is cut into the table. Stationary tables utilize wooden work surfaces, and the saw actually cuts into the table surface with each cut. Both designs function well, however wooden tables will need to be replaced periodically as they become worn. Being able to replace the table actually may be an advantage at times, since you are able to minimize the splintering tendency on the bottom of the work by

providing a table kerf which fits the blade closely.

The system used to provide for angle adjustment varies slightly from one manufacturer to another. All saws will have a protractor scale of some type to use for angle

---

A miter saw is a simple tool consisting of a small circular saw mounted on a hinged arm, which allows the tool to cut with a chopping action.

---

reference. Some units come with positive stops at 22½, 45, and 90 degrees and others have no stops. Both designs function well, but positive stops make the set-up easier for the most common cuts.

SAFETY

All saws are equipped with some type of sliding guard to shield the blade. In spite of the guarding, miter saws have the reputation of being "finger getters". Guards, even though they are usually made from clear plastic, do make it harder to see the exact

---

The quality of the blade on a circular saw is directly related to the quality of work it will produce—the better the blade the better the work.

---

point of cut and for this reason some people remove them to improve visibility. It is much better to adapt your sawing technique to a guarded blade rather than remove the guard.

Miter saw tables are short and you will need to make provisions to support long pieces on both ends. Some saw injuries occur because the operator tries to hold a long, unsupported piece while sawing and something slips.

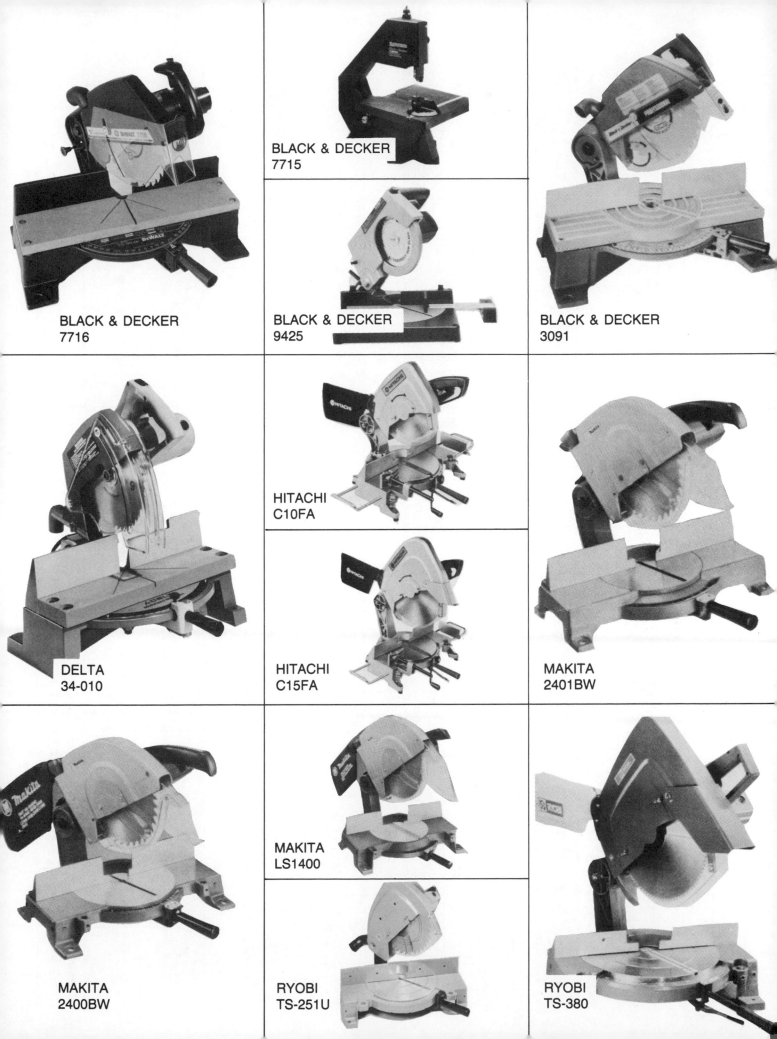

BLACK & DECKER
7715

BLACK & DECKER
7716

BLACK & DECKER
9425

BLACK & DECKER
3091

DELTA
34-010

HITACHI
C10FA

HITACHI
C15FA

MAKITA
2401BW

MAKITA
2400BW

MAKITA
LS1400

RYOBI
TS-251U

RYOBI
TS-380

MITER SAW

Brand *No Photo Available	Model	Motor**	Special Features***	Options****	Blade Diameter	Arbor Size	Cutting Capacity At 90°	Cutting Capacity At 45°	Amps	Voltage	No Load Speed (RPM)	Dust Bag (Yes or No)	Shipping Weight	Suggested Retail Price
BLACK & DECKER	7716	1.5 HP 1	1-21-22 23-24-25	—	10″	—	—	—	10.5	120	5500	No	41	$231
BLACK & DECKER	7715	2 HP 2	16-24 25-26-27	—	9″	⅝″	$2\frac{15}{16} \times 4$	$2\frac{15}{16} \times 3\frac{1}{2}$	9	120	5300	No	37	228^{95}
BLACK & DECKER	9425	1.25 HP 3	5-16-26-28	—	8¼″	⅝″	2¼ × 5¼	2¼ × 3¾	8	120	3600	No	17.5	179^{95}
BLACK & DECKER	3091	2 HP	5-16-24 26-29-30	—	10″	⅝″	3¼ × 4⅜	—	10	—	5300	No	39	249
*CRAFTSMAN	2374N	—	5-31	—	7½″	—	2½ × 8¾	$2\frac{1}{2} \times 6\frac{3}{16}$	—	—	—	No	65	269^{99}
*CRAFTSMAN	23355C	—	5-32	—	8¼″	—	2¼ × 5¼	2¼ × 3¾	—	—	—	—	20	144^{99}
DELTA	34-010	1.6 HP	12-16-19-20-21	11	9″	⅝″	2½ × 4	2½ × 3⅝	10.5	115	5000 Under load	No	39	231
*HITACHI	C10FB	Maximum 2.2 HP	3-5-8 11-12-33	1-2-3-4	10″	⅝″	$3\frac{1}{8} \times 4\frac{5}{16}$	3⅛ × 3⅛	12	115	4100	No	48	349
HITACHI	C10FA	Maximum 2.7 HP	3-5-8-11 12-13-14	4	10″	⅝″	$3\frac{1}{8} \times 4\frac{5}{16}$	3⅛ × 3⅛	15	115	4500	Yes	44	419
HITACHI	C15FA	Maximum 2.7 HP	3-5-8-11 12-13-14-15	—	15″	¾″ & 1″	4¾ × 6⅜	4¾ × 4¾	15	115	3400	Yes	55	599
MAKITA	2401BW	—	1-2-3-4-5 6-7-8-33	—	10″	⅝″	2⅞ × 4¾	2⅞ × 3½	12	115	4100	No	63	329
MAKITA	2400BW	—	1-2-3-4-5 6-7-8-9-10	—	10″	⅝″	2⅞ × 4¾	2⅞ × 3½	12	115	4100	Yes	64	369
MAKITA	LS1400	—	1-2-3-4 5-6-7-8-33	—	14″	25mm	4¾ × 6	4¾ × 4½	12	115	3200	Yes	92.6	578
RYOBI	TS-251U	—	1-3-5-8-16	5-6	10″	⅝″	3⅛ × 4¾	3⅛ × 4⅜	12.5	120	5000	No	33.5 Net	300
RYOBI	TS-380	—	1-3-5 8-16-17	7-8-9-10	14″	1″	$4\frac{13}{16} \times 6\frac{3}{16}$	$4\frac{13}{16} \times 4\frac{3}{8}$	14	120	3400	Yes	50.6	550

****Motor**

1. Ball Bearing
2. Ball and Sleeve Bearing
3. Ball and Roller Bearing

***SPECIAL FEATURES

1. Double insulated.
2. Ball bearing and needle bearing construction.
3. Electric brake.
4. Cast base.
5. Rotating, slotted cutting table; turns with the blade.
6. Externally located motor brushes for easy inspection and replacement.
7. Motor head locks down for transporting.
8. Shaft lock for blade changes.
9. Positive stops at 15°, 22½°, 30°, 45°, and 90° right and left.
10. Inset table is precision machined aluminum.
11. Safety switch lock.
12. Ball bearing construction.
13. Includes vice assembly and extension holder assembly.
14. Positive stops at 0°, 22½°, 30°, and 45°, right and left.
15. Includes collar for 1" arbor.
16. Positive stops at 90°, 22½°, and 45°, right and left.
17. Miter cuts up to 52° right and left.
18. 4" × 17" table size.
19. Manual pushbutton brake.
20. Specially designed arbor permits quick blade removal.
21. Retractable, clear blade guide.
22. Manual brake.
23. Removable on/off key.
24. Miter cuts up to 47° right and left.
25. Calibrated in half degrees plus veneer scale for ¼° sections.
26. Gear driven blade.
27. 4" × 21¼" table with fence.
28. Bevel post adjusts to 45°.
29. Pushbutton brake.
30. 41⅜" × 21¼" table.
31. Aluminum table, 5⅝" × 20⅛".
32. Aluminum table, 7¼" × 13½".
33. Positive stops at 90° and 45° right and left.

****OPTIONS

1. #974580, dust bag, no price available.
2. #974662Z, vice assembly, no price available.
3. #974661Z, extension holder assembly, no price available.
4. #9764451, collar for 1" arbor, no price available.
5. #X2247, dust bag, $7.60.
6. #X2300, vice assembly, extensions, stop and dust bag, $20.
7. #X2244, vice assembly, no price available.
8. #X2527, dust bag, $5.
9. #X2304, 7" extension, $40.80.
10. #X2284, vice assembly extensions and stops, $33.20.
11. #50-508, steel stand, $69.30.

PORTABLE ROUTERS

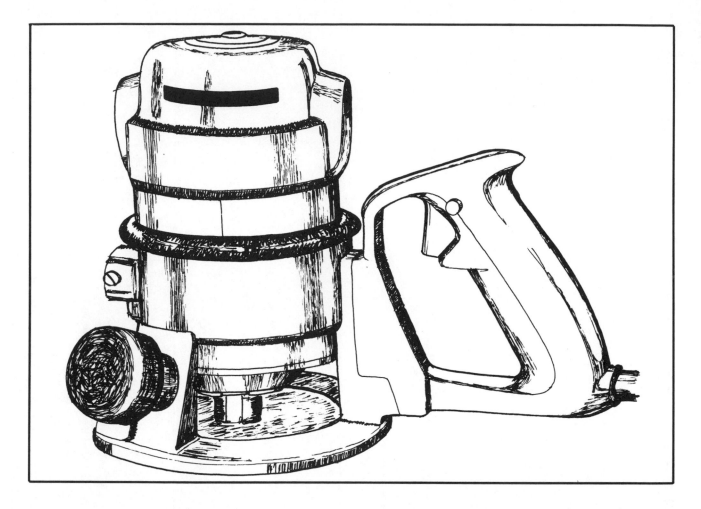

Portable routers are common tools in most wood shops today. They are used for a wide variety of operations including the following: cutting moldings, grooves, rabbets, dados, dovetails; making signs; and cutting recesses for inlay. It isn't uncommon for woodworkers to have several routers of different sizes for various operations. Before selecting one of these tools, carefully analyze your needs and select a tool which will do the jobs you need to do. Don't buy the tool simply based on price.

Routers are simple tools consisting basically of a high speed motor and an adjustable base. The size of a router is usually referred to in terms of the horsepower of the motor with sizes ranging from less than ½ HP to over 3 HP. RPM range, motor amps, and chuck capacity are other size specifications. Spindle speeds range from approximately 20,000 to 30,000 RPM. Motor amperage ranges from approximately one amp for Dremel tools through 12 amps for some of the larger models. Standard chuck capacities range from ⅛″ to ½″ with ¼″ being most common.

MOTORS AND CHUCKS

The quality of a router depends largely upon the quality of the motor and its bearings. Router motors are small high speed universal motors. Motors of this type have carbon brushes which must be checked and replaced periodically. Failure to main-

---

Routers are simple tools consisting basically of a high speed motor and an adjustable base.

---

tain the brushes is a common router problem. If the brushes are allowed to wear down too short, the motor armature can be scored, leading to major repair. The size and quality of the bearings is important. Ball bearings are usually used, however, some of the smaller units will have sleeve bearings. Ball bearings are typically sealed units requiring no lubrication, however, sleeve bearings will need oil regularly. Ball bearings will usually last longer than sleeve bearings. Better routers will have large, heavy duty ball bearings.

Since routers operate at such high speeds noise becomes a possible problem. Some routers are simply louder than others. Usually the cheaper models will be the noisy ones, however, all routers are loud. Be sure to turn the router on and listen to it before you buy it. The sound and feel of the running router can tell you quite a bit about quality. Poorly made units will frequently be loudest and actually feel somewhat rough or vibrate in your hand. On a quality tool you will notice little if any excessive vibration and the unit will sound smooth (no "grinding like" noises).

Some routers are made with permanently mounted handles on the motor or base. Router users frequently complain that these fixed knobs get in the way at times. Removable handles or knobs offer the most versatility.

Generally there are two things which can

be said about router horsepower, the higher the horsepower the more it will cost and the more it will weigh. The weight of a stationary tool is frequently used as an index of quality. It isn't necessarily best to select a heavy portable router. Heavier units are, in fact, sometimes awkward and fatiguing to use. Some woodworkers prefer good smaller units because of the added freedom they have in maneuvering the tool. If your interests depend upon router maneuverability, a ½ to 1½ HP unit may be a good choice. If you are planning to use the tool for heavy molding work or plunge routing, a 1½ to 2 HP might be best.

It is important to realize that all routers do not perform well when inverted and mounted to a table. Some manufacturers recommend that some of their tools not be used this way. Most people agree that it is best to use heavy duty routers on router tables. This

---

Since routers operate at such high speeds noise becomes a possible problem. Some routers are simply louder than others.

---

method of router use puts added strain on the bearings, and smaller tools won't hold up.

The chucking system used to hold bits will vary slightly from one brand to the next. Essentially, they are of the split collet type which provides the most accurate means of holding straight shanks. Some collet designs are easier to use than others. Cheaper chucks will have a split collet and a separate collet retaining ring. Chucks of this design have an annoying tendency to lock themselves to the bit (the collet ring gets jammed to the collet). The best chucks are one piece units which utilize a tapered hole in the end of the router spindle for tightening.

The method used for bit removal varies.

Some routers have built-in locking mechanisms which can be engaged to fix the spindle while a single wrench is used to loosen or tighten the collet. Others will have no locking device but require the use of two wrenches for bit removal. The one wrench system works, but on occasions, the locking system breaks down. The two wrench system is a bit more awkward, but it is better in the long run. Speaking of wrenches, the quality of the wrenches supplied with some routers is very low. Don't be surprised if these tools break or bend completely out of shape. It is a good idea to plan to use quality open-end wrenches for your router.

ROUTER BASE

The router base is actually an adjustable unit which fits around the motor and forms the work surface for tool support. The base must be adjusted repeatedly during the life of the tool, and it is important that it be simple to change. The base will usually have some type of depth adjustment gauge. One router even has a digital read out option which will show the precise depth setting of the bit. You will find that many woodworkers ignore the gauge and rely on measuring the bit projection by hand. There are times, such as in plunge routing, when

---

Some routers have built-in locking mechanisms which can be engaged to fix the spindle while a single wrench is used to loosen or tighten the collet.

---

accurate gauges and stops are vital to efficient tool use.

The actual working surface of the base is usually made from plastic. We sometimes think of plastic as an inferior material for some machine parts; that isn't the case here. Plastic bases are light weight, have a low coefficient of friction (slide easily), and will not mar wood surfaces. Unfortunately, manufacturers typically use opaque (black or gray) plastic for bases. A good clear polycarbonate would certainly improve visibility. No manufacturers use these transparent bases yet.

ACCESSORIES AND BITS

Routers are usually sold without bits, and the tool is useless without them. You will need to immediately start a bit collection, and there are many to choose from. Bits are sold individually or in sets. Sets are a temptation, but people find that they sometimes only use a few bits in a set, so this may not be the best way to start. It is probably best to begin with the bits that are most versatile and fit your immediate needs.

The router base is actually an adjustable unit which fits around the motor and forms the work surface for tool support.

Router bits are either made from high speed steel or carbide tipped. High speed steel tools are less expensive and perform well but do not hold an edge as long as carbide tipped tools. Carbide tipped cutters cost about twice as much as high speed steel bits, but the added edge life really makes a difference. Once you use a high quality, carbide tipped bit, you will probably not want to use any other type.

A wide assortment of accessories is available for routers. Accessories are not always interchangeable between router brands, so it is important to understand exactly what accessories are available for the tool you are considering. Typical accessories include dovetailing jigs, router tables, guides of various sorts, hinge and lock templets, stair templets, and a host of other special jigs.

BLACK & DECKER
3335

BLACK & DECKER
3310

BLACK & DECKER
7615

BLACK & DECKER
7614

BLACK & DECKER
7604

BLACK & DECKER
7600

BOSCH
90300

BOSCH
90303

BOSCH
1600

BOSCH
1604

BOSCH
1606

BOSCH
1602

BOSCH
1603

BOSCH
1601

CRAFTSMAN
ELECTRONIC
1750

HITACHI
TR-8

HITACHI
TR-12

MAKITA
3608BK

MAKITA
3601B

MAKITA
3612BR

MILWAUKEE

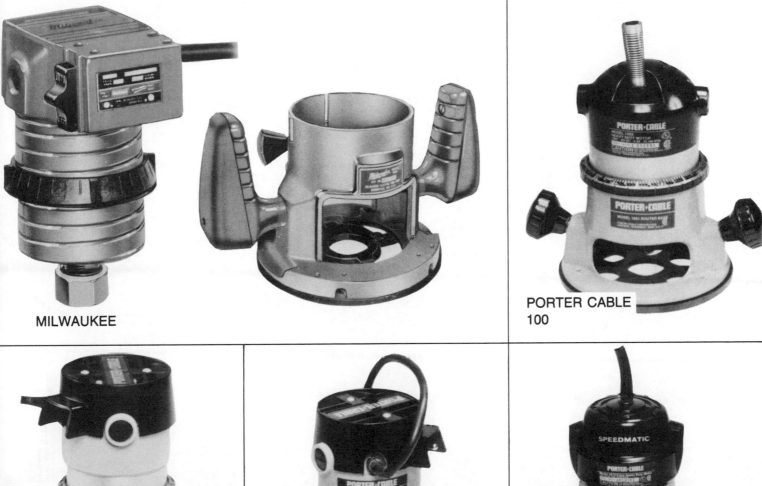

MILWAUKEE

PORTER CABLE
100

PORTER CABLE
630

PORTER CABLE
690

PORTER CABLE
536 SPEEDMATIC

PORTER CABLE
537 SPEEDMATIC

PORTER CABLE
518 SPEEDTRONIC

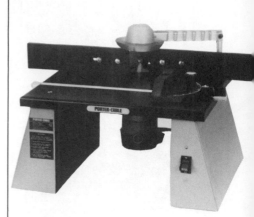

PORTER CABLE
695
ROUTER/SHAPER

PORTER CABLE
5537

PORTER CABLE
5675

PORTER CABLE
5020
DUST COLLECTOR

RYOBI
R-150

RYOBI
R-330

RYOBI
R-500

PORTABLE ROUTER

Brand *No Photo Available	Model	Horse-Power	Amps	Voltage	Motor Diameter	Special Features**	Options***	RPM	Standard Collets	Available Collets	Collet Type	Height	Base	Net Weight	Suggested Retail Price
BLACK & DECKER	3335	5.0	13.0	—	4½″	—	4	18,000	½″	—	Split	9.4″	8″ dia.	14¼	$468
BLACK & DECKER	3310	1.5	8.0	—	3½″	—	4	25,000	⅜″	—	Split	6¾″	6″ dia.	7¼	209
BLACK & DECKER	7615	1.5	9.0	120	—	—	4-17	25,000	—	—	—	—	—	8¼	111^{95}
*BLACK & DECKER	7613	1.25	8.5	120	—	—	4	25,000	—	—	—	—	—	7 13/16	79^{95}
BLACK & DECKER	7604	1.0	5.0	—	—	—	4	30,000	—	—	—	—	—	4	67^{95}
BLACK & DECKER	7600	.75	4.5	—	—	—	4	30,000	—	—	—	—	—	3⅞	52^{95}
BOSCH	90300	3.25	—	120	4¼″	25-26-27-28	4-5-6-7	22,000	½″	¼″, ⅜″	Split	—	7½″ dia.	15½	500
BOSCH	90303	3.25	—	120	4¼″	27-29 30-31-32	4	22,000	½″	¼″, ⅜″	Split	—	7½″ dia.	19¼	675
BOSCH	1600	2.25	—	115	4¼″	8-33-34	4	26,000	½″	¼″, ⅜″	Split	—	7″ dia.	12¾	349
BOSCH	1604	1.75	—	115	3½″	35-36-37	4	25,000	¼″, ½″	⅜″	Split	—	6″ dia.	7¼	199
BOSCH	1606	1.75	—	115	3½″	8-35 37-38-39	4	25,000	¼″, ½″	⅜″	Split	—	6″ dia.	7.8	223
BOSCH	1602	1.5	—	115	3½″	36-37-39-40	4	25,000	¼″	⅜″	Split	—	6″ dia.	7	175
BOSCH	1603	1.5	—	115	3½″	8-35-37-39	4	25,000	¼″	⅜″	Split	—	6″ dia.	7½	199
BOSCH	1601	1.0	—	115	3½″	35-36-37-40	4	25,000	¼″	—	Split	—	6″ dia.	6¼	145
CRAFTSMAN	1750	—	—	—	—	7-42-44 45-46-47	4-14-15-16	11,000 to 25,000	¼″	—	Split	—	—	—	149^{99}
*CRAFTSMAN	1743	1.5	—	—	—	47-48-49 50-51-52	4-14-15-16	25,000	¼″	—	Split	—	—	—	109^{99}
*CRAFTSMAN	1755	1.0	—	—	—	47-52-53	4-14-15-16	25,000	¼″	—	Split	—	—	—	79^{99}
*CRAFTSMAN	1730	⅝	—	—	—	54	4-14-15-16	25,000	¼″	—	Split	—	—	—	39^{99}
HITACHI	TR-8 Heavy Duty	—	6.9	115	—	47-57-79-80	4	24,000	¼″	—	—	9″	—	6.6	206
HITACHI	TR-12 Super Duty	—	12.2	115	—	47-57-79-80	4	22,000	½″	—	—	10⅝″	Round	12.3	299

PORTABLE ROUTER

Brand *No Photo Available	Model	Horse-Power	Amps	Voltage	Motor Diameter	Special Features**	Options***	RPM	Standard Collets	Available Collets	Collet Type	Height	Base	Net Weight	Suggested Retail Price
MAKITA	3608BK	.75	4.8	115	—	47-56 66-67-70	4	23,000	⅜″, ¼″	—	Split	6⅞″	—	5	$132
MAKITA	3601B Heavy Duty	1⅜	8.5	115	—	8-47-50-67	4	23,000	½″, ⅜″, ¼″	—	Split	7½″	—	8	168
MAKITA	3612BR Super Duty	3.0	14.0	115	—	47-53-68-69	4	23,000	½″, ⅜″, ¼″	—	Split	11 5/16″	—	12½	286
MILWAUKEE	5620	1.0	8.0	—	—	7-41-42-43	4-9-10-13	23,000	¼″	⅜″	Split	8″	6″ dia.	8	245
MILWAUKEE	5660	1.5	10.0	—	—	7-41-42-43	4-8-9-11-13	24,500	¼″	⅜″, ½″	Split	8″	6″ dia.	8½	256
MILWAUKEE	5680	2.0	12.0	—	—	7-41-42-43	4-9-12-13	26,000	½″	¼″, ⅜″	Split	8″	6″ dia.	8¾	314
PORTER CABLE	100	⅞	6.5	115	3½″	1-2-3-4-5	1-3-4	22,000	¼″	—	Split	7″	Round	7	134
PORTER CABLE	630	1.0	6.8	115	3½″	1-2-3-6-7	1-3-4	22,000	¼″	—	Split	8″	Round	8¼	145
PORTER CABLE	690	1.5	8.0	115	3½″	1-2-3-5-6-7	1-3-4	22,000	½″	⅜″, ¼″	Split	8″	Round	8¾	189
*PORTER CABLE	691	1.5	8.0	115	3½″	1-2-3-6-7-8	1-3-4	22,000	½″, ¼″	⅜″	Split	8″	Round	10	213
PORTER CABLE	536 Speedmatic	1.5	8.0	115	3 4/5″	1-2-3-4-5-6	1-3-4	23,000	½″	¼″	Split	9⅜″	Round	12	295
PORTER CABLE	537 Speedmatic	1.5	8.0	115	3 4/5″	1-2-3-4-6-8	1-3-4	23,000	½″	¼″	Split	9⅜″	Round	14	310
PORTER CABLE	518 Speedtronic	3.0	15.0	120	4½″	1-3-4-6-9-10 11-12-13-14	1-3-4	See Special Feature 81	½″	¼″	Split	12¾″	Round	18¾	475
PORTER CABLE	695	1.5	8.0	115	3½″	15-16-17-18 19-20-21-22	2-4	22,000	½″, ¼″	—	Split	10″	—	38.8	278
PORTER CABLE	5537	1.5	8.0	115	3 4/5″	23	4	23,000	½″	¼″	Split	9¾″	Round	17¼	399
PORTER CABLE	5675	1.25	7.5	115	3½″	24	4	22,000	⅜″	¼″	Split	8⅜″	Round	13¼	255
RYOBI	R-150	1.0	6.5	120	—	47-57 71-72-73	4	24,000	¼″	—	Split	9½″	—	13.4	220
RYOBI	R-330	2.0	12.1	120	—	74-75-76	4	24,000	½″	¼″, ⅜″	Split	9 1/16″	6⅛″ dia.	9.7	265
RYOBI	R-500	3.0	13.3	120	—	47-57-73 75-76-77-78	4	22,000	½″	¼″, ⅜″	—	10⅝″	—		

**SPECIAL FEATURES

1. Permanently sealed, precision ball bearings.
2. Failure protected motor with high torque power.
3. Replaceable non-marking base.
4. Heavy duty strain relief cord.
5. Knobs placed close to base for accurate control.
6. Micrometer depth of control cut.
7. Flat top design for fast, easy bit changes.
8. Has D-handle design with trigger switch.
9. Microprocessor electronics.
10. Larger cutters can be used at lower speeds to obtain proper SFPM.
11. Motor is monitored 30 times per second to maintain desired speed.
12. "Soft start" provides 50-75% less reaction torque at start-up.
13. Up to 10 decibels quieter than a standard router at lower speeds.
14. Includes tool-mounted routing data chart for proper speed selection.
15. Combination router/shaper.
16. Individually adjusted split fence with micro adjustment.
17. Fence adjustable to cutter size.
18. Starting pins in two different locations.
19. Quick-adjust guard.
20. Overall dimensions: Width 20½", Depth 16", Height 10".
21. Table size is 16" × 18".
22. Table insert openings: 3", 2" and 1¼".
23. Includes #537 D-handle router and #5020 routo-vac dust collector attachment.
24. Includes #675 D-handle router and #5020 routo-vac dust collector attachment.
25. Designed for heavy woodworking operations.
26. Micromatic ring allows fast, accurate, depth setting.
27. Base has squared-off side for close quarter routing and straight line guiding.
28. Large, contoured handles.
29. Plunge router.
30. Designed for production routing and thick materials.
31. Motor inserts into base with no adjustments required.
32. Instant depth setting changes up to 2".
33. Two auxiliary handles.
34. Precision adjustments made easy.
35. Captive template guide for quick, easy seating.
36. Raised index pointer.
37. Large sub-base, center opening.
38. One auxiliary handle.
39. Spiral depth adjustment with raised 1/32" index marks.
40. Removable side handles.
41. Heavy-duty sub-base with large openings for maximum visibility.
42. Depth adjustment graduated in 1/64" increments.
43. Functional trigger-handle grouping.
44. Overload protector and slow starting feature.
45. Electronic feedback maintains selected speeds under load conditions.
46. Dual monitoring system indicates proper pressure.
47. 100% ball bearing.
48. Dust pick-up system.
49. Two chip deflectors.
50. Locking trigger on handle.
51. Work light.
52. Depth set for repetitive cuts.
53. One chip deflector.
54. Ball and sleeve bearings.
55. Electronic motor control for easier start up.
56. Trigger-handle switch.
57. Plunge cut router.
58. Rack and pinion plunge with a 2" range.
59. Removable chip deflector.
60. Rack and pinion depth adjustment of 1½".
61. Spindle lock; only one wrench needed; wrench stores in router base.
62. Side mounted switch.
63. Ring depth adjustment of 1½".
64. Motor switch is shut off when router is resting on its top.
65. Directed air exhaust clears chips from working area.
66. Contoured, double handle design.
67. Large, calibrated depth control ring.
68. 2½" plunge depth capacity.
69. Shaft locks for quick change of bits with one wrench.
70. Includes carrying case.
71. Capacity of 2".
72. Plunge depth is set by simple thumb action.
73. Stopper block can be adjusted for three different cutting levels.
74. Exclusive design allows bit to be clearly visible when cutting.
75. Thumb reach off/on lever without removing hands from handle.
76. Comfortable handles for less fatigue.
77. Capacity of 2³/₈".
78. Self-disconnecting brushes prevent commutator damage.
79. Three stages of cutting depth; easily selectable.
80. Quick change of cutting depth.
81. Six speeds: 10,000, 13,000, 16,000, 19,000, and 22,000.

***OPTIONS

1. #26793, steel carrying case, $40.60.
2. #696, shaper table, same as #695 except without router, $149.50.
3. #5020, dust collector attachment, fits any standard vacuum with 1½" intake, $99.50.
4. See catalog for various bits, cutters, arbors, spindles and other standard router accessories.
5. #93905, router table, fits most Bosch routers, $99.85.
6. #82989, 1½" × 10' vacuum hose, dustless router system, 6", fits most Bosch routers, $99.50.
7. #82990, 1½" × 10' vacuum hose, dustless router system, 7⅜", fits most Bosch routers, $117.45.
8. #5660-2, also available with 240V motor, $269.
9. #48-55-0810, steel carrying case, $38.40.
10. #5610, motor only, includes ¼" collet, $209.
11. #5650, motor only, includes ¼" collet, $219.
12. #5670, motor only, includes ½" collet, $279.
13. #48-10-0070, base assembly only, includes base, two handles and wing locking nut, $46.90.
14. #25443, router table, transparent hinge guard, mitre gauge, adjustable fences, die-cast aluminum top, 1¼" diameter vacuum hose hookup, $69.99.
15. #25444, same as #25443 without sawdust collector, $59.99.
16. #25457, light duty router table, structural foam top and fences, transparent hinge guard, and mitre gauge, $39.99.
17. #7614, same as #7615, except is not a plunge cut router; rack and pinion depth adjustment of 1½", $94.95.

PORTABLE DRILLS

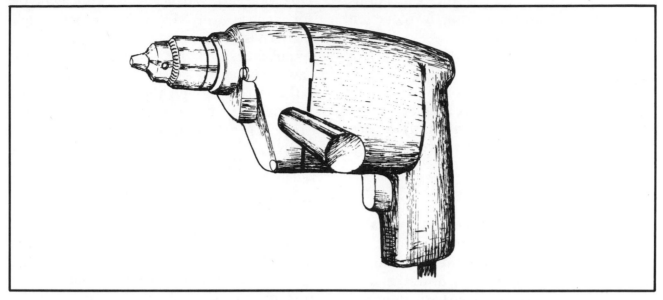

The portable electric drill is probably the most common of all power tools, and many times, is the first power tool acquired by a woodworker. They are simple tools consisting of a small motor with a gear drive system to transfer the power from the motor to the chuck. They typically have a "pistol" grip with a simple trigger control switch.

All portable drills operate in essentially the same way, however, there are differences from one tool to the next. These differences include chuck design and capacity, material used to make the housing and reduction gears, bearings, speed and speed control features, reversing switch, motor amperage, weight, overall size, and cordless options.

CHUCKS

When you are shopping for a drill, be sure to examine the chuck carefully. Most portable drills have geared chucks which require a key for adjustment, however, there are some keyless "auto-chucks" on the market. Jacobs brand chucks are considered by many to be best, and you will usually find them on the better drills. Chuck capacities

generally range from ¼" to ¾" with ¼", ⅜" and ½" being most common. Check the operating smoothness of the chuck by opening it to its maximum capacity and then closing it completely, the jaws should move smoothly and accurately. The size capacity should be marked on the outside of the chuck somewhere. A chuck with a 0-½" capacity will hold the smallest numbered drills and shanks up to ½" in diameter.

When trying to decide what size chuck to buy, think of the ways you intend to use the tool. Most woodworkers use portable drills for small hole work. A ¼" chuck capacity will often be sufficient, however, a ⅜" capacity offers more versatility and is the most popular size today. If you are like most woodworkers you will seldom need a ½" capacity in a portable tool. As chuck sizes increase so does the overall size of the tool. Larger drills are sometimes awkward to use and are fatiguing in long runs.

HOUSING DESIGN

Drill housings are either made from plastic or a combination of plastic and metal. One hundred percent metal housings are a thing of the past. Plastic handles offer added electrical insulation and increase the overall safety of the tool. Some of the better drills have a metal housing covering the reduction gears and a plastic handle.

The overall design of the motor and housing will determine the weight, length, balance, and feel of the tool. Some of the newer models are using smaller, more efficient motors which significantly reduce the bulk of the tool and improve handling.

SPEED

Drills are available in single or variable speed models. Variable speed tools are most versatile and are probably the best choice. There is a bit of a "trade-off", however, with any variable speed tool. Since variable speed options require complex electrical systems, you may experience more frequent switch or speed control problems. Single speed units usually present fewer electrical problems.

A wide variety of speed options are available. The top speed is directly related to the chuck capacity, 1/4" drills have the highest top speeds, and 1/2" drills have the slowest. Approximate average speed ranges for variable speed drills are 1/4" capacity, 0-1800 RPM; 3/8" capacity, 0-1400 RPM; 1/2" capacity, 0-500 RPM.

SPECIAL SWITCH FEATURES

Drills will be equipped with a trigger switch, and most have a locking pin which can be engaged to hold the trigger in an "on" position. The switch on variable speed models also controls the RPM. Some variable speed models have an adjustable stop on the trigger so the same RPM can be obtained each time.

Some drills are equipped with a reversing switch, a feature which is useful when you are using the tool to install and remove screws.

ACCESSORIES

A wide variety of accessories are available for electric drills. With the proper attachments it is possible to use the tool as a buffer or polisher, a grinder, a saber saw, a circular saw, a plane, a sander, and even a small lathe. Even though these varied uses are possible, a drill performs best as a drill, and you will get the longest, trouble free service from the tool if it is used primarily as a hole making tool.

PRICES

Drill prices vary with quality and features offered. It is possible to buy a 1/4" single speed drill for less than $20.00, and it's also possible to spend almost $150.00 for a 1/4" variable speed model. Aside from the variable speed feature, the biggest overall quality difference between these tools would be in engineering, including bearing and gear design. The higher priced units will have ball bearings throughout and metal reduction gears, whereas, cheaper models will have sleeve bearings and plastic gears. Some people consider the low priced models to be disposable tools; they use them until they experience trouble, then discard them and buy a new one. You will find that you may never wear out a high quality drill.

CORDLESS DRILLS

There are a number of cordless drills on the market today, and these tools are truly portable. Not having to worry about a convenient electric outlet or a long extension cord really improves the overall versatility of the electric drill. There is some "trade-off", however. Cordless drills are generally slower in RPM, vary in power holding capabilities, and are bulky. Even with these limitations, if you have a need for a completely portable tool, cordless is the way to go.

AEG
BE 8RL

AEG
BE 10RL

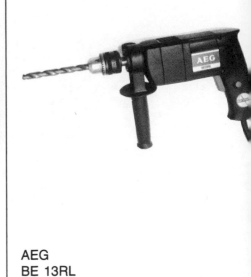

AEG
BE 13RL

BLACK & DECKER
1182

BLACK & DECKER
1180

BLACK & DECKER
1181

BLACK & DECKER
1170

BLACK & DECKER
1575

BLACK & DECKER
7145

BLACK & DECKER
7190

BLACK & DECKER
7144

BLACK & DECKER
1040

BLACK & DECKER
1042

BLACK & DECKER
7043

BLACK & DECKER
1311

BOSCH
1158 VSR

BOSCH
1160 VSR

BOSCH
91064

BOSCH
1157 VSR

BOSCH
91066

BOSCH
1920 VSRK

CRAFTSMAN

CRAFTSMAN
ELECTRONIC

HITACHI
D 6V

HITACHI
D 10VC

HITACHI
D 10V

HITACHI
D 13V

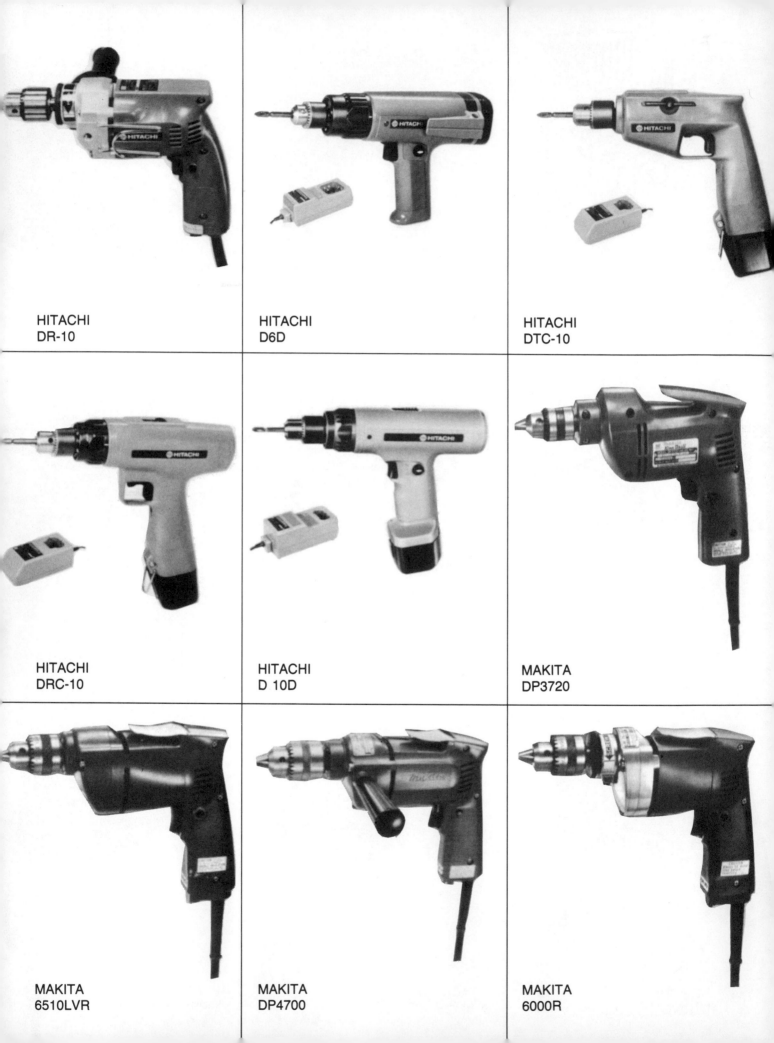

HITACHI
DR-10

HITACHI
D6D

HITACHI
DTC-10

HITACHI
DRC-10

HITACHI
D 10D

MAKITA
DP3720

MAKITA
6510LVR

MAKITA
DP4700

MAKITA
6000R

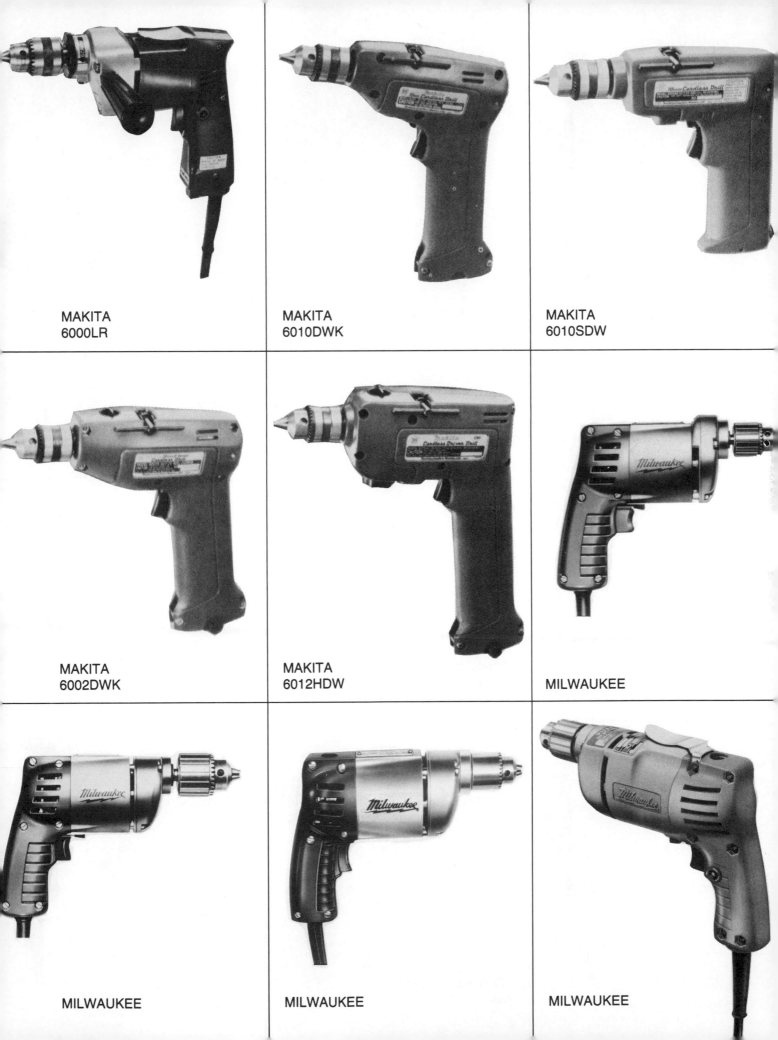

MAKITA
6000LR

MAKITA
6010DWK

MAKITA
6010SDW

MAKITA
6002DWK

MAKITA
6012HDW

MILWAUKEE

MILWAUKEE

MILWAUKEE

MILWAUKEE

PORTER CABLE
7501

PORTER CABLE
7503

PORTER CABLE
664

PORTER CABLE
7510

PORTER CABLE
7511

PORTER CABLE
620

PORTER CABLE
621

PORTER CABLE
666

PORTER CABLE
7514

PORTER CABLE
622

RYOBI
D-100VR

RYOBI
D-1320R

SKIL
6125

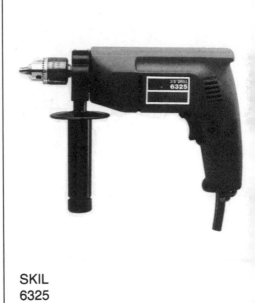

SKIL
6325

SKIL
6345

SKIL
6505

SKIL
6545

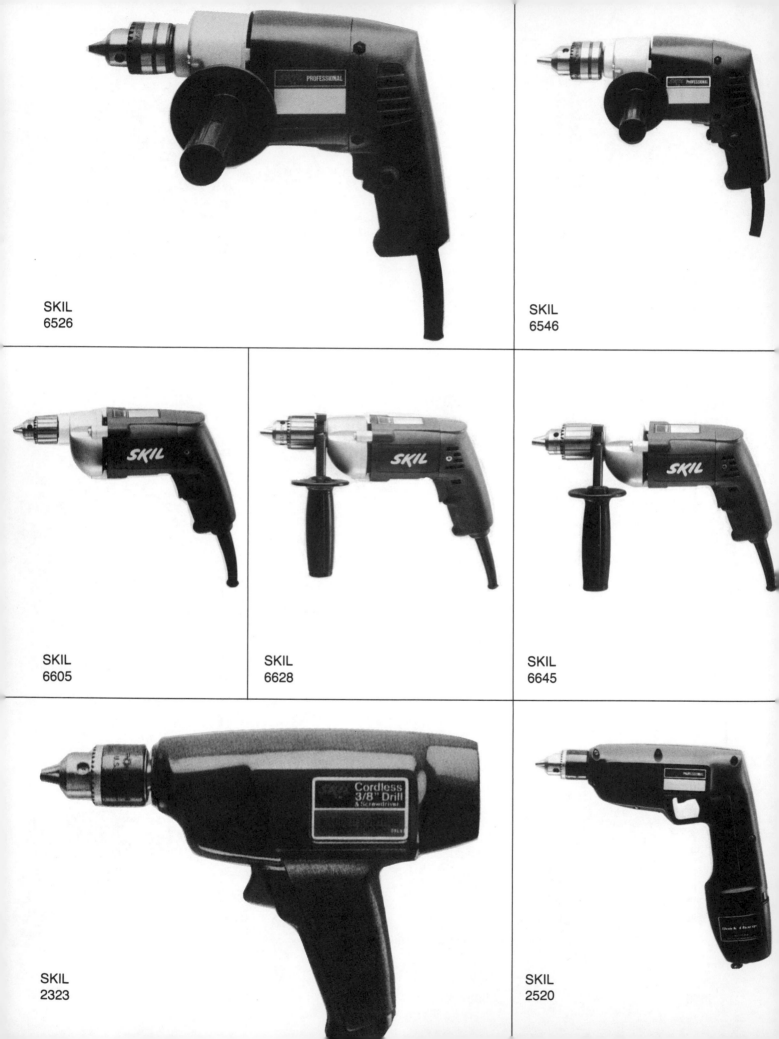

SKIL
6526

SKIL
6546

SKIL
6605

SKIL
6628

SKIL
6645

SKIL
2323

SKIL
2520

PORTABLE DRILL

Brand *No photo Available	Model	Size	Voltage	Amps	Watts In	Watts Out	Special Features**	Options***	Drilling Capacity In Steel	Drilling Capacity In Wood	Bearings	Speed	RPM	Length	Reversible	Net Weight	Suggested Retail Price
AEG	BE8RL	3/8"	115	3.8	400	215	16-27 44-50-51	–	3/8"	3/4"	Ball	Variable	0-2200	–	Yes	3	$ 86
AEG	BE10RL	3/8"	115	5.0	525	270	16-27 44-52	–	3/8"	1 1/2"	Ball & Needle	Variable	0-1400	–	Yes	3 1/2	125
AEG	BE13RL	1/2"	115	4.5	475	260	28-38 44-51-53	–	1/2"	1 1/2"	–	Variable	0-550	–	Yes	4.2	139
*AEG	EZ505	3/8"	–	–	–	–	7-12 39-54-55	–		3/4"	–	Two	300/600	11 3/4"	Yes	2 2/3	139
*AEG	EZ506	3/8"	–	–	–	–	7-12-39 44-55-56-57	–		3/4"	–	Variable	100-500	11 3/4"	Yes	3	159
BLACK & DECKER	1182	3/8"	–	4.5	–	–	16-17-18	–	3/8"	1 1/4"	Ball & Roller	Variable	0-1200	10 3/4"	Yes	3 3/4	175
BLACK & DECKER	1180	3/8"	–	4.5	–	–	18-19	–	3/8"	1 1/4"	Ball & Roller	Variable	0-1200	9 3/4"	Yes	3 5/8	157
BLACK & DECKER	1181	3/8"	–	4.5	–	–	18-19	–	3/8"	1"	Ball & Roller	Variable	0-1800	9 3/4"	Yes	3 5/8	157
*BLACK & DECKER	1179	3/8"	–	4.5	–	–	18-19	–	3/8"	1 1/4"	Ball	Variable	0-1200	9 5/8"	Yes	3 1/2	122
BLACK & DECKER	1170	3/8"	–	4.5	–	–	18-19-20	–	3/8"-LO 1/4"-HI	1 1/4"-LO 3/4"-HI	Ball	Dual Range Variable	0-1200 0-2500	10 1/2"	Yes	3 3/4	169
*BLACK & DECKER	1175	3/8"	–	3.5	–	–	2-18	–	3/8"	1"	Ball & Roller	Variable	0-2000	9 5/8"	Yes	3 1/2	96
BLACK & DECKER	1575	3/8"	–	4.5	–	–	6-18	–	3/8"	1 1/4"	Ball	Variable	0-1200	10 1/2"	Yes	3 1/4	180
BLACK & DECKER	7145	3/8"	120	3.0	–	–	21-22-23	–	3/8"	3/4"	Ball-thrust & Sleeve	Variable	0-1200	–	Yes	2 1/2	67.95
BLACK & DECKER	7190	3/8"	120	3.0	–	–	18-23	–	3/8"	3/4"	Ball-thrust & Sleeve	Variable	0-1200	–	Yes	2 3/4	58.95
BLACK & DECKER	7144	3/8"	120	2.2	–	–	24	3-4	3/8"	3/4"	Ball-thrust & Sleeve	Variable	0-1200	–	Yes	2 1/2	–

PORTABLE DRILL

Brand *No photo Available	Model	Size	Voltage	Amps	Watts In	Watts Out	Special Features**	Options***	Drilling Capacity In Steel	Drilling Capacity In Wood	Bearings	Speed	RPM	Length	Reversible	Net Weight	Suggested Retail Price
BLACK & DECKER	1040	¼″	—	4.5	—	—	19	—	¼″	1″	Ball & Roller	Variable	0-1800	9⅜″	Yes	3¼	$152
*BLACK & DECKER	1046	¼″	—	4.5	—	—	18-19	—	¼″	1″	Ball & Roller	Variable	0-2500	9⅜″	Yes	3¼	152
BLACK & DECKER	1042	¼″	—	4.5	—	—	18-19	—	¼″	¾″	Ball & Roller	Variable	0-4000	9⅜″	Yes	3¼	152
BLACK & DECKER	7043	¼″	120	2.2	—	—	—	—	¼″	½″	Ball-thrust & Sleeve	Single	2500	—	—	1⅞	26^{95}
BLACK & DECKER	1311	½″	—	4.5	—	—	17-25	—	½″	1½″	Ball & Roller	Variable	0-600	10⅞″	—	4⅝	170
*BOSCH	1161VSR	¼″	115	—	350	—	63-64	—	¼″	⅝″	—	Variable	0-1900	10¼″	Yes	3¼	145
BOSCH	1158VSR	⅜″	115	—	280	—	64	—	⅜″	1″	—	Variable	0-2100	10″	Yes	3¼	85
BOSCH	1160VSR	⅜″	115	—	350	—	63-64	—	⅜″	1″	—	Variable	0-1000	10¼″	Yes	3¼	135
BOSCH	91064	⅜″	120	—	370	—	16-58	—	⅜″	1″	—	Variable	0-1000	7¾″	Yes	3¼	169
BOSCH	1157VSR	⅜″	115	—	350	—	63-64	—	⅜″-LO $^{3}/_{16}$″-HI	¾″-LO ½″-HI	—	Two Range Variable	0-1400 0-2400	11⅜″	Yes	3¼	159
BOSCH	91066	½″	120	—	330	—	16-58	—	½″	1¼″	—	Variable	0-650	8½″	Yes	3¾	185
*BOSCH	1163VSR	½″	115	—	500	—	28-63-64	—	½″	1¼″	—	Variable	0-800	11¾″	Yes	5	149
BOSCH	1920VSRK	⅜″	—	—	—	—	12-39	12	¼″	$^{9}/_{16}$″	—	Two Range Variable	0-300 0-650	9.6″	Yes	2¾	159
CRAFTSMAN	1030	⅜″	—	—	—	—	16-17-27-35 44-45-46	—	—	—	Ball, sleeve & Roller	Variable	0-1200	—	Yes	—	99^{99}
CRAFTSMAN	1027	½″	—	—	—	—	16-22-25-27	—	—	—	Sleeve	Single	600	—	Yes	—	59^{99}
CRAFTSMAN	1001	⅜″	—	—	—	—	16-18	—	—	—	Sleeve	Single	1200	—	Yes	—	24^{99}
CRAFTSMAN	1004	⅜″	—	—	—	—	16-27-71	—	—	—	Sleeve	Variable	0-1200	—	Yes	—	59^{99}

PORTABLE DRILL

Brand *No photo Available	Model	Size	Voltage	Amps	Watts In	Watts Out	Special Features**	Options***	Drilling Capacity In Steel	Drilling Capacity In Wood	Bearings	Speed	RPM	Length	Reversible	Net Weight	Suggested Retail Price
CRAFTSMAN	1051	3/8"	–	–	–	–	16-35	–	–	–	Ball & Sleeve	Variable	0-1200	–	Yes	–	$69.99
CRAFTSMAN	10419	3/8"	–	–	–	–	16-27-34 35-72	–	–	–	Ball, sleeve & Roller	Variable	0-1200	–	Yes	–	89.99
CRAFTSMAN	1116	3/8"	110/120	–	–	–	7-16-18-39	16	–	–	Ball-thrust & Sleeve	Two	100 & 300	–	Yes	–	69.99
CRAFTSMAN	27101	3/8"	–	4.5	–	–	18-73	–	–	–	Ball & Roller	Variable	0-1200	–	Yes	–	109.99
CRAFTSMAN	27102	3/8"	–	4.5	–	–	18-73	–	–	–	Ball & Roller	Two Range Variable	0-1200 0-2500	–	Yes	–	119.99
CRAFTSMAN	27100	3/8"	–	3.5	–	–	18-73	–	–	–	Ball & Roller	Variable	0-2000	–	Yes	–	79.99
CRAFTSMAN	27121	1/2"	–	4.5	–	–	25-73	–	–	–	Ball & Roller	Variable	0-550	–	–	–	119.99
CRAFTSMAN	27124	1/2"	–	6.0	–	–	25-73	–	–	–	Ball & Roller	Single	450	–	–	–	129.99
HITACHI	D6V Heavy Duty	1/4"	115	2.7	–	–	1-2-3	–	1/4"	1/2"	Ball	Variable	0-2300	8 3/4"	Yes	2.9	110
HITACHI	D10VC Medium Duty	3/8"	115	3.2	–	–	1	–	3/8"	5/8"	–	Variable	0-1800	9 1/2"	Yes	3	90
HITACHI	D10V Heavy Duty	3/8"	115	3.3	–	–	1-2-3-4	–	3/8"	1"	Ball & Needle	Variable	0-1100	9 2/3"	Yes	3.3	118
HITACHI	D13V Heavy Duty	1/2"	115	4.7	–	–	1-3-4	–	1/2"	1 3/8"	Ball & Needle	Variable	0-600	11 3/8"	Yes	4.4	155
HITACHI	DR10	3/8"	115	3.1	–	–	3-5-6	–	3/8"	5/8"	–	Variable	0-2600	10"	Yes	4.2	173
HITACHI	D6D	1/4"	–	–	–	–	7-8-9 10-11-14	–	0.138"	3/8"	–	Single	320	9 7/8"	Yes	2.2	130
HITACHI	DTC10	3/8"	–	–	–	–	11-12-14	1	3/8"	19/32"	–	Two	280/700	9 7/8"	Yes	2.6	143

PORTABLE DRILL

Brand *No photo Available	Model	Size	Voltage	Amps	Watts In	Watts Out	Special Features**	Options***	Drilling Capacity In Steel	Drilling Capacity In Wood	Bearings	Speed	RPM	Length	Reversible	Net Weight	Suggested Retail Price
HITACHI	DRC10	3/8"	—	—	—	—	9-11 12-13-14	2	3/8"	19/32"	—	Two	300/650	10⅝"	Yes	3.3	$159
HITACHI	D10D	3/8"	—	—	—	—	9-11 13-14-15	—	3/8"	23/32"	—	Two	300/1000	10 13/32"	Yes	3.5	185
MAKITA	DP3720	3/8"	115	2.7	—	—	2-16	—	3/8"	5/8"	Ball	Variable	0-1800	9½"	Yes	3.3	90
MAKITA	6510LVR Heavy Duty	3/8"	115	3.0	—	—	4-16-18	—	3/8"	3/4"	Ball	Variable	0-1050	9½"	Yes	3.3	116
MAKITA	DP4700 Heavy Duty	1/2"	115	4.8	—	—	2-16	—	1/2"	1 3/8"	Ball & Needle	Variable	0-550	10⅞"	Yes	4.4	154
MAKITA	6000R UNI Drill	3/8"	115	3.3	—	—	6-16	—	3/8"	5/8"	Ball & Needle	Variable	0-2600	10⅞"	Yes	3.5	168
MAKITA	6000LR UNI Drill	3/8"	115	3.3	—	—	6-16-22	—	3/8"	3/4"	—	Variable	0-1200	10¼"	Yes	4.2	178
MAKITA	6010DWK	3/8"	—	—	—	—	7-11-12-14 26-58-59	—	—	3/8"	—	Single	600	9"	Yes	2.4	152
MAKITA	6010SDW	3/8"	—	—	—	—	6-7-12-26 58-60-61	—	3/8"	3/8"	—	Single	600	8"	Yes	2.1	84
MAKITA	6002DWK	3/8"	—	—	—	—	7-11-12 26-58-59	10	3/8"	5/8"	—	Two	600/2500	9¼"	—	2.6	154
MAKITA	6012HDW	3/8"	—	—	—	—	7-15-26 39-59-62	11	1/4"	5/8"	—	Two	400/1100	9"	Yes	3.5	178
MILWAUKEE	0101	1/4"	120	3.0	—	—	—	—	—	—	Ball & Roller	Single	2500	8⅜"	No	3½	125
MILWAUKEE	0102-1	1/4"	120	3.0	—	—	—	—	—	—	Ball & Roller	Variable	0-2500	8⅜"	Yes	3½	129
MILWAUKEE	0122-1	1/4"	120	3.3	—	—	—	—	—	—	Ball & Roller	Variable	0-2000	8¾"	Yes	3¾	145

PORTABLE DRILL

Brand *No photo Available	Model	Size	Voltage	Amps	Watts In	Watts Out	Special Features**	Options***	Drilling Capacity In Steel	Drilling Capacity In Wood	Bearings	Speed	RPM	Length	Reversible	Net Weight	Suggested Retail Price
MILWAUKEE	0141	¼"	120	3.3	–	–	–	–	–	–	Ball & Roller	Single	3500	8¾"	No	3¾	$149
MILWAUKEE	0181	¼"	120	3.3	–	–	–	–	–	–	Ball & Roller	Single	2500	8¾"	No	3¾	149
MILWAUKEE	0221	3/8"	120	3.3	–	–	–	–	–	–	Ball & Roller	Single	650	9½"	No	4	159
MILWAUKEE	0222-1	3/8"	120	3.3	–	–	–	–	–	–	Ball & Roller	Variable	0-1000	9½"	Yes	4	146
MILWAUKEE	0228-1	3/8"	120	3.3	–	–	3-4-30-65	13	–	–	Ball & Roller	Variable	0-1000	9¼"	Yes	3¾	129
*MILWAUKEE	0124-1 Magnum	¼"	120	4.5	–	–	22-65-66-67	14	–	–	Ball & Roller	Variable	0-2000	10"	Yes	4	159
*MILWAUKEE	0224-1 Magnum	3/8"	120	4.5	–	–	22-65-66-67	–	–	–	Ball & Roller	Variable	0-1200	10½"	Yes	4¾	159
*MILWAUKEE	0234-1 Magnum	½"	120	4.5	–	–	4-22 65-66-67	15	–	–	Ball & Roller	Variable	0-850	10¼"	Yes	4¾	159
*MILWAUKEE	0244-1 Magnum	½"	120	4.5	–	–	22-65-66-67	–	–	–	Ball & Roller	Variable	0-600	10½"	Yes	4¾	159
PORTER CABLE	7501	¼"	115	5.2	598	–	16-18-68-19	–	¼"	1"	Ball & Needle	Variable	0-1700	9⅝"	Yes	3¼	140
PORTER CABLE	7503	¼"	115	5.2	598	–	16-18-68-69	–	¼"	3/4"	Ball & Needle	Single	2500	9⅝"	No	3¼	140
PORTER CABLE	664	¼"	115	4.0	460	–	16-18 68-69-70	–	¼"	½"	Ball & Needle	Variable	0-2000	8½"	Yes	3½	150
PORTER CABLE	7510	3/8"	115	5.2	598	–	16-22 25-68-69	–	3/8"	1¼"	Ball & Needle	Single	1000	10"	No	4	150
PORTER CABLE	7511	3/8"	115	5.2	598	–	16-22 25-68-69	–	3/8"	1¼"	Ball & Needle	Variable	0-1000	10"	Yes	4	154

PORTABLE DRILL

Brand *No photo Available	Model	Size	Voltage	Amps	Watts In	Watts Out	Special Features**	Options***	Drilling Capacity In Steel	Drilling Capacity In Wood	Bearings	Speed	RPM	Length	Reversible	Net Weight	Suggested Retail Price
PORTER CABLE	620	3/8"	115	4.0	460	—	16-18-68-69	—	3/8"	3/4"	Ball & Needle	Single	1000	9½"	No	3¼	$114.50
PORTER CABLE	621	3/8"	115	4.0	460	—	16-18-68-69	—	3/8"	3/4"	Ball & Needle	Variable	0-1000	9½"	Yes	3¼	120
PORTER CABLE	666	3/8"	115	4.0	460	—	16-18 68-69-70	—	3/8"	3/4"	Ball & Needle	Variable	0-1200	8½"	Yes	3¾	155
PORTER CABLE	7514	1/2"	115	5.2	598	—	16-22 25-68-69	—	1/2"	1½"	Ball & Needle	Variable	0-750	11½"	Yes	4	159
PORTER CABLE	622	3/8"	115	4.0	460	—	6-68	—	—	—	Ball & Needle	Variable	0-1000	11"	Yes	4	165
RYOBI	D-100VR	3/8"	120	3.2	—	—	2-17 27-47-48	—	3/4"	3/8"	—	Variable	0-1200	9⅝"	Yes	3.1	91
*RYOBI	D-1010	3/8"	120	3.3	—	—	2-27	—	—	—	—	Variable	0-1300	—	Yes	3.0	118
RYOBI	D-1320R	1/2"	120	6.8	—	—	28-30	—	1/2"	1⅛"	—	Two	700/1400	—	Yes	6.6	145
*RYOBI	D-1015A	3/8"	120	3.3	—	—	2-6	—	—	—	—	Variable	0-2600	—	Yes	3.0	No Price Available
*RYOBI	BD-1020R	3/8"	—	—	—	—	7-12 26-39-49	—	3/8"	1/2"	—	Two	300/600	—	Yes	—	148
SKIL	6125	3/8"	120	3.0	—	—	16-26-27	6	3/8"	3/4"	Ball-thrust & bronze	Single	2500	—	Yes	3½	34.99
SKIL	6325	3/8"	120	3.2	—	—	16-18 26-27-28	—	3/8"	3/4"	Ball-thrust	Variable	0-1300	—	Yes	3¾	45.99
SKIL	6345	1/2"	120	3.2	—	—	16-18 26-27-28	—	1/2"	1"	Ball-thrust & bronze	Variable	0-800	—	Yes	4	49.99
SKIL	6505	1/4"	120	3.5	—	—	16-27-29 30-31-32	—	1/4"	1/2"	Ball & Needle	Variable	0-2000	—	Yes	3¾	88

PORTABLE DRILL

Brand *No photo Available	Model	Size	Voltage	Amps	Watts In	Watts Out	Special Features**	Options***	Drilling Capacity In Steel	Drilling Capacity In Wood	Bearings	Speed	RPM	Length	Reversible	Net Weight	Suggested Retail Price
*SKIL	6525	3/8"	120	3.5	–	–	16-27-29 30-31-33-34	–	3/8"	3/4"	Ball & Needle	Variable	0-750	–	Yes	3¾	$96
SKIL	6545	1/2"	120	3.5	–	–	16-27-29 30-31-33	–	1/2"	1"	Ball & Needle	Variable	0-500	–	Yes	4	103
*SKIL	6506	1/4"	120	3.8	–	–	16-27-29 30-31-32-34	–	1/4"	1/2"	Ball & Needle	Variable	0-2100	–	Yes	4 1/16	104
SKIL	6526	3/8"	120	3.8	–	–	16-27-30 31-34-35	7	3/8"	3/4"	Ball & Needle	Single	1200	–	No	3¾	105
SKIL	6546	1/2"	120	3.8	–	–	16-27-29 30-31-33-34	–	1/2"	1"	Ball & Needle	Variable	0-550	–	Yes	4 1/8	119
SKIL	6605	1/4"	120	4.5	–	–	16-27-30 31-33-36-37	8	1/4"	1/2"	Ball & Needle	Variable	0-2900	–	Yes	4¾	137
SKIL	6628	3/8"	120	4.5	–	–	16-27-28-30 31-33-36-37	8	3/8"	3/4"	Ball & Needle	Variable	0-1300	–	Yes	4 1/8	139
SKIL	6645	1/2"	120	4.5	–	–	16-27-28-30 31-36-37-38	–	1/2"	1"	Ball & Needle	Variable	0-850	–	Yes	4 5/8	149
*SKIL	2323	3/8"	–	–	–	–	7-18-26-27 39-40-41-42	–	3/8"	3/4"	–	Two	100/300	–	Yes	2 1/5	82⁹⁵
SKIL	2520	3/8"	–	–	–	–	11-12 27-39-43	9	3/8"	3/4"	–	Single	600	–	Yes	3¾	99

**SPECIAL FEATURES

1. All insulation construction.
2. Belt clip for easy carrying.
3. Auto-stop carbon brush for longer armature life.
4. Industrial drive chuck.
5. Side hook.
6. Positive clutch, can be used as screwdriver.
7. Cordless.
8. Includes battery pack of 4.8 volts and charger.
9. Two mode action, adjustable screwdriving and drilling.
10. Three stage adjustable clutch for screw drilling.
11. Removable 60 minute rechargable battery pack system.
12. Includes battery pack of 7.2 volts and charger.
13. Five stage adjustable clutch for screw drilling.
14. Automatic cutoff, 1 hour charger.
15. Includes battery pack of 9.7 volts and charger.
16. Double insulated.
17. Auxiliary handle.
18. Double gear reduction.
19. Two finger trigger switch.
20. Mechanical two speed gear shift.
21. Electronic drill with infinite speed lock.
22. Includes side handle.
23. Infinite speed trigger locks at selected speed.
24. Back of drill designed so greater hand pressure can be applied to drill bit.
25. Triple gear reduction.
26. Built in key storage.
27. Trigger lock-on.
28. 360° rotating assist handle.
29. Pre-set speed adjustment and trigger.
30. Die-cast aluminum gear housing.
31. Reinforced motor housing.
32. Single reduction helical gearing.
33. Double reduction helical gearing.
34. Removable side handle.
35. Double reduction helical and spur gearing.
36. Constant force brush spring.
37. Reversing switch on both sides of handle.
38. Triple reduction helical gearing.
39. 1 hour recharge cycle.
40. Ready light indicates full charge.
41. Nickel cadium batteries.
42. Includes 120V charger.
43. Charge indicator light-charger.
44. Electronic.
45. Keyless chuck.
46. Analog feedback control keeps speed constant.
47. Hardened steel gears.
48. High impact glass-reinforced polycarbonate housing.
49. Three clutch settings plus straight drive.
50. 24 bar welded commutator.
51. Glass reinforced nylon housing.
52. Helical, hardened gear train.
53. Aluminum gear box is nylon encapsulated for safety.
54. Four stage torque control.
55. Bit storage in handle.
56. Micro-processor system to control speed regardless of load.
57. Six independent clutch settings.
58. Overload protected.
59. Includes carrying case.
60. 3 hour recharge cycle.
61. Built in power pack.
62. Five stage torque setting.
63. Variable speed switch with adjusting knob allows pre-setting to desired speed.
64. Fully insulated.
65. Trigger speed control.
66. Exclusive brush cartridge system.
67. Kuik-lok detachable cords.
68. Precision gearing with helical pinion.
69. Positive brush stops.
70. "T" handle design.
71. Double reduction spur gearing.
72. Auto-chuck for quick bit change without a key.
73. Industrial model.

***OPTIONS

1. #D10DB, variable version of #DTC10, 0-300/650, $155.
2. #D10DC, variable version of #DRC10, 0-300/650, $170.
3. #7147, same drill except is non-reversing, $37.95.
4. #7143, same as #7147, with single speed of 1200, $33.95.
5. #1312, same as #1311 except with variable speed of 0-900, $170.
6. #6225, same as #6125 except has variable speed of 0-2500, $42.99.
7. #6530, same as #6526 except has variable speed of 0-1200 and a reversing switch, $109.
8. #6625, same as #6628 except has single speed of 1300, non-reversing, $96.
9. #2725, same as #2520 except has dual range variable speeds of 0-250 and 0-750, $139.
10. #6002D, same as #6002DWK except without carrying case and charger, $118.
11. #6012HD, same as #6012HDW except without carrying case and charger, $146.
12. #1920RK, same as #1920VSRK except with two speeds of 300 and 650, non-reversing, $139.
13. Also available in 240V AC.
14. Also available in 220V.
15. Also available in 240V.
16. #1112, same as #1116 except has two range, variable speeds of 0-250 and 0-750, $99.99.

PORTABLE JIG SAWS OR SABER SAWS

Portable jig saws or saber saws have probably one of the worst reputations of all portable power tools, and they don't deserve this distinction. Jig saws certainly aren't the answer to all of a woodworker's sawing needs, but when properly chosen and used, they are quite versatile and can be used for operations which are not possible with other power tools. They are used for rough cut-off work, scroll cutting, internal curved sawing even on very large panels; and they will plunge cut without a pilot hole. When equipped with the proper blade, they can be used for cutting a variety of materials including solid wood, plywood, particle board, hardboard, plastics, tile, leather, carpet, and metals. Woodworkers, especially carpenters, find these tools invaluable in making curved cuts on large plywood sheets. Basically a jig saw consists of a motor, gear system, housing, base, blade, blade or ram shaft, and an electrical control.

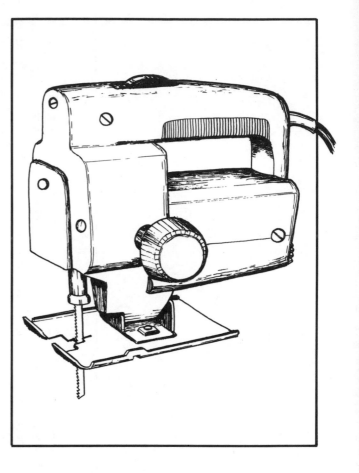

HOUSING

Plastic is the principal material used to make jig saw housings because of the added electrical insulation it provides. The entire unit may be plastic, but occasionally, metal gear housings are used at the front of the tool.

Housings frequently include some type of handle design on top of the saw. The two most common handle shapes are closed loop and open-end designs. The handle will include a start/stop control, and sometimes, a variable speed control. Handles should be comfortable to your hand and should be located to provide for well balanced handling. Unfortunately most jig saw handles put the operators hand far above the work surface and tool manipulation is awkward. It would be easier to control the tool if the grip and center of gravity were lower. Some manufacturers have realized this advantage, and on some of the more recent saw designs, the operator actually grips the motor housing. The tool may or may not have a knob located above the gear housing for the other hand. These improved handles are referred to as "barrel" or "barrel and knob" grips and should result in much better tool control. Unfortunately you will find this handle design on only a few of the more expensive saws.

BLADE, BLADE GUIDE, AND CLAMP

When you really think about the design and function of the jig saw blade and the shaft it is attached to, it doesn't take long to realize that the blade itself is a fragile thing and the ram shaft is subjected to some rather severe loads. A single guide roller behind the blade is used on many saws to provide back support for the blade and relieve some of the stress on the ram shaft. One manufacturer carries the roller design one step further by providing side rollers for the blade to improve side support. Guide rollers should definitely prolong the life of the tool. Jig saws with an "auto-scroll" head, a head which will allow you to rotate the ram shaft 360 degrees, cannot have a back up roller.

Unfortunately all jig saws do not use the same type of blade. Almost 90% of the saws sold today will accommodate a blade with a universal end; it's the other 10% you need to be careful about. It's something like not being able to use a router bit because your router has some kind of special chuck design. Thank goodness routers don't have this problem. Universal blades are readily available at most hardware stores, but you may have trouble finding some of the special designs. The safest way to go is buy a tool with universal blade capabilities. If everyone did this, we would probably soon find that universal blades would fit all jig saws.

The blade clamping system should be simple and easy to use since you will be changing blades often. Many saws use straight slotted screws to tighten the clamp. This is probably because a straight screwdriver is a much more common tool than an allen wrench. Allen head screws actually have a longer life expectancy and are probably best, if you can keep up with the wrench. Speaking of wrenches, it sure is nice if the tool used to tighten the chuck is the same tool needed to adjust the saw's base. It is really inconvenient if it isn't.

The cutting stroke on jig saws ranges from ½" to 1⅛" with 1" being most common. The longer the stroke, the more teeth you have working for you. This results in a faster cutting tool and better blade life.

CUTTING FEATURES & SPEED

Jig saws cut on the up-stroke, and you should be prepared for a certain amount of splintering on top of the work piece, especially on panels with thin face veneers. Splintering is more of a problem with orbital action saws rather than those with a straight up and down movement. Some orbital units come with an anti-splinter insert which can be attached to the base to help overcome the problem. Orbital saws cut faster than straight action models, so if speed is what you want and the added splintering tendency isn't a problem, orbital may be the way to go.

The majority of the jig saws on the market today are either variable speed or dual speed units. Only a few single speed models are available. Available speeds range from 0 to 4500 strokes per minute with 0 to 3100 SPM being about average for variable speed saws. If you want the maximum versatility, you should definitely consider a variable speed model which will allow you to change speeds as materials and material thickness change.

BASES

Jig saw bases are small, sometimes almost too small for good stability. Generally the larger the base the easier the tool is to control. Bases are usually adjustable so that bevel cuts up to 45 degrees, left and right, can be made. The accuracy of most base angle indicators is marginal. Actually, precision is usually required only at 90 degrees and 45 degrees, so slight inaccuracies at other angles may not necessarily be a problem. The best way to be sure the base and blade are set at the angle you want is to use a square or a protractor.

AEG
FSP60

AEG
FSPE60

AEG
BSPE60

BLACK & DECKER
3159

BLACK & DECKER
3157

BLACK & DECKER
3153

BLACK & DECKER
7580

BLACK & DECKER
7548

BLACK & DECKER
7530

BLACK & DECKER
CORDLESS 3140

BOSCH
1581 & 1581VS

BOSCH
1582 & 1582VS

BOSCH
7551 100

BOSCH
1922

BOSCH
3230 & 3238 VS

CRAFTSMAN
ELECTRONIC
1840

HITACHI
JHV-60

HITACHI
CJ65V

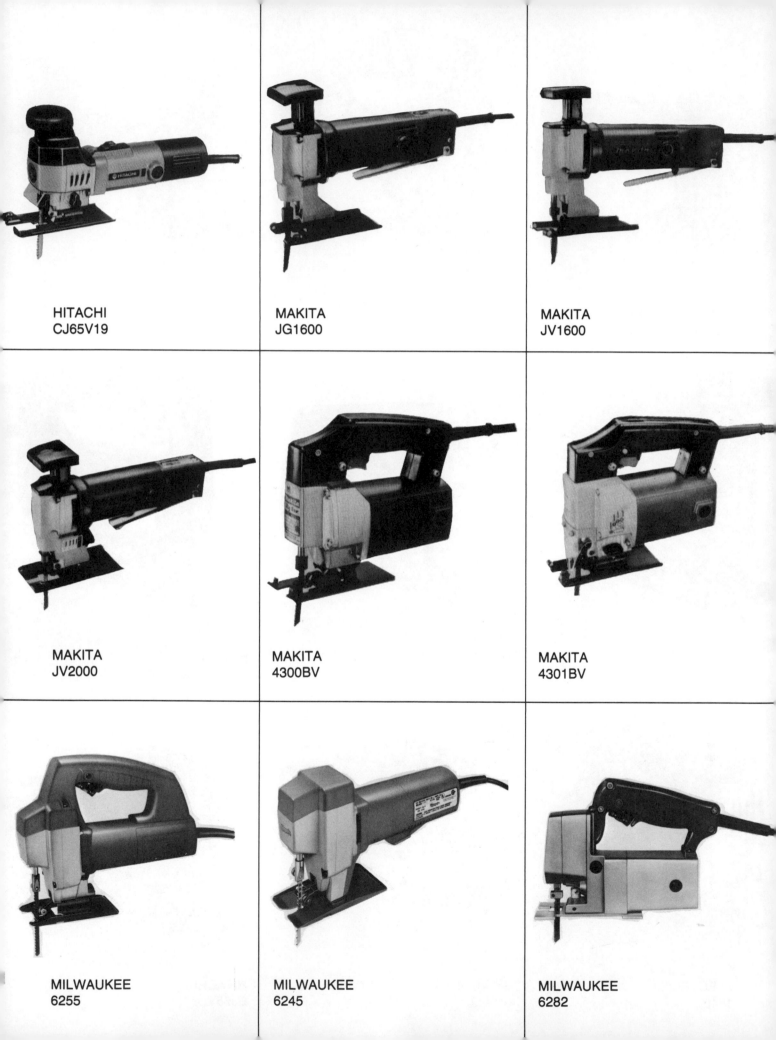

HITACHI
CJ65V19

MAKITA
JG1600

MAKITA
JV1600

MAKITA
JV2000

MAKITA
4300BV

MAKITA
4301BV

MILWAUKEE
6255

MILWAUKEE
6245

MILWAUKEE
6282

**PORTER CABLE
548 & 8548**

**PORTER CABLE
648**

**PORTER CABLE
348**

**RYOBI
JS-60**

**RYOBI
JSE-60**

**SKIL
4115**

**SKIL
4235**

**SKIL
4535**

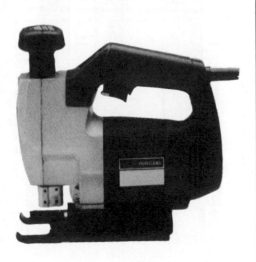

**SKIL
4555**

**SKIL
4575**

JIG SAW

Brand *No photo Available	Model	Amps	Voltage	Special Features**	Options***	Speed (Strokes per Minute)	Length of Stroke	Dimensions H × W	Length	Base Tilt	Bearings	Net Weight	Suggested Retail Price
AEG	FSP60	4.6	115	3-7-15 33 thru 38	—	3200	1″	—	—	45° R&L	—	4½	$158
AEG	FSPE60	4.6	115	3-7-15 33 thru 39	—	300 to 3200	1″	—	—	45° R&L	—	4½	178
AEG	BSPE60	4.6	115	3-7-13-15-39 33 thru 37	—	300 to 3200	1″	—	—	45° R&L	—	4½	198
BLACK & DECKER	3159	4.5	—	7-15-52	—	2100 & 3100	1″	7¼ × —	10¼″	—	Ball & Roller	6¼	183
BLACK & DECKER	3157	4.5	—	7-15-52-65	—	0 to 3100	1″	8$^{1}/_{16}$ × —	8¾″	—	Ball & Roller	6¼	183
BLACK & DECKER	3153	4.5	—	52-65	—	0 to 3100	1″	8$^{1}/_{16}$ × —	8¾″	—	Ball & Roller	6¼	172
*BLACK & DECKER	7571	3.0	120	66-67-68-69	—	2500 & 3200	⅝″	—	—	45° R&L	Sleeve	4¼	59^{95}
BLACK & DECKER	7580	3.0	120	3-11	—	0 to 3200	⅝″	—	—	45° R&L	Sleeve	3½	51^{95}
BLACK & DECKER	7548	2.2	120	70-71	—	0 to 3200	⅝″	—	—	45° R&L	Sleeve	2⅞	44^{95}
BLACK & DECKER	7530	3.0	120	3	—	2500 & 3200	⅝″	—	—	45° R&L	Sleeve	6⅜	37^{95}
*BLACK & DECKER	7543	2.2	120	3-70-71	—	3200	⅝″	—	—	45° R&L	Sleeve	2⅝	29^{95}
BLACK & DECKER	3140	—	—	7-27-45 52-72-73-74	—	2400	¾″	6⅞ × —	12⅛″	—	Ball	4.3	175
*BLACK & DECKER	3141	—	—	7-27-45 52-72-73-75	—	2400	¾″	6⅞ × —	12⅛″	—	Ball	4.3	152
BOSCH	1581	—	115	3-7-8-13-14 15-16-22	—	3100	1″	—	10⅝″	45° R&L	—	5¾	195
BOSCH	1582	—	115	3-7-15-19 20-21-22	—	3100	1″	—	10⅝″	45° R&L	—	5½	179
BOSCH	7551-100	—	—	18-23-24 25-26	—	0 to 3000	1″	—	9¼″	—	—	4.3	329

JIG SAW

Brand *No photo Available	Model	Amps	Voltage	Special Features**	Options***	Speed (Strokes per Minute)	Length of Stroke	Dimensions H × W	Length	Base Tilt	Bearings	Net Weight	Suggested Retail Price
BOSCH	1922	—	—	3-7-27-28 29-30-31-32	—	1700	3/4"	—	—	—	—	5	$199
BOSCH	3230	—	115	7-8-28-33	5	3000	3/4"	—	9¾"	45° R&L	—	4½	79
CRAFTSMAN	1840	—	—	48-76-77-78 79-80-81	—	—	1"	—	—	45° R&L	Ball & Sleeve	—	99⁹⁹
*CRAFTSMAN	17209	—	—	3-48-78-82	—	0 to 3000	3/4"		—	45° R&L	—	—	79⁹⁹
*CRAFTSMAN	1072	—	—	3-78-81-83	—	0 to 3000	5/8"	—	—	45° R&L	Sleeve	—	69⁹⁹
*CRAFTSMAN	1070	—	—	3-78-81	—	0 to 3000	5/8"	—	—	45° R&L	Sleeve	—	59⁹⁹
*CRAFTSMAN	1716	—	—	3-81-84	—	0 to 3000	1/2"	—	—	45° R&L	Sleeve	—	39⁹⁹
*CRAFTSMAN	1714	—	—	3-84	—	2600 & 3000	1/2"	—	—	45° R&L	Sleeve	—	24⁹⁹
HITACHI	JHV-60	3.5	115	7-41 7-15	—	0 to 3200	1"	—	8¼"	45° R&L	—	5.2	208
HITACHI	CJ65V	3.7	115	57-58-59	—	700 to 3200	1"	—	9¾"	45° R&L	—	5.5	192
HITACHI	CJ65VA	3.7	115	7-15-38 60-61-62	—	700 to 3200	1"	—	11³/₁₆"	45° R&L	—	5.8	192
MAKITA	JG1600	2.6	115	3-8 40-41-42	—	3700	5/8"	—	9½"	45° R&L	—	3.7	138
MAKITA	JV1600	2.6	115	3-8 40-41-42	—	0 to 3700	5/8"	—	10"	45° R&L	—	3.3	148
MAKITA	JV2000	3.2	115	3-7-8 15-41	—	0 to 3400	3/4"	—	10⅜"	45° R&L	—	3.5	165
MAKITA	4300 BV Super Duty	3.5	115	8-41-43	—	0 to 3100	1"	—	8⅞"	45° R&L	—	5.5	192
MAKITA	4301 BV Super Duty	3.5	115	3-7-8-15	—	0 to 3100	1"	—	8⅞"	—	—	6	208
MILWAUKEE	6255	3.8	120	3-7-8-17	1-2	0 to 3100	1"	8½ × 3½	9¹⁵/₁₆"	45° R&L	Ball & Roller	6	199

JIG SAW

Brand *No photo Available	Model	Amps	Voltage	Special Features**	Options***	Speed (Strokes per Minute)	Length of Stroke	Dimensions H × W	Length	Base Tilt	Bearings	Net Weight	Suggested Retail Price
MILWAUKEE	6245 Heavy Duty	3.8	120	3-7-8-17	1-2	3100	1″	$5^{1}/_{16} \times 3\frac{1}{2}$	$9^{15}/_{16}$″	—	—	4¾	$175
MILWAUKEE	6282 Heavy Duty	2.3	120	10-11-12	2	0 to 3900	¾″	6½ × 3½	8½″	—	Ball & Roller	5	No Price Available
PORTERCABLE	548 Heavy Duty	3.2	115	1-2-3-4-5	—	0 to 4500	$^{7}/_{16}$″	—	7⅛″	—	Ball & Needle	6	235
PORTERCABLE	8548	1.75	220	1-2-3-4-5	—	4500	$^{7}/_{16}$″	—	7⅛″	—	Ball & Needle	6	258
PORTERCABLE	648 Heavy Duty	3.0	115	3-6-7-8	—	3200	1″	—	8¾″	—	Ball & Needle	5	186
PORTERCABLE	348 Heavy Duty	3.0	115	5-9-18	—	3500	$^{9}/_{16}$″	—	8″	45° R&L	Ball & Bronze	5	143
RYOBI	JS-60	3.5	120	7-8-15 53-63	—	3000	1″	—	$10^{7}/_{16}$″	45° R&L	—	5½	172
RYOBI	JSE-60	3.5	120	7-15-53 63-64	—	1000 to 2700	1″	—	$10^{7}/_{16}$″	45° R&L	—	5½	198
SKIL	4115	3.0	120	8-35 44-45-46	—	LO 2600 HI 3200	⅝″	—	—	—	—	3⅝	38^{99}
SKIL	4235	3.0	120	8-44 45-46	7-8-9	0 to 3200	⅝″	—	—	—	—	3⅝	43^{99}
*SKIL	4355	3.0	120	8-35 44 thru 49	7-8-9	0 to 3200	⅝″	—	—	—	—	3⅞	49^{99}
*SKIL	4395	3.2	120	8-35 44 thru 51	7-8-9	0 to 3200	⅝″	—	—	—	—	4	54^{99}
SKIL	4535	3.5	120	3-8-35-41 52-53-54	7-8-9	0 to 3200	$^{13}/_{16}$″	—	—	45° R&L	—	5½	80
SKIL	4555	3.5	120	3-8-35-41 48-52-54-55	7-8-9	0 to 3200	$^{13}/_{16}$″	—	—	45° R&L	Ball & Needle	5½	90
SKIL	4575	3.5	120	3-8-35-41-48 50-52-54-56	7-8-9	0 to 3200	$^{13}/_{16}$″	—	—	45° R&L	Ball & Needle	5⅝	102

1. Worm gear drive.
2. Top handle design with auxiliary side handle.
3. Built in sawdust blower.
4. 24 square inch base for stable tool support.
5. "Magic circle" base insert eliminates chipping and splintering.
6. Wrap-around blade clamp automatically positions blade at proper cutting angle.
7. Roller bearing blade support.
8. Double insulated.
9. Base is 15½" square.
10. Pivoting head, 45° right or left.
11. Includes combination circle and rip guide.
12. Shoe quickly adjusts for straight, miter, or flush cuts.
13. Top handle design.
14. Internal weights dynamically balance the cutting mechanism.
15. Four position blade orbital action.
16. Will cut from straight line reciprocating to full orbital.
17. Exclusive blade clamp; blade changed with screwdriver.
18. Orbital blade cutting action.
19. Six position speed control.
20. Barrel grip removable, rotating handle.
21. Industrial duty.
22. Bayonet blade lock eliminates set-screw mounting hole, which is the most common breaking point on universal mounting jig saw blades.
23. Explosion proof.
24. No room air is drawn through the unit.
25. Air supply requirement is 90 psi.
26. Air consumption: no load, 20.1 cfm; full load, 27.5 cfm.
27. Cordless; battery powered.
28. Three position orbital action.
29. Footplate adjusts for 45° bevel cuts and retracts for close edge cutting.
30. Takes one hour to charge batteries.
31. Uses 24V DC battery.
32. Includes battery and charger.
33. Anti-splintering device.
34. Universal blade retention system.
35. Counterbalance system.
36. Safety guard for plunger.
37. Blade key clip on shoe.
38. Barrel grip.
39. Electronic, full wave feedback speed control assures precise blade speed.
40. Motor housing grip and paddle switch.
41. Universal blade clamp.
42. Includes circular guide and rip fence.
43. Non-conductive polycarbonate housing.
44. Precision machined steel plunger.
45. Blade storage compartment in body.
46. Storage slot for blade and foot wrench.
47. Front assist knob.
48. Auto-scrolling has the blade positioned behind the plunger; allows easy tracking for even the most intricate patterns.
49. Manual mode blade lock 0, 90, 180, and 270 degrees.
50. Vari-orbit scroll provides auto scrolling along with orbital action in a single unit.
51. Five vari-orbit ranges.
52. Professional model.
53. Ball bearing construction.
54. Aluminum die-cast gear housing.
55. Three mode operation: auto scroll, manual scroll, and straight line cutting.
56. Six position adjustable vari-orbit.
57. Electronic feedback system automatically.
58. Anti-abrasion design.
59. Moving base, front to rear.
60. Moving base, front and rear side.
61. Auto-stop carbon brush for longer armature life.
62. Electronic control variable speed.
63. Hardened steel gears.
64. Electrode module provides constant speed and torque.
65. Fan motor cools gripping surfaces and clears dust for visibility.
66. Auto-scrolling pivots blade in direction saw is guided.
67. Manual scrolling top knob can rotate blade 360° by hand.
68. Scrolling action may be locked out for use as regular jig saw.
69. Includes chip deflector, rip fence/circle guide.
70. Two position shoe.
71. Rectangular drive shaft.
72. Includes 100 watt DC motor.
73. Thick, flat aluminum shoe.
74. Includes #3141 power unit, #98003 detachable energy pack, charger.
75. Includes #3141 power unit, #98003 detachable energy pack.
76. Electronic.
77. Includes chip shield.
78. Trigger locking switch.
79. Analog feedback automatically maintains selected speed.
80. Speed can be set at 20 different increments to obtain up to 3,000 strokes per minute.
81. Includes edge guide.
82. Includes circle cutting and straight edge attachment.
83. Manual scrolling mechanism.
84. Slide-type switch.

1. #49-22-4090, rip fence, $3.45.
2. #48-55-1076, steel carrying case, $28.45.
3. #1581VS, also available with variable speed of 500-3100, $225.
4. #1 607 000 159, suction fixture and hose, no price available.
5. #3238VS, also available with variable speed of 0-3000, $119.
6. #1582VS, also available with variable speed of 500-3100, $209.
7. #25281, rip fence, $4.74.
8. #13802, universal miter gauge, $15.89.
9. #71026, jig saw table, $28.54.

PORTABLE SANDERS

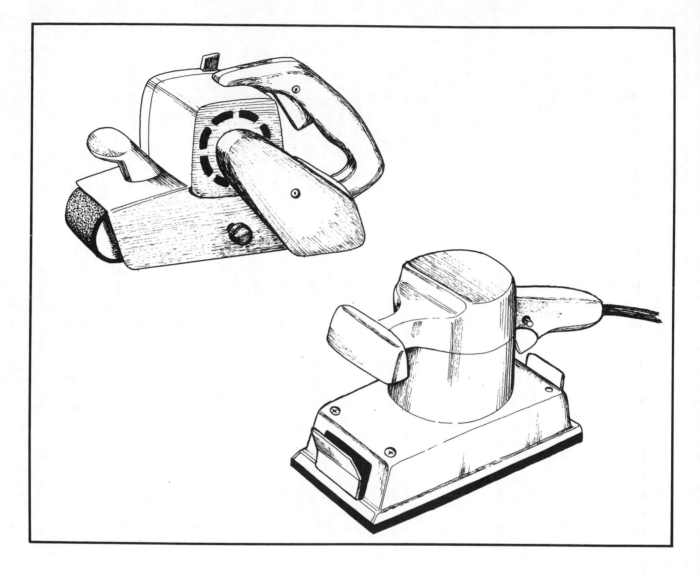

Portable sanders can be grouped into three general categories: belt sanders, pad (orbital or in-line) sanders, and disc sanders. These are all useful tools with each having its own unique characteristics. Woodworkers may have all three types in their tool collection.

PORTABLE BELT SANDERS

Portable belt sanders are primarily used for sanding flat surfaces. The belt design makes it possible to remove wood quickly, and this tool is frequently used in the early stages of sanding. While it is possible to sand flat surfaces with this tool, it takes practice. Skillful operators make the job look easy, but inexperienced workers will find that it is somewhat difficult to produce a dip free surface.

Belt sanders are sized by the width and length of the belt with common sizes being 3" × 21", 3" × 24", and 4" × 24". Small sanders with 2" to 2½" wide belts are available and convenient for small work. These light weight tools are not a good choice for large jobs, and you may experience problems finding belts to fit them.

Three inch wide sanders are most common. This width is actually a compromise

Portable belt sanders are primarily used for sanding flat surfaces.

between the 2″ and 4″ models. Two common belt lengths (21″ and 24″) are available on 3″ sanders. The longer belt will provide a longer sanding surface or platen and this improves the stability of the tool. Longer belts also have a larger abrasive surface which speeds up the work and improves belt life.

Four inch sanders are best suited for large jobs. The wider belt makes surface sanding quicker and easier, but the added expense limits the use of sanders of this size in small shops.

The parts of a belt sander include abrasive belt, two rollers or pulleys (idler and drive), sanding plate or platen, drive system, and motor. Most of these tools have a belt/gear drive system. A toothed belt connects the motor to a set of reduction gears which are attached to the rear pulley. On some of the most expensive models the belt is replaced with a chain.

Four inch sanders are best suited for large jobs.

The horsepower of portable sander motors usually isn't included in the tool's specifications. You must use the motor amperage as an index of power. The higher the amp rating the more powerful the tool will be, and generally, the more expensive it

is. It is usually best to buy as much amperage as you can afford.

The best belt sanders will be heavy enough to cut effectively without having to apply down pressure. This will give the operator better overall tool control.

Using a belt sander without a dust collection system is a mistake. This tool generates an enormous amount of dust which can create serious health and fire hazards. Be sure to purchase a tool which has a dust bag attached or one which can be attached to a shop vacuum. The attached dust bag design is most versatile.

The best belt sanders will be heavy enough to cut effectively without having to apply down pressure.

When you are shopping for a belt sander also consider the following details.

1. How is the belt changed and tracked? These are the most often used adjustments on a belt sander and should be simple and convenient to use.

2. What kind of switch does the unit have? One of the oldest belt sander problems has to do with a switch system which can be locked in an "on" position. If this is the case, it is possible to plug-in the sander while it's sitting on a bench and watch it run off to the floor. A lot of belt sanders have been damaged this way. The switch should be designed so it cannot be locked in an "on" position.

3. What kind of accessories or design features are available to convert the tool into a bench sander? Some sander housings are designed so they can be held in a clamp or vise for bench use. Others can be fitted to small tool stands. The added versatility of bench use is a desirable feature.

4. Is the tool balanced and do the handles and knobs feel comfortable?

PAD SANDERS

Pad sanders or finishing sanders are used primarily for final sanding operations. These tools are either orbital, straight-line or multi-action in design, and are available with pad sizes ranging from $\frac{1}{6}$ to $\frac{1}{2}$ of a sheet of abrasive paper.

ORBITAL SANDERS

Orbital action is best for rapid stock removal, however, tools of this design can leave swirl marks that can show up under a finish. Swirl marks are more of a problem with tools with fewer orbits per minute (opm). Speeds range from 3000 to 12,000 opm. It is probably best not to consider tools with fewer than 10,000 opm if you want efficient, smooth sanding.

In recent years small, $\frac{1}{4}$ sheet, orbital sanders (sometimes called palm sanders)

Most orbital sanders and other pad sanders will have a soft felt or foam pad under the sandpaper.

---

have become popular. Tools of this type have been used for a long time in industry, but only during the last ten years have manufacturers produced tools of this size for the home craftsman or small shop. These small sanders typically operate at approximately 12,000 opm and can produce smooth surfaces. Because of the small pad size, they are inefficient when sanding large surfaces. The abrasive sheets wear-out rather quickly.

Most orbital sanders and other pad sanders will have a soft felt or foam pad under the sandpaper. The softer this pad is, the more of a problem it can present. Soft pads can actually cause an exaggeration of the annual ring pattern on the wood. Each annual ring is composed of soft early wood and harder late wood. The soft pad will cut away the soft portion faster than the harder

areas, leaving the hard, late wood in relief. This becomes apparent after the finish is applied. It is actually best to sand the surface with a hard flat block or pad if you want to produce a flat surface.

STRAIGHT LINE ACTION

Straight line pad sanders are designed to produce a sanding action similar to hand sanding, the orbital scratches are eliminated. Tools of this type remove stock more slowly than orbital units and are usually used after an orbital sander. Some sanders are made with two kinds of pad action built in and can be changed from orbital to straight line by simply flipping a switch.

PORTABLE DISC SANDERS

Portable disc sanders are very common in auto body shops but are somewhat uncommon in wood shops. Auto body craftsmen use these tools for all sorts of smoothing and contouring operations. They have the same potential with wood. Many woodworkers consider this tool to be a shaping and forming tool rather than a finishing tool. Small 5″ disc sanders are most convenient for woodworking. In the hands of a skilled person, these tools can do a wonderful job of contour shaping.

ELECTRIC OR PNEUMATIC

Portable sanders are commonly available as electric tools, however, there are a number of pneumatically operated pad and disc sanders on the market. Industry will use pneumatic tools more often than their electric cousins. Pneumatic tools are usually smaller, easier to maintain, and generally perform better under continuous industrial use than electric tools. If you plan to use a sander under production conditions, it would be best to consider pneumatic options.

160

AEG
HBSE 75S

BLACK & DECKER
4030-10

BLACK & DECKER
4026

BLACK & DECKER
4025-10

BLACK & DECKER
7451

BLACK & DECKER
7496

BLACK & DECKER
7447

BOSCH
1272

BOSCH
1272D

BOSCH
3270D

BOSCH
1273

BOSCH
1273D

HITACHI
SB-75

HITACHI
SB-8T

HITACHI
SB-8TA

HITACHI
SB-110

MAKITA
9030

MAKITA
9900B

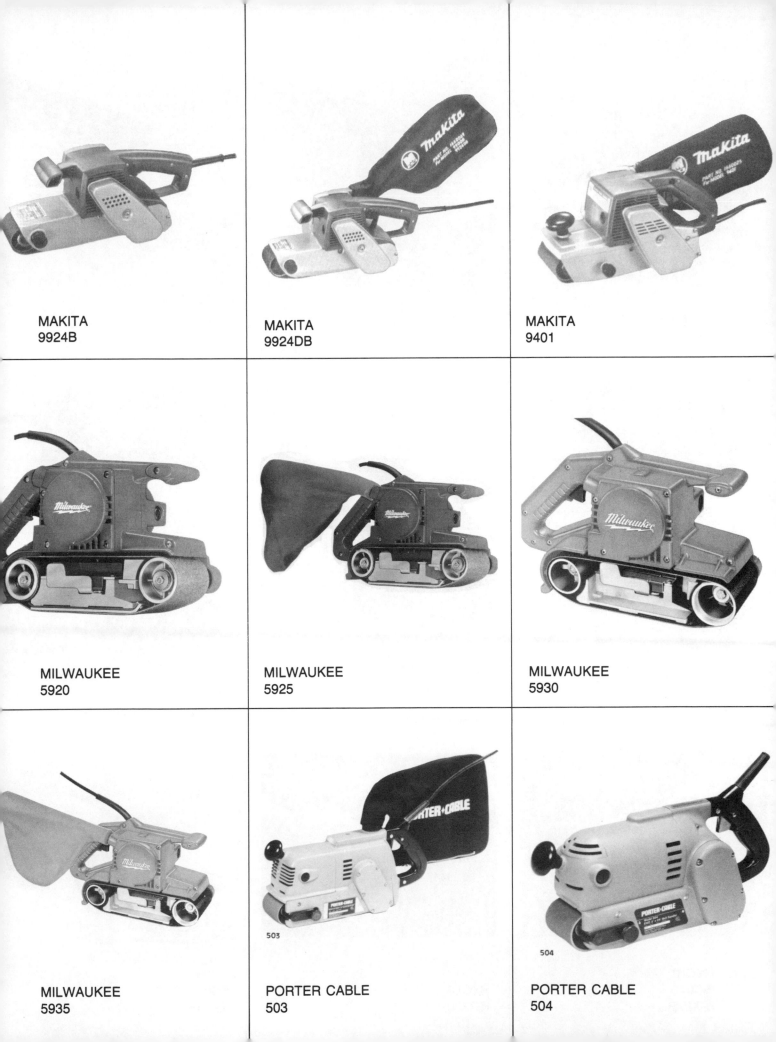

MAKITA
9924B

MAKITA
9924DB

MAKITA
9401

MILWAUKEE
5920

MILWAUKEE
5925

MILWAUKEE
5930

MILWAUKEE
5935

PORTER CABLE
503

PORTER CABLE
504

PORTER CABLE
336

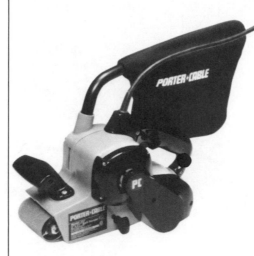

PORTER CABLE
337

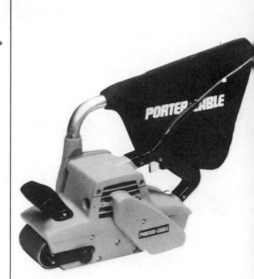

PORTER CABLE
360

PORTER CABLE
361

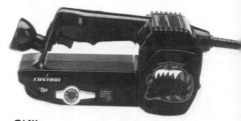

SKIL
7212

PORTER CABLE
363

PORTER CABLE
362

SKIL
7313

RYOBI
B-7075
B-7100

RYOBI
B-7200A

SKIL
595

PORTABLE BELT SANDER

Brand *No Photo Available	Model	Voltage	Amps	Special Features**	Options***	Belt Size	Surface Feet Per Minute (SFPM)	Length	Dust Collector	Drive	Bearings	Net Weight	Suggested Retail Price
AEG	HBSE 755	115	7.8	13-14-15	–	3×21	490-1040	16"	Yes	Belt/Gear	Ball	8.4	$199
BLACK & DECKER	4030-10 Professional	–	8.7	12	–	4×24	1150	14¾"	Yes	Belt/Gear	Ball & Sleeve	16.5	282
BLACK & DECKER	4026 Professional	–	8.4	17	–	3×24	1500	14"	Yes	Belt/Gear	Ball & Sleeve	10.5	212
BLACK & DECKER	4025-10 Professional	–	8.4	17	–	3×21	1180	12½"	Yes	Belt/Gear	Ball & Sleeve	9.6	201
BLACK & DECKER	7451	120	5.2	19	–	3×24	1200	–	Yes	Gear	Ball & Sleeve	8.75	169⁹⁵
BLACK & DECKER	7496	120	4.75	20	–	2½×16	600	–	Yes	Belt/Gear	Ball, Sleeve & Roller	5.25	78⁹⁵
BLACK & DECKER	7447	120	3.4	21	–	3×21	600	–	No	Belt	Ball & Sleeve	7	67⁹⁵
BOSCH	1272	115	10.5	1-2-3-7	1-5	3×24	1550	14"	No	Belt/Gear	Ball	13.8	259
BOSCH	32700	115	6.3	4-5-6	2-3-5	3×21	1080	17½"	Yes	Belt/Gear	Ball & Needle	7.9	175
BOSCH	1273	115	10.5	1-2-3-7	4-6	4×24	1550	14"	No	Belt/Gear	Ball	14.6	274
*CRAFTSMAN	11791C	–	–	12-27-28	–	4×21	1300	–	Yes	Belt/Gear	Ball & Roller	–	129⁹⁹
*CRAFTSMAN	11715	–	–	21-29	–	3×21	1300	–	Yes	Belt/Gear	Ball, Roller & Sleeve	–	99⁹⁹
*CRAFTSMAN	11713	–	–	21-29	–	3×21	1300	–	No	Belt/Gear	Ball, Roller & Sleeve	–	89⁹⁹
*CRAFTSMAN	1170	–	–	21-30	–	3×21	1300	–	No	Belt/Gear	Ball, Roller & Sleeve	–	69⁹⁹
*CRAFTSMAN	11722	–	–	21-31	–	3×21	600	–	No	Belt/Gear	Ball & Sleeve	–	59⁹⁹

PORTABLE BELT SANDER

Brand *No Photo Available	Model	Voltage	Amps	Special Features**	Options***	Belt Size	Surface Feet Per Minute (SFPM)	Length	Dust Collector	Drive	Bearings	Net Weight	Suggested Retail Price
HITACHI	SB-75	115	8.7	12	10	3×21	LO 1180 HI 1475	12¹⁵/₁₆"	Yes	Belt/Gear	Ball & Sleeve	10.8	$198
HITACHI	SB-8T	115	8.7	12	11	3×24	LO 1180 HI 1475	14⁹/₁₆"	Yes	Belt/Gear	Ball & Sleeve	11.4	219
HITACHI	SB-110	115	8.7	12-22	12	4¼×24⅜	LO 985 HI 1150	15⁷/₁₆"	Yes	Belt/Gear	Ball & Sleeve	17.1	280
MAKITA	9030	115	4.2	23	—	1⅛×21	3280	14⅛"	No	—	Ball & Needle	4	185
MAKITA	9900B	115	7.8	12-24	—	3×21	1180	12½"	Yes	Belt/Gear	Ball & Needle	10	198
MAKITA	9924B	115	7.8	12-24	—	3×24	1300	14"	No	Belt/Gear	Ball & Needle	10.2	188
MAKITA	99240B	115	7.8	12	—	3×24	1300	14"	Yes	Belt/Gear	Ball	10.5	214
MAKITA	9401	115	8.5	12	13	4×24	1148	14¾"	Yes	Belt/Gear	Ball & Needle	16	248
MILWAUKEE	5920	120	10.0	8-9-10-11	7	3×24	1400	—	No	Belt	—	13.5	289
MILWAUKEE	5930	120	10.0	8-9-10-11-12	8	4×24	1400	—	No	Belt	—	14.25	299
PORTER CABLE	503	115	9.0	—	—	3×24	1500	16¾"	Yes	Worm Gear & Chain	Ball & Needle	15	495
PORTER CABLE	504	115	9.0	—	—	3×24	1600	16"	No	Worm Gear & Chain	Ball & Needle	14	480
PORTER CABLE	336	115	6.5	—	—	3×21	1300	11¾"	No	Belt/Gear	Ball & Needle	9.5	171
PORTER CABLE	337	115	6.5	—	—	3×21	1300	11¾"	Yes	Belt/Gear	Ball & Needle	10	181
PORTER CABLE	360	115	10.5	—	—	3×24	1500	14"	Yes	Belt/Gear	Ball & Needle	16	275

PORTABLE BELT SANDER

Brand *No Photo Available	Model	Voltage	Amps	Special Features**	Options***	Belt Size	Surface Feet Per Minute (SFPM)	Length	Dust Collector	Drive	Bearings	Net Weight	Suggested Retail Price
PORTER CABLE	361	115	10.5	—	—	3×24	1550	14"	No	Belt/Gear	Ball & Needle	14	$255
PORTER CABLE	362	115	10.5	—	—	4×24	1500	14"	Yes	Belt/Gear	Ball & Needle	15.25	290
PORTER CABLE	363	115	10.5	—	—	4×24	1550	14"	No	Belt/Gear	Ball & Needle	14.5	275
RYOBI	B-7075	120	8.4	12-16-17	—	3×21	1181	12¼"	Yes	Belt/Gear	Ball	9.6	179
RYOBI	B-7100	120	8.4	12-16-17	—	3×24	1500	14"	Yes	Belt/Gear	Ball	9.7	208
RYOBI	B-7200A	120	8.7	12-16-18	9	4×24	1148	14¾"	Yes	Belt/Gear	Ball	16.7	269
*SKIL	7102	120	2.8	12	—	2½×16	600	—	No	Gear	Ball & Needle	4.5	59⁹⁹
SKIL	7212	120	3.3	12	—	3×18	700	—	No	Gear	Ball & Needle	6	83⁹⁵
SKIL	7313	120	4.5	12-17-25	—	3×18	700	—	Yes	Belt/Gear	Ball & Needle	5.5	76⁹⁹
SKIL	595	120	5.5	12	—	3×21	1000	—	Yes	Belt/Gear	Ball	8.25	180
*SKIL	7845	120	9.0	12-17-26	—	4×22	1000	—	Yes	Belt/Gear	Ball & Needle	10⅜	225

SPECIAL FEATURES

1. Rated for production sanding.
2. Unique tracking/tensioning system keeps belt centered.
3. Carbide wear-inserts protect housing from belt damage.
4. Spring steel belt support.
5. Detachable front handle.
6. Fine adjustment for exact belt tracking.
7. Pinch point guard for operator safety.
8. Rubber coated rear pulley wheel.
9. Positive brush stop prevents spring from damaging commutator.
10. Independent, ventilating and exhaust fan.
11. Strong fiberglass construction.
12. Sands flush.
13. Electronic model.
14. Electronic speed regulation.
15. Two die-cast aluminum stationary supports allow sander to be mounted upside down for bench use.
16. D-type handle provides operator control in all positions.
17. Can be used as a bench sander by turning upside down.
18. Can be used as a bench sander with accessory #X2065.
19. 13.8 square inches of sanding surface.
20. 10.7 square inches of sanding surface.
21. 14 square inches of sanding surface.
22. Can also use a 4 × 24 belt.
23. Removable multi-position side handle.
24. Externally accessable brushes.
25. 15 square inches of sanding surface.
26. 20½ square inches of sanding surface.
27. 29 square inches of sanding surface.
28. 1.25 HP motor.
29. 1 HP motor.
30. .75 HP motor.
31. ⅓ HP motor.

OPTIONS

1. #1272D, same as #1272 except has dust collector, $274.
2. #1608132007, bevel fence/width guide, $14.80.
3. #1167007164, vacuum hose connector, no price available.
4. #1273D, same as #1273 except has dust collector, $289.
5. #3601010504, platen protectors, 3", $2.40.
6. #3601010503, platen protectors, 4", $2.90.
7. #5925, same as #5920 except has dust collector, $309.
8. #5935, same as #5930 except has dust collector, $319.
9. #X2065, bench stand, $2.
10. #SB75S, bench stand, $35.
11. #SB-8TA, same as #SB-8T except without dust collector, $209.
12. #SB110S, bench stand, $45.
13. #342332-2, bench stand, $2.20.

AEG
VS130

AEG
VS260

BLACK & DECKER
4015

BLACK & DECKER
4018

BLACK & DECKER
4010

BLACK & DECKER
7480

BLACK & DECKER
7438

BLACK & DECKER
7445

BOSCH
1288D

BOSCH
1288

BOSCH
3254

HITACHI
SV12SA

HITACHI
SO110A

MAKITA
BO4510

MAKITA
BO4530

MAKITA
9035

MAKITA
9045B

MAKITA
9045N

MILWAUKEE
6014
SHOWN WITH DUST COLLECTOR

PORTER CABLE
505 & 8505

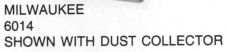

PORTER CABLE
330 & 8330

RYOBI
S-500A

RYOBI
SU-6200

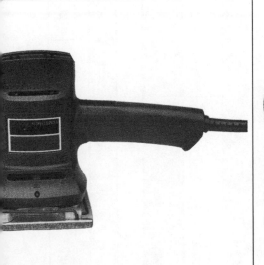

SKIL
7182

SKIL
7372

SKIL
7382

FINISHING SANDER

Brand *No Photo Available	Model	Voltage	Amps	Special Features**	Options***	Orbits Per Minute	Orbit Diameter	Paper Size	Height	Length × Width	Dust Collector	Bearings	Net Weight	Suggested Retail Price
AEG	VS130	115	1.3	1	—	20,000	3/32"	3⅜ × 9	6¾"	—	No	—	3½	$ 75
AEG	VS260	115	2.4	2-3	—	25,000	5/64"	4½ × 11	7¼"	—	No	—	5¾	156
*AEG	VSS260	115	2.4	2-4	—	25,000	5/64"	4½ × 11	7¾"	—	Yes	—	6½	189
BLACK & DECKER	4015 Professional	—	3.0	5-6	—	10,000	—	4½ × 11	7"	11½ × 4½	No	Ball	7½	172
BLACK & DECKER	4018 Professional	—	2.4	6-7	—	10,000	—	4½ × 11	7⅜"	11½ × 4½	No	Ball	5	149
BLACK & DECKER	4010 Professional	—	1.2	6-7-8-9	1	12,000	—	4½ × 5½	4¼"	5¼ × 4½	Yes	Ball	2⅝	88
*BLACK & DECKER	7456	120	3.0	6-10-11	—	4,000	—	4½ × 11	—	—	Yes	Ball & Sleeve	5⁷/₁₆	84⁹⁵
BLACK & DECKER	7480	120	3.0	6-11	—	4,000	—	4½ × 11	—	—	No	Ball & Sleeve	5	73⁹⁵
BLACK & DECKER	7438	120	2.8	6-10-11	—	4,200	—	3⅝ × 9	—	—	Yes	Ball & Sleeve	3½	74⁹⁵
BLACK & DECKER	7445	120	1.7	6-8-11	—	15,000	—	4¼ × 5½	—	—	No	Ball	1⅞	51⁹⁵
*BLACK & DECKER	7436	120	2.8	6-10-11	—	4,200	—	3⅝ × 9	—	—	No	Ball & Sleeve	3½	59⁹⁵
*BLACK & DECKER	7443	120	1.5	6-7-8	—	13,000	—	4¼ × 5½	—	—	No	Ball & Sleeve	1⅞	39⁹⁵
*BLACK & DECKER	7448	120	1.7	6-11	—	13,000	—	3⅝ × 9	—	—	No	Ball & Sleeve	2⅛	35⁹⁵
BOSCH	1288D	115	—	12-13	2	10,000	3/32"	4½ × 11	7⅜"	12 × 5⅞	Yes	—	6	179
BOSCH	3254	115	—	12-13-14	—	10,000	3/32"	3⅝ × 9	6¾"	9½ × 3¾	No	—	4¼	99
*CRAFTSMAN	1068	—	—	10-11	—	4,000	—	4½ × 11	—	—	Yes	Ball & Roller	—	89⁹⁹

FINISHING SANDER

Brand *No Photo Available	Model	Voltage	Amps	Special Features**	Options***	Orbits Per Minute	Orbit Diameter	Paper Size	Height	Length × Width	Dust Collector	Bearings	Net Weight	Suggested Retail Price
*CRAFTSMAN	1169	—	—	10-11	—	4,000	—	4½ × 11	—	—	No	Ball & Sleeve	—	$\$59^{99}$
*CRAFTSMAN	1165	—	—	10-11	—	4,000	—	3⅔ × 9	—	—	Yes	Ball & Sleeve	—	69^{99}
*CRAFTSMAN	1163	—	—	10-11	—	4,000	—	3⅔ × 9	—	—	No	Ball & Sleeve	—	39^{99}
*CRAFTSMAN	1062	—	—	11	—	9,200	—	3⅔ × 9	—	—	No	Ball & Sleeve	—	24^{99}
*CRAFTSMAN	11601	—	—	8	—	12,000	—	3⅔ × 9	—	—	No	Ball	—	69^{99}
*CRAFTSMAN	1066	—	—	8-15	—	N/A	—	3⅔ × 9	—	—	No	Ball	—	69^{99}
HITACHI	SV12SA	115	1.7	8-16-17	3	12,000	—	4⅜ × 4	—	4½ × __	No	Ball	3.3	79
HITACHI	S0110A	115	3.2	—	4-5	10,000	—	4½ × 9	—	11¼ × __	No	Ball	5.9	164
MAKITA	B04510	115	1.8	6-8-11-18	—	12,000	—	4⅜ × 4	5″	4½ × 4⅜	No	Ball	2.4	79
MAKITA	B04530	115	1.8	8-18-19	6	12,000	—	6″ round	5″	4½ × 6	No	Ball	2.4	84
MAKITA	9035	115	1.7	—	—	10,000	—	3⅝ × 7¼	—	9¼ × __	No	Ball	3	79
MAKITA	9045B Heavy Duty	115	4.0	11-20	7	10,000	—	4½ × 9¼	—	9¼ × __	No	Ball	6.2	156
*MILWAUKEE	6012 Heavy Duty	120	5.0	21-22	—	12,000	⅛″	3⅝ × 7⅜	7″	10½ × 3⅝	No	Ball	6	159
MILWAUKEE	6014 Heavy Duty	120	5.0	21-22	8	12,000	⅛″	4½ × 9¼	7″	11½ × 4½	No	Ball	7	169
PORTER CABLE	505 Heavy Duty	115	2.3	6	—	10,000	⅛″	4½ × 11	—	11½ × __	No	Ball	7¾	165
PORTER CABLE	8505 Heavy Duty	220	1.15	6	—	10,000	⅛″	4½ × 11	—	11½ × __	No	Ball	7½	170
PORTER CABLE	330	115	1.2	8	—	12,000	5/64″	4½ × 5½	—	4½ × __	No	Ball	3¾	87^{50}

FINISHING SANDER

Brand *No Photo Available	Model	Voltage	Amps	Special Features**	Options***	Orbits Per Minute	Orbit Diameter	Paper Size	Height	Length × Width	Dust Collector	Bearings	Net Weight	Suggested Retail Price
PORTER CABLE	8330	220	0.6	6-8	9-10	12,000	5/64"	4½×5½	—	4½×__	No	Ball	3¾	$94
RYOBI	S-500A	120	1.5	6-8	—	12,000	—	3×5½	—	—	No	Ball	2.16	70
*RYOBI	LS-35	120	1.45	—	—	10,000	5/64"	3×5½	5 9/16"	9×3⅝	No	Ball	2.9	78
RYOBI	SU-6200	120	2.9	6-23	—	10,000	⅛"	4½×11	—	—	No	Ball	8	142
SKIL	7182	120	1.2	6-17	—	8,400	1/16"	4½×5½	—	—	No	—	2½	38.99
SKIL	7372	120	2.5	6-10-24	—	4,000	3/16"	3⅝×9	—	—	No	Ball	5½	61.99
SKIL	7382	120	1.6	6-21	—	10,000	3/32"	3⅝×9	—	—	Yes	Ball	3.7	59.99
*SKIL	7582	120	2.0	6-24	—	10,000	⅛"	3⅝×9	—	—	No	Ball	4¼	98

SPECIAL FEATURES

1. Dust suction through base using external vacuum.
2. Auxiliary handle.
3. Detachable dust frame.
4. Rubber sanding plate conforms to contours.
5. Metal construction.
6. Flush sanding.
7. Needs no tools for paper changing.
8. Palm grip sander.
9. Includes paper punch and template.
10. Also acts as a straight line sander.
11. Lever actuated paper clamps.
12. Counter balanced vibration free.
13. Bearings and drive mechanism completely sealed against dust contamination.
14. Pushbutton clamping system allows quick sandpaper change.
15. Straight line sanding only; no orbital action.
16. Dust proof construction.
17. Spring wire clamping system for replacing sandpaper.
18. Designed for heavy duty use.
19. Uses pressure sensitive sandpaper.
20. Externally accessible brushes for easy inspection and replacement.
21. Low vibration.
22. 40% glass reinforced nylon housing and handles.
23. Water protection cover is designed for wet sanding.
24. Front assist handle.

OPTIONS

1. #4008, same as #4010 except without dust collector, $85.
2. #1288, same as #1288D except without dust collector; dust collector cannot be added to #1288, 5 lbs., $159.
3. #987177, 5" round pad, no price available.
4. #953365, dust bag, no price available.
5. #953364, dust cover, no price available.
6. 5" round and 4" square pads available.
7. #9045N, same as #9045B except with dust collector, $158.
8. #48-09-0300, dust pick-up kit, $14.40.
9. #47699, rubbing pad, $5.40.
10. #47696, sponge rubber pad, $6.75.

GRINDERS

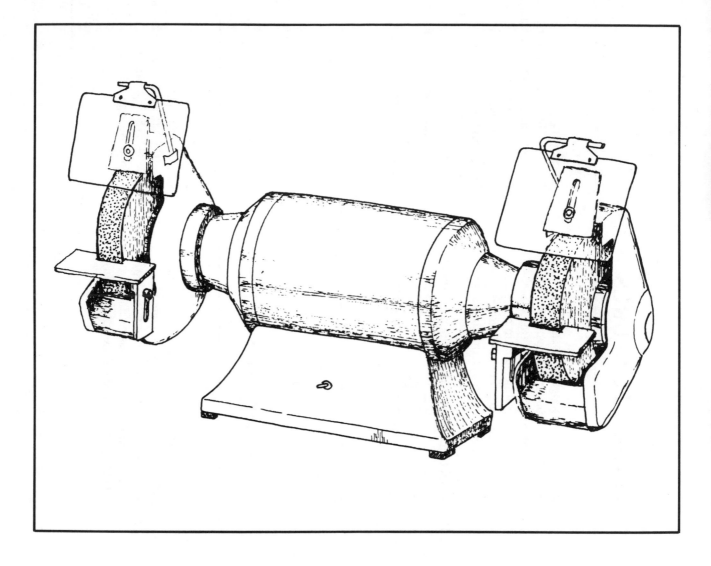

A woodworking shop isn't really complete without a bench grinder. Tool sharpening is an absolute must for the woodworker and the grinder plays a vital role in sharpening. Grinders are also used for cleaning, buffing and polishing when equipped with the proper wire or cloth wheels.

Grinders are available as either bench or pedestal models, and bench models are usually sufficient for most work done in the typical wood shop. Bench grinders are simple machines consisting basically of a small fractional horse power motor with extended shafts on each end. Grinding wheels will be mounted on these spindles and the wheels will be covered with guards. Tool rests and eye shields will be attached to housing of each wheel guard.

It is possible to purchase a belt driven grinder or grinder head. In this case the motor drives the grinder spindle with a single v-belt from the rear or under the head through an opening in the bench. Belt driven grinders can be used just like any other except that they may occupy more bench space.

SIZES

The size of a grinder is generally referred to in terms of the maximum diameter of the wheels. Sizes range from 6″ to 10″ with 6″ being most common. The horse power of the motor may also be included in a size designation, especially if the unit is direct drive. Horse power generally ranges from ¼ to 1 HP, with ¼ to ⅓ HP being common for 6″ machines. Grinder motors should be totally enclosed and fan cooled, and most units have sealed bearings requiring no lubrication. Motor speed will typically be either 1725 or 3450 RPM. Some craftsmen prefer 1725 RPM since it is somewhat easier to control grinding operations at this speed.

WHEEL GUARDS

Small bench grinders are very innocent looking tools, but they can be very dangerous if they are poorly guarded or improperly used. Good grinders will be equipped with

---

A woodworking shop isn't really complete without a bench grinder.

---

wheel guards which cover all of the wheel on both sides except for approximately one fourth of the wheel in front. Guards of this type will have outside covers which are bolted to a fixed wheel guard. Adjustable spark deflectors should be attached to the upper part of each wheel guard. The deflectors should be adjusted so they are as close to the wheel as possible before using the machine, and they will need to be readjusted periodically as the wheels wear down.

TOOL RESTS

The design of the tool rests is an important consideration in grinder selection. Quality grinders will have sturdy, fully adjustable tool rests. Some of the cheaper models will have small, poor quality, stamped steel rests which are awkward to adjust and use, and believe it or not, a few grinders are sold without tool rests. It is hard to believe that anyone would buy such a tool.

The size of a grinder is generally referred to in terms of the maximum diameter of the wheels.

Quality tool rests are made from relatively heavy steel or cast iron, and should be easily adjusted to a wide variety of angle settings. The best rests will be "U" shaped so a portion of the rest extends down the sides of the wheel, however, a well made straight tool rest will function very well.

EYE SHIELDS

It is more common to find grinders sold without eye shields than you might think. No one should ever use a grinder without eye protection in the form of safety glasses or a face shield. Eye shields attached to the grinder offer an additional protective device. Shields range from small adjustable plastic units to fairly large lighted designs.

The design of the tool rests is an important consideration in grinder selection. Quality grinders will have sturdy, fully adjustable tool rests.

The poorest excuses for eye shields are the flimsy ones made entirely from thin injection molded plastic. You will find these on some of the cheaper grinders, and they frequently break after a few hours use. You are better off to discard them immediately and install a quality shield to begin with.

Before you buy, be sure to inspect the eye shield carefully. It should have metal adjustments throughout, the shield itself can be plastic but not the entire assembly.

GRINDING WHEELS

New grinders should be equipped with two grinding wheels and be ready to use. Most tool sharpening can be done with medium hardness, aluminum oxide wheels. It is usually best to have a coarse wheel (approximately 36 grit) on one arbor and a finer wheel (approximately 60 grit) on the other. This is frequently the way new grinders are sold and offers the most

---

The poorest excuses for eye shields are the flimsy ones made entirely from thin injection molded plastic.

---

versatility. You will find that ¾" width wheels are sufficient for most work, but occasionally you might need special narrow wheels.

WORK LAMP

Good light is essential in grinding. The very nature of the grinding operation makes shadows a problem. The best eye shields are equipped with individual lights for each wheel. These shields are really nice, but they are expensive. A less expensive option is a single adjustable work lamp which can be mounted behind the grinder with a "goose neck" light extending over the motor.

Some grinders come with work lamps as standard items, on others it is an option, and on others it isn't available. A lamp of some type is certainly worth considering when shopping for grinders.

ALIGNMENT & ACCURACY

The accuracy of the grinder spindle and wheel flanges is controlled by the manufacturer of the unit. A new grinder should run smoothly at the proper speed and the spindle should have little or no end play.

When checking out a new grinder, be sure to check the spindle for end play and "run

---

Good light is essential in grinding. The very nature of the grinding operation makes shadows a problem.

---

out". You can easily check "run out" by simply spinning the wheels by hand and watching the relationship between the wheels and the wheel guard/tool rest. The wheels should move smoothly, without wobble.

It is really best to actually run the grinder before buying. A quality grinder should operate smoothly at full speed with little, if any, vibration. Don't buy a grinder if it vibrates badly, it was probably poorly manufactured.

ACCESSORIES

A wheel dresser, a device used to clean and true up grinding wheels, is the only accessory you need to maintain a grinder.

It is really best to actually run the grinder before buying.

These are either abrasive sticks, mounted industrial diamonds or mechanical wheels. Diamond dressers are actually best, but they are most expensive. You can get satisfactory results from mechanical dressers or abrasive sticks, and you should plan to buy a dresser of some type when you purchase a grinder.

BALDOR 6"
612

BALDOR 7"
7306DP

BALDOR 10"
1022WD

BLACK & DECKER
6818

BLACK & DECKER
6816

BLACKER & DECKER
7901

BOSCH
1961

CRAFTSMAN 6"
VARIABLE-SPEED
19213

DELTA
23-750

DELTA
23-850

DELTA
23-901

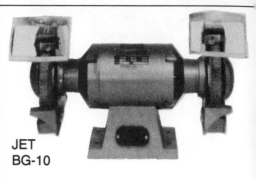

SCANGRIND
150

JET
BG-10

JET
BGS-8

MAKITA
9300

MILWAUKEE

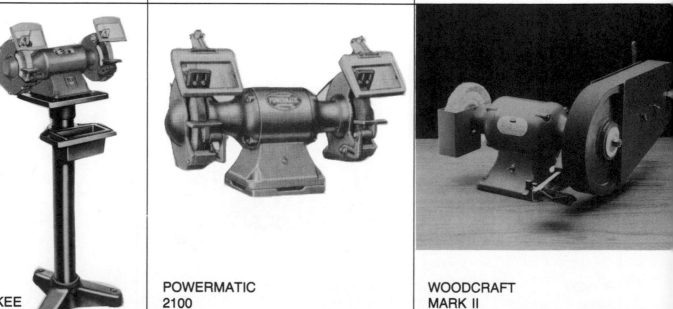

MILWAUKEE

POWERMATIC
2100

WOODCRAFT
MARK II

GRINDER

Brand *No Photo Available	Model	Size	Motor**	Horse-Power	Phase	Voltage	RPM	Amps	Special Features***	Options****	Distance Between Wheels	Wheel Size	Arbor Size	Tool Rest Construction	Clear Eye Shields	Lighted	Shipping Weight	Suggested Retail Price
BALDOR	612 Standard	6"	–	⅓	Single	115	3450	–	1-2	1-23 24-25-26	12¼"	6×¾	½"	PS	Yes	No	28	$139
*BALDOR	612E Deluxe	6"	1	⅓	Split	115	3450	–	1-2-3	2-3-23 24-25-26	14⅝"	6×¾	½"	PS	Yes	No	46	165
*BALDOR	632E Deluxe	6"	1	¼	Single	115	1725	–	1-2-3	23-24-25-26	14⅝"	6×¾	½"	CI	Yes	No	46	185
*BALDOR	673E Deluxe	6"	1	⅓	Single	115	3450	–	1-2-3-4	23-24-25-26	14⅝"	6×¾	½"	CI	Yes	No	42	185
*BALDOR	7306	7"	1	½	Single	115/230	1725	–	2-6-7	4-5-6-7 23-24-25-26	16½"	7×1	⅝"	CI	Yes	No	70	244
*BALDOR	762	7"	1	½	Single	115	3450	–	2-4	8-23 24-25-26	16¼"	7×1	⅝"	PS	Yes	No	67	199
BALDOR	7306DP	7"	1	½	Single	115/230	1725	–	2-7-9-10	9-10-11-12 23-24-26	–	7×1	⅝"	CI	Yes	Yes	88	406
*BALDOR	7312B	7"	1	⅓—Lo ½—Hi	Single	115/230	1725 Lo 3450 Hi	–	2-7-9-10	23-24-26	–	7×1	⅝"	CI	Yes	Yes	94	485
*BALDOR	8100W	8"	1	¾	Single	115/230	1725	–	2-6 11-12-13	13-14-15 23-24-25-26	17¾"	8×1	¾"	CI	Yes	No	97	395
*BALDOR	8250W	8"	1	¾	Single	115/230	3450	–	2-4-6 11-12-14	16-23 24-25-26	17¾"	8×1	¾"	CI	Yes	No	93	395
*BALDOR	8100WD	8"	1	¾	Single	115/230	1725	–	2-10 11-12-13	17-18-19 23-24-26	17¾"	8×1	¾"	CI	Yes	Yes	114	450
*BALDOR	1022W	10"	1	1	Single	115/230	1725	–	2-11-15	20-21-23 24-25-26	18"	10×1	⅞"	CI	Yes	No	115	498
BALDOR	1022WD	10"	1	1	Single	115/230	1725	–	2-10-15	22-23-24-26	18"	10×1	⅞"	CI	Yes	Yes	136	570
BLACK & DECKER	6818 Professional	8"	3-5	1	–	–	3580	7.2	2-34	–	16"	8×1	⅝"	PS	Yes	No	37	260

GRINDER

Brand *No Photo Available	Model	Size	Motor**	Horse-Power	Phase	Voltage	RPM	Amps	Special Features***	Options****	Distance Between Wheels	Wheel Size	Arbor Size	Tool Rest Construction	Clear Eye Shields	Lighted	Shipping Weight	Suggested Retail Price
BLACK & DECKER	6816 Professional	6"/7"	3-5	½	—	—	3580	4.8	2-34	—	13"	6×¾	½"	PS	Yes	No	27	$176
BLACK & DECKER	7901	5"	4	—	—	120	3600	2.2	2	—	10"	5×½	½"	PS	Yes	No	9¾	48⁹⁵
*BLACK & DECKER	9412	—	4	—	—	120	3600	2.8	35-36-37 38-39	—	—	5×¾	—	PS	Yes	No	12	85⁹⁵
BOSCH	1961	6"	—	⅓	—	115	3450	—	1-2-17	—	—	6×¾	½"	PS	Yes	No	26¾	169
CRAFTSMAN	19213	6"	2-6-7	—	—	110/115	0 to 3800	—	2-40	31-55-56 57-58-59	—	6×½	—	—	Yes	No	12	79⁹⁹
*CRAFTSMAN	19219C	8"	4	1	—	—	—	—	2-41-42-43	31-55-56 57-58-59	—	—	—	PS	Yes	No	44	249⁹⁹
*DELTA	23-650	6"	2	⅓	Single	—	3450	—	2-6 17-21-22	31-42-43	—	6×¾	½"	CI	Yes	No	29	173
DELTA	23-750	7"	2	½	Single	115	3450	—	2-6-17 21-22-23	31-34-37-38 39-40-41	—	7×1	⅝"	CI	Yes	No	41	283
DELTA	23-850	8"	2	¾	Single	115	3450	—	2-6-17 21-22-23	31-35-37-38 39-40-41	—	8×1	¾"	CI	Yes	No	65	330
DELTA	23-901	10"	2	1	Single	115/230	1725	—	2-6-17 21-22-23	31-36-37-38 39-40-41	—	10×1	¾"	CI	Yes	No	96	501
F&H MACHINERY (MFG-SCANGRIND)	150	6"	—	—	—	110 or 220/440	196	—	2-18-19-20	32-33	—	6×1½	—	—	No	No	12	125 PPD
*GRIZZLY	G1036	—	—	⅕	Single	110	60	2.0	2-20-27	—	—	10×2	—	—	No	—	32	129⁵⁰ PPD
*GRIZZLY	G1090	—	—	⅓	—	—	3600	—	2-22	—	—	6×1½	—	PS	Yes	—	—	79⁹⁵ PPD
*JET	BG-6	6"	1-3	½	—	115/230	3450	—	2-28	—	—	6×¾	½"	CI	Yes	No	35	67⁹⁵
*JET	BG-8	8"	1-3	¾	—	115/230	3450	—	2-28	—	—	8×¾	⅝"	CI	Yes	No	57	103⁹⁵
JET	BG-10	10"	1-3	2	—	115/230	1720	—	2-28	—	—	10×1	1"	CI	Yes	No	124	199⁹⁵
*JET	BG-12	12"	1-3	2½	—	115/230	1720	—	2-28	—	—	12×1	1"	CI	Yes	No	208	289⁹⁵

GRINDER

Brand *No Photo Available	Model	Size	Motor**	Horse-Power	Phase	Voltage	RPM	Amps	Special Features***	Options****	Distance Between Wheels	Wheel Size	Arbor Size	Tool Rest Construction	Clear Eye Shields	Lighted	Shipping Weight	Suggested Retail Price
JET*	BGS-6	6"	1-3	½	–	115/220	–	–	29	–	–	–	–	PS	Yes	No	48	$144⁹⁵
JET	BGS-8	8"	1-3	¾	–	115/220	–	–	30	–	–	–	–	PS	Yes	No	78	279⁹⁵
MAKITA	9300	5"	1-2-3-4	–	–	115	3600	1.7	33	54	–	5×½	–	–	Yes	No	35.2	222
MILWAUKEE	4901	6"	–	¼	Single	115	3450	2.6	1-2 6-12-·6	28-29-30-31	9⅞"	6×⅝	⅝"	CI	Yes	No	26	159
MILWAUKEE	4921	6"	–	⅓	Single	115	3450	2.9	–	28-29-30-31	11¹³⁄₁₆"	6×¾	⅝"	CI	Yes	No	28	179
MILWAUKEE	4981	7"	–	½	Single	115	3450	4.0	–	27-28 29-30-31	13⅝"	7×1	⅝"	CI	Yes	No	43	279
MILWAUKEE	5041	8"	–	¾	Single	115	3450	8.2	–	27-28 29-30-31	17⅜"	8×1	⅝"	CI	Yes	No	60	379
MILWAUKEE	5081	10"	–	1	Single	115	1725	12.8	–	27-28 29-30-31	18⅛"	10×1	¾"	CI	Yes	No	90	479
POWERMATIC	2100 1210010	7"	2	½	Single	115/230	1800	–	2-24-25-26	44-45-46 49-51-52-53	15½"	7×1	⅝"	CI	No	–	71	538
POWERMATIC	2100 1210050	8"	2	¾	Single	115/230	3600	–	2-24-25-26	47-49 51-52-53	16½"	8×1	⅝"	CI	No	–	109	777
POWERMATIC	2100 1210070	10"	2	1	Single	115/230	1800	–	2-24-25-26	48-49 51-52-53	18"	10×1	⅞"	CI	No	–	140	994
POWERMATIC	2100 1210140	12"	2	2	Three	230/460	1800	–	2-24-25-26	50-51-52-53	23¾"	12×2	1¼"	CI	No	–	276	2190
WOODCRAFT	Mark II	8"	2-3	½	Single	110	1725	–	2-22-31-32	–	–	–	–	–	No	–	100	550

**MOTOR

1. Capacitor-start, capacitor-run
2. Totally enclosed
3. Ball bearing
4. Induction motor
5. Overload protection
6. Variable speed, 0-3800 RPM
7. Permanent magnet

**SPECIAL FEATURES

1. Removable wheel guards and covers allow unit to be used as a buffer or polisher.
2. Includes two piece tool rest; adjustable vertical and horizontal.
3. Exhaust type guards accomodate 2" diameter vent pipe.
4. Combination buffer/grinder.
5. Includes 36 grit wheel and .012 gauge wire brush.
6. Specially made for heavy duty grinding.
7. Exhaust type guards accomodate 3" diameter vent pipe.
8. Includes grinding wheel and wire brush; non-exhaust type guards.
9. Includes edge tool grinding attachment.
10. Water pot and tool tray mounted on swivel type arm.
11. Oversized 206 ball bearings.
12. Heavy cast iron base.
13. Exhaust type guards.
14. Includes grinding wheel and wire brush; exhaust type guards.
15. Guards designed to accomodate 1¼" wide wheels.
16. All ball and roller bearings.
17. Built-in water pot.
18. Double insulated.
19. Runs forward or reverse.
20. Grinding wheel runs in a tray of water as a coolant.
21. Lifetime, sealed ball bearing construction.
22. Removable wheel guards.
23. Adaptor for connecting dust collector.
24. Shaft is mounted in oversized sealed ball bearings.
25. Guards are heavy gauge steel construction, easily removed for wheel change.
26. Machines are not sold without eye shields.
27. Includes a second wheel of 4½" × ¾"; turns at 3,000 RPM, has clear eye shield.
28. Cast iron body, wheel guards and dust vents.
29. Combination grinder/belt sander; belt is 2 × 48.
30. Combination grinder/belt sander; belt is 4 × 36 or 38.
31. Combination grinder/belt sander; belt is 2½ × 60.
32. Idler arm, motor base and sides are heavy castings.
33. Comes complete with attachments to sharpen saw and planer blades.
34. Extra wide wheel guards.
35. Bench sander/grinder.
36. Has 6" sanding disc.
37. Adjustable table and mitre gauge on disc sander.
38. Includes 15 watt ball swivel lamp.
39. Removable water tray.
40. ABS thermoplastic housing and quench tray.
41. Die cast aluminum housing and wheel covers.
42. Dust chutes.
43. Includes quench tray, gooseneck lamp.

****OPTIONS

1. #662, same as #612, combination buffer/grinder with 36 grit wheel and .012 gauge wire brush, $139.
2. #623E, same as #612E, except has cast iron tool rest, single phase motor, $185.
3. #662E, same as #612E, except has pressed steel tool rest, combination buffer/grinder with 36 grit wheel and .012 gauge wire brush, 38 lbs., $165.
4. #712, same as #7306, except has pressed steel tool rest, 115V motor, 3,450 RPM, 68 lbs., $199.
5. #7307, same as #7306, except with 3,450 RPM, $244.
6. #7308, same as #7306, except with 208/230/460V three phase motor, $242.
7. #7309, same as #7306, except has 208/230/460V three phase motor, 3,450 RPM, $242.
8. #7351, same as #762, except has 115/230V, 3" diameter exhaust guard, grinding wheel and wire brush, cast iron tool rest, $244.
9. #7308DP, same as #7306DP, except has 208/230/460V three phase motor, $403.
10. #7306D, same as #7306DP, except does not have edge tool grinding attachment, $315.
11. #7307D, same as #7306DP, except has 3,450 RPM motor, does not have edge tool grinding attachment, 82 lbs, $315.
12. #7309D, same as #7306DP, except has 208/230/460V three phase motor, 3,450 RPM, 82 lbs., $312.
13. #8107W, same as #8100W, except has 3,450 RPM, motor, $395.
14. #8102W, same as #8100W, except has 208/230/460V three phase motor, $375.
15. #8123W, same as #8100W, except has 208/230/460V three phase motor, 3,450 RPM, $375.

****OPTIONS (CON'T)

16. #8252W, same as #8250W, except has 208/230/460V three phase motor, $375.

17. #8107WD, same as #8100WD, except has 3,450 RPM motor, $450.

18. #8102WD, same as #8100WD, except has 208/230/460V three phase motor, $435.

19. #8123WD, same as #8100WD, except has 208/230/460V three phase motor, 3,450 RPM, $435.

20. #1021W, same as #1022W, except has 1.5 HP, 208/230/460V three phase motor, $483.

21. #105W, same as #1022W, except has 1.5 HP, 575V three phase motor, $483.

22. #1021WD, same as #1022WD, except has 1.5 HP, 208/230/460V three phase motor, $555.

23. #GA16, pedestal, 32⅞" H × 15¾" W × 14" D; for 6", 7", 8" and 10" grinders, 58 lbs., $120.

24. #GA14, pedestal, 34½" H, formed steel with three shelves, for 6", 7", 8" and 10" grinders, 60 lbs., $92.

25. #GA9, lighted eye shield, $56.

26. Also available are larger industrial type grinders, buffers, dust control units and carbide tool grinders. See Baldor catalog for prices and specifications.

27. #49-62-0050, illuminated eye shield, 4 × 6 glass window, lighted, available for .5 HP, .75 HP and 1 HP grinders only; sold as a separate unit; if pair required, specify two units, $66.50.

28. #49-39-0050, grinder pedestal, heavy gray iron casting with tubular steel column. Removable water pot; adaptable to all models, 34" high, shipping wt. 54 lbs., $129.85.

29. #49-62-0100, plastic eye shields, supplied as a pair, $21.

30. #49-62-0060, glass eye shields, supplied as a pair, $31.05.

31. Also available are wire brushes, grinding wheels and buffing wheels. See catalog for prices and specifications.

32. Different grit stones are available.

33. Scangrind #200, same as #150, except has 120 RPM, wheel is 8 × 1½, 19 lbs., $160 PPD.

34. #23-751, same as #23-750, except has 230/460V three phase motor, $283.

35. #23-851, same as #23-850, except has 230/460V three phase motor, $330.

36. #23-902, same as #23-901, except has 1.5 HP three phase motor, 230/460V, $501.

37. #23-294, edge tool grinding attachment, $108.15.

38. #23-035, lighted safety shield, one only, $67.50.

39. #23-312, diamond pointed wheel dresser, $79.10.

40. #23-664, holder for diamond wheel dresser, $46.

41. #23-805, pedestal for bench models, $209.35.

42. #23-845, edge tool grinding attachment, $80.95.

43. #25-857, lamp attachment, $28.

44. #1210020, same as #1210010, except has three phase motor, 230/460V, $595.

45. #1210030, same as #1210010, except has 3,600 RPM motor, $538.

46. #1210040, same as #1210020, except has 3,600 RPM motor, $595.

47. #1210060, same as #1210050, except has three phase motor, 230/460V, $805.

48. #1210080, same as #1210070, except has three phase motor, 230/460V, $1,014.

49. #258801, steel pedestal with water pot and tool rest, for .5 HP, .75 HP, and 1 HP grinders, $124.

50. #2588002, cast iron pedestal with water pot and tool rest for 2 HP grinder, $659.

51. #6028005, grinding wheel dresser, $188.

52. #6805001, set of two shatterproof eye shields, $38.

53. #6805002, set of two shatterproof eye shields, illuminated, $102.

54. Tool rest optional, no price available.

55. #2963C, grinder stand, $39.99.

56. #19244, gooseneck light, $19.99.

57. #64856, disc sander attachment with table, $19.99.

58. #19596, tool holder for sharpening chisels and screwdrivers, $29.99.

59. #6677, bit grinder attachment, $15.99.

SPRAY EQUIPMENT

Spraying is the most common method used to apply finishes in the furniture industry. Many small cabinet shops and home craftsmen also prefer spray finishing. With spraying you are able to quickly cover items with uniform coatings. Even inexperienced operators can achieve acceptable results with very little practice.

Spray finishing can be divided into three broad classifications: conventional air, airless, and electrostatic. Woodworkers are generally concerned with air or airless units, however, electrostatic spraying does have industrial wood applications.

AIR ATOMIZED EQUIPMENT

Conventional air atomization is the oldest method used in spray finishing. Equipment of this type is still probably most common, especially in small shops. It consists of the following basic components: air source (air compressor), air hose, air regulator/filter, spray gun and exhaust system (spray booth). Getting into spraying isn't simply a matter of buying a spray gun, you must have a number of other items to make the system work, and a good compressor is a must.

COMPRESSORS

Compressed air is a very convenient service to have in a wood shop. It can be used not only in spray painting but for operating portable pneumatic tools and for cleaning, not to mention pumping up bicycle tires.

When selecting a compressor you should consider all of the air needs you have or will have in the shop. Each air consuming tool, including a spray gun, will be rated according to the amount of air required (cfm) at a

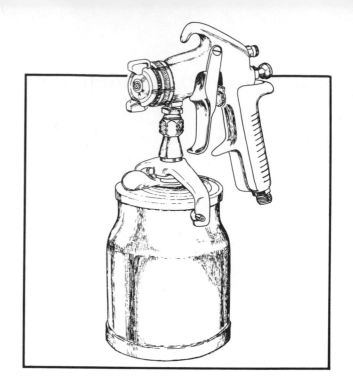

given pressure. Cfm requirements for spray guns vary widely depending upon the design of the air cap, fluid tip, and the gun itself. One spray gun manufacturer, for example, offers guns with cfm requirements ranging from 2.9 to 10.1 cfm at 30 psi or 4.4 to 14.8 cfm at 50 psi. Be sure to choose a gun which matches your compressor. A common rule of thumb for estimating the actual volume of air (cfm) delivered by a compressor at 100 psi is 3 to 5 cfm per horsepower for electric motor driven units.

Air compressors typically used in small shops are either diaphragm or piston type. Diaphragm units typically do not have air storage tanks and will operate continuously. These units are small and portable. The maximum pressure for a diaphragm compressor is approximately 30 to 40 psi. They do supply enough air for spray painting if the spray gun is carefully chosen, but they will not supply enough air for some of the larger production guns. Since these units do not have storage tanks you will notice an occasional air pressure drop while you are using the gun. This can cause problems, especially in some tricky staining operations.

Piston compressors can be either single or two stage units. A single stage compressor will compress the air to full pressure with one stroke of the piston. These units will produce pressures up to 100 psi. Two stage units compress the air twice and are used when air pressure is required in excess of 100 psi and normally not more than 200 psi. Single-stage compressors are common in small shops with two-stage being found most often in larger cabinet shops and industry.

AIR REGULATORS AND FILTERS

The air supplied to a spray gun must be pressure regulated, clean, and dry. Most compressors will have an air pressure regulator which can be used to accurately set the air pressure for spraying, but air filters and moisture traps are often not provided and must be purchased as an option. If you plan to do serious finishing, an air filter and moisture trap is essential.

SPRAY GUNS

Air atomized spray guns range from tiny air brushes to heavy duty production guns. The guns found most often in home shops or small cabinet shops are the external mix, siphon feed type. These guns are excellent for refinishing, touch-up or situations which do not require large quantities of paint or high production rates. The average siphon feed gun will have a one quart cup capacity.

Pressure feed spray guns are used in cabinet shops and industry. They yield a much higher production rate and can have large paint tanks (3 to 60 gallons). Pressure feed systems are expensive, but they are essential in production situations.

Spray guns are similar to many other items in the sense that you tend to get what you pay for. Cheaper guns will spray paint but often do not meet the standards needed for high quality finishing. These guns will frequently lack accurate pattern and fluid control and tend to produce a fairly coarse atomized pattern. More expensive guns will be easier to control and offer greater versatility.

AIRLESS SPRAYING

Airless spraying utilizes a specially designed hydraulic pump to deliver the paint to the gun under high pressure. When the fluid is released through the gun's nozzle orifice, it is atomized. Airless spraying is probably best suited for maintenance applications where large areas need to be covered, however, a number of large furniture companies now use airless equipment. Small portable airless units for the hobbyist and home owner have been on the market for several years. These units will function well for general painting but do not offer the control required for high quality furniture finishing. One of the chief limitations of airless spraying is the fact that the spray pattern is fixed and can only be changed by changing tips. This fact alone significantly limits versatility. Airless units are efficient, and less fluid is wasted in overfog or overspray.

SPRAY BOOTH

Spray finishing requires an efficient exhaust system for the overspray and solvent vapors. Some hobbyists spray outside when the weather permits, unfortunately the weather often doesn't permit. A small spray booth with a suitable exhaust fan will make it possible to spray regardless of the weather. It is possible to purchase spray booths or make your own. The booth should be constructed from non-combustible materials. The exhaust fan should be one designed especially for spraying installations. The motor and electrical controls for the booth must be approved for hazardous locations. Any lights used in the booth must be special, explosion proof lamps. A good spray booth can be expensive, but if you are really serious about spray finishing, a booth is a must. If you are in a product situation, OSHA regulations related to spraying installations must be followed.

SPRAY EQUIPMENT

Brand	Gun (Part No.)	Gun Price	Suggested Usage	Regulator (Part No.)	Regulator Capacity (CFM)	Dials	Regulator Price	Cup (Part No.)	Cup Capacity	Cup Price	
BINKS	7	$169	Refinishing; general use	86-836	8	None	$49^{50}	81-350 Drip proof	1 Qt.	$27	
	26	135	Smaller projects; small & lt. wt.	86-940	30	Single	87	81-550	1 Qt.	24^{75}	
	18	169	High quality production work	86-945	40	Single	116	81-520	1 Pt.	—	
	62	161	General production use	86-974	40	Two	183	81-540	8 oz.	25^{50}	
	370A	99	Lt. to med. production use	86-980	45	None	—				
	2001	120	Newest production model	86-948	60	Two	204				
				86-964	100	None	—				
DeVILBISS	JGK-501	$179	High volume production	HAR-501	15	None	$43^{50}	KR-566	1 Qt.	$35^{25}	
	JGA-502	119	Heavy duty production spraying	HAR-504	40	None	25	KS-525	25 oz.	30^{25}	Use only with MGB or TGA
	MBC-510	199^{50}	High production heavy duty use	HLE-501	50	Single	198^{50}	KS-524	8 oz.	27^{50}	Use only with MGB or TGA
	TGA-510	142^{50}	Medium volume spraying	HLF-501	40	Single	78				
	CGA-501-FF	with cup	Light duty refinishing	HAA-504	80	None	67				
				HLG-501	100	Two	324^{50}				
				HLT-510	100	Single	119				

SPRAY EQUIPMENT

Brand	Gun (Part No.)	Gun Price	Suggested Usage	Regulator (Part No.)	Regulator Capacity (CFM)	Dials	Regulator Price	Cup (Part No.)	Cup Capacity	Cup Price	
PAASCHE	AUF	$80^{60}	Light duty	RC-¼"-12'M	27	—	$123^{45}	1 SL	1 Qt.	$34	
	BUF	89^{60}	Medium duty	RC-⅜"-12'M	70	—	131^{30}	30SC	1 Qt.	19^{50}	
	D2UF	111^{15}	High production	RC-¼"-12'M	27	—	132^{60}				
	211	115	General use	R3-⅜"-12'M	70	—	137^{80}				
	LSC-QT	—	General use & touch up								
CRAFTSMAN	9 HT 15635	$119^{99}	Light to medium duty					Drip proof	1 Qt.	—	All Craftsmen guns come
	9 HT 15501	99^{99}	Touch-up use					CAM-lock	8 oz.	—	complete with cup;
	9 HT 15624	89^{99}	General purpose					Drip proof	1 Qt.	—	regulator not included
	9 HT 15614	59^{99}	General purpose; medium duty					Drip proof	1 Qt.	—	
	9 HT 15583	39^{99}	All purpose; medium duty					Drip proof	1 Qt.	—	
				9 HT 16023	175 psi maximum	—	$136^{99}				
STEWART-WARNER	7839	$—	High capacity	7928	60	Single	$252^{90}	7940 Agitator	1 Qt.	$91^{75}	
	7856	149^{90}	Medium capacity	7927	30	Single	157^{05}	7945 Drip proof	1 Qt.	35^{95}	
	7848	212^{45}	Designed for heavy materials	7926	60	None	131^{40}				
				7923	30	None	106^{75}				
				7935	20-40	Single	98^{60}				

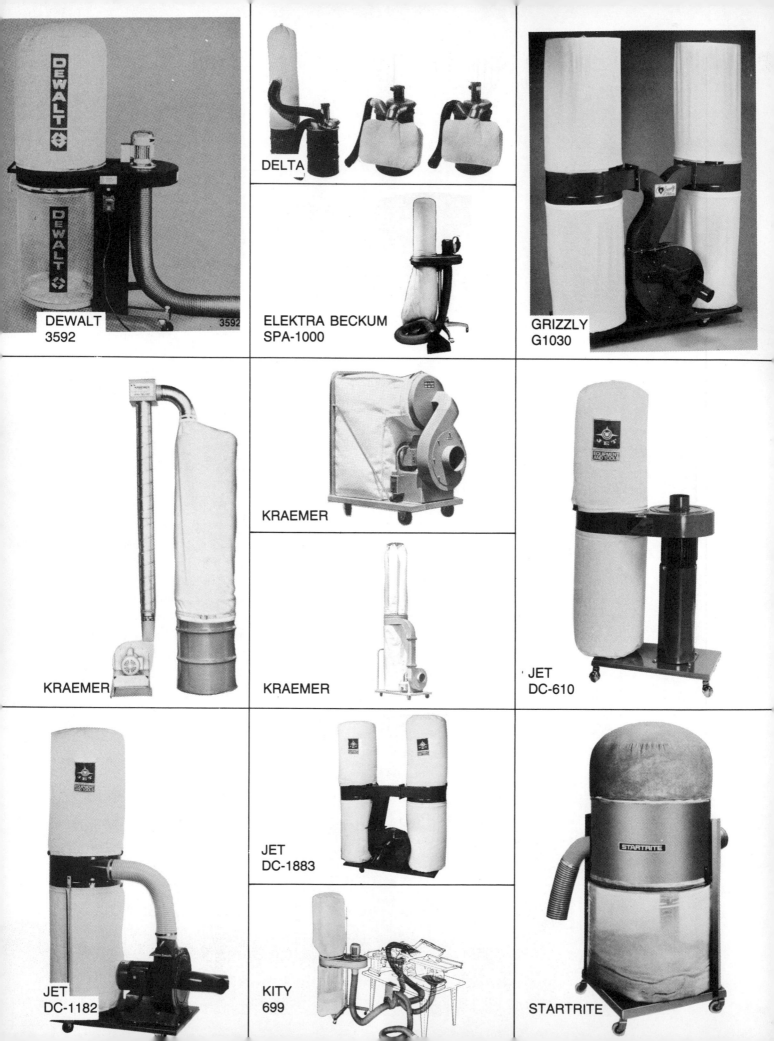

DEWALT
3592

DELTA

ELEKTRA BECKUM
SPA-1000

GRIZZLY
G1030

KRAEMER

KRAEMER

KRAEMER

JET
DC-610

JET
DC-1182

JET
DC-1883

KITY
699

STARTRITE

DUST COLLECTOR

Brand *No Photo Available	Model	Phase	Horse-Power	Voltage	Special Features**	Options***	Maximum Cubic Ft. Per Minute	Bag Area (Sq. Ft.) or Bag Size	Number of Bags	Drum Size (Gallons)	Hose Size	Number of Hose Connections	Net Weight	Suggested Retail Price
BLACK & DECKER (MFG-DEWALT)	3592	NO SPECIFICATIONS AVAILABLE AT TIME OF PUBLICATION											—	$616
DELTA	50-180	1	1	115/230	1-2-4	1	700	19.0	1	55	5×60	1	72	463
DELTA	50-181	1	2	230	1-2-4	1	1100	19.0	1	55	6×60	1	97	658
DELTA	50-182	3	3	230/460	1-3-4	1	1300	50.0	1	55	6×60	1	113	766
ELEKTRA BECKUM	SPA-1000	—	¾	110	6-19	25	765	—	2	None	4×98	1	54	450
*GRIZZLY	G1028	1	1	—	5-6	—	498	19×35	2	—	—	2	140	295
*GRIZZLY	G1029	1	2	—	5-6	—	960	19×35	2	—	—	2	150	355
GRIZZLY	G1030	1	3	—	5-6	—	1515	19×35	4	—	—	3	209	455
J. PHILIP HUMFREY (MFG-KRAEMER)	S1	1	1	110/220	6-15-16-17	8	810	—	1	None	—	1-6"	95	990
J. PHILIP HUMFREY (MFG-KRAEMER)	S2N	1	2	110/220	6-15-16-17	9	1200	—	2	None	—	1-7"	186	1495
J. PHILIP HUMFREY (MFG-KRAEMER)	S3	1	3	110/220	6-15-16-17	10	1605	—	2	None	—	1-7"	212	1867.50
J. PHILIP HUMFREY (MFG-KRAEMER)	S5	1	5	110/220	6-15-16-17	11	2137	—	2	None	—	1-8"	237	2593.80
J. PHILIP HUMFREY (MFG-KRAEMER)	S22-12N	1	2	110/220	6-15-16-17	12	1200	—	4	None	—	1-7"	256	1947.60
J. PHILIP HUMFREY (MFG-KRAEMER)	E11	1	1	110/220	15-16-18	13	810	39	1	45-55	—	1-6"	90	698
J. PHILIP HUMFREY (MFG-KRAEMER)	E21	1	2	110/220	15-16-18	14	1200	39	1	45-55	—	1-7"	110	900.90
J. PHILIP HUMFREY (MFG-KRAEMER)	E31	1	3	110/220	15-16-18	15	1604	39	1	45-55	—	1-7"	151	1193

DUST COLLECTOR

Brand *No Photo Available	Model	Phase	Horse-Power	Voltage	Special Features**	Options***	Maximum Cubic Ft. Per Minute	Bag Area (Sq. Ft.) or Bag Size	Number of Bags	Drum Size (Gallons)	Hose Size	Number of Hose Connections	Net Weight	Suggested Retail Price
J. PHILIP HUMFREY (MFG-KRAEMER)	E51	1	5	110/220	15-16-18	16	2137	39	1	45-55	—	1-8"	179	$1638.50
J. PHILIP HUMFREY (MFG-KRAEMER)	E12	1	1	110/220	15-16-18	17	810	78	2	45-55	—	1-6"	97	994.50
J. PHILIP HUMFREY (MFG-KRAEMER)	E22	1	2	110/220	15-16-18	18	1200	78	2	45-55	—	1-7"	117	1197.90
J. PHILIP HUMFREY (MFG-KRAEMER)	E32	1	3	110/220	15-16-18	19	1604	78	2	45-55	—	1-7"	158	1490
J. PHILIP HUMFREY (MFG-KRAEMER)	E52	1	5	110/220	15-16-18	20	2137	78	2	45-55	—	1-8"	182	1935
J. PHILIP HUMFREY (MFG-KRAEMER)	E13	1	1	110/220	15-16-18	21	810	117	3	45-55	—	1-6"	104	1292
J. PHILIP HUMFREY (MFG-KRAEMER)	E23	1	2	110/220	15-16-18	22	1200	117	3	45-55	—	1-7"	124	1494.90
J. PHILIP HUMFREY (MFG-KRAEMER)	E33	1	3	110/220	15-16-18	23	1604	117	3	45-55	—	1-7"	165	1787
J. PHILIP HUMFREY (MFG-KRAEMER)	E53	1	5	110/220	15-16-18	24	2137	117	3	45-55	—	1-8"	193	2232
JET	DC-610	1	1	115/230	6-7	—	610	—	2	None	—	1	83	406
JET	DC-1182	1	2	115/230	6-8	—	1182	—	2	None	—	1-5" 1-4"	190	570
JET	DC-1883	1	3	115/230	6-9	—	1883	—	4	None	—	2-4" 1-6"	194	963
KITY	699	NO SPECIFICATIONS AVAILABLE AT TIME OF PUBLICATION											70	634.90
STARTRITE	55	—	3	—	6-10-11 13-14	3-5-7	565	—	1	None	4½×96	1	125	774
STARTRITE	75	—	1	—	6-11-12 13-14	4-6-7	1045	—	1	None	6¼×96	1	145	1051

DUST COLLECTOR

Brand *No Photo Available	Model	Phase	Horse-Power	Voltage	Special Features**	Options***	Maximum Cubic Ft. Per Minute	Bag Area (Sq. Ft.) or Bag Size	Number of Bags	Drum Size (Gallons)	Hose Size	Number of Hose Connections	Net Weight	Suggested Retail Price
*SUNHILL (MFG-SEN KONG)	UFO-90	1	1	—	6	—	550	—	2	None	4×__	1	145	$385
*SUNHILL (MFG-SEN KONG)	UFO-101	1	2	—	6	—	1182	—	2	None	5×__	1	200	450
*SUNHILL (MFG-SEN KONG)	UFO-102B	1	3	—	6	—	1883	—	4	None	5×__	1	250	595
*SUNHILL (MFG-SEN KONG)	UFO-104	3	5	—	6	—	2960	—	8	None	4×__	5	600	1650
*WOODMASTER	620	—	⅓	115	20-21-22	—	—	—	—	55	4×60	—	—	197⁵⁰

(PRICES INCLUDE FREIGHT TO NEAREST TERMINAL OF OUR HOUSE CARRIER [SUNHILL])

SPECIAL FEATURES

1. Self-cleaning cast aluminum radial pressure fan.
2. Heavy duty fiberglass drum lid and 14 gauge steel blower housing.
3. Cast aluminum drum lid and 14 gauge steel blower housing.
4. All models fit any 55 gallon open end steel drum; not included.
5. Blowers are squirrel cage type mounted directly on motor shaft.
6. Mounted on portable base with casters.
7. Has a 10" blower wheel.
8. Has a 12¼" blower wheel.
9. Has a 14$^{5}/_{16}$" blower wheel.
10. Has a collection capacity of 5 cubic feet.
11. Unit is intended for collection of sawdust and chippings from woodworking machinery; should not be used with abrasive or sanding machines.
12. Has a collection capacity of 9 cubic feet.
13. Overload and no volt protection motor.
14. Uses polythene collection bags. Ten supplied with machine.
15. Direct coupling of motor provides maintenance-free service.
16. When dust from sanders is a primary material to be handled, multiple top bags should be chosen.
17. Portable models (except S1) have the option to be set up as stationary units substituting barrels for bottom bags.
18. Stationary models require the use of your own 45-55 gallon drum.
19. Accepts any standard trash bag.
20. Direct drive.
21. Fits on 55 gallon drum; not provided.
22. Solid 9" diameter wide blower wheel.

OPTIONS

1. #50-185, extra bags, $97.30.
2. #G1027, extra bags, $25 each, PPD.
3. Also available with three phase, 220/440V motor, same price.
4. Also available with three phase, 220/440V motor, $948.
5. #W55B, extra collection bags, 10 for $29.
6. #W75B, extra collection bags, 10 for $38.
7. #5583, linen filter bag, $79.
8. Also available with three phase, 220/440/575V motor, same price.
9. Also available with three phase, 220/440/575V motor, $1,382.40.
10. Also available with three phase, 220/440/575V motor, $1,556.10.
11. Also available with three phase, 220/440/575V motor, $2,130.30.
12. Also available with three phase, 220/440/575V motor, $1,835.10.
13. Also available with three phase, 220/440/575V motor, $683.10.
14. Also available with three phase, 220/440/575V motor, $792.
15. Also available with three phase, 220/440/575V motor, $810.
16. Also available with three phase, 220/440/575V motor, $1,188.50.
17. Also available with three phase, 220/440/575V motor, $980.10.
18. Also available with three phase, 220/440/575V motor, $1,089.
19. Also available with three phase, 220/440/575V motor, $1,180.
20. Also available with three phase, 220/440/575V motor, $1,488.
21. Also available with three phase, 220/440/575V motor, $1,277.10.
22. Also available with three phase, 220/440/575V motor, $1,386.
23. Also available with three phase, 220/440/575V motor, $1,485.
24. Also available with three phase, 220/440/575V motor, $1,782.
25. Also available with ¾ HP, 220V motor, $425.

MISCELLANEOUS

In the woodworking field there are many unusual and one-of-a-kind specialty items. There are also items that are not manufactured by a wide variety of companies. It is for this reason that we have included this miscellaneous section. In it you will find items of great interest to woodworkers. Further information on each item can be obtained by writing to the manufacturer.

BOWL TURNER
BRAND: TOOLMARK CO.
MODEL: 709A

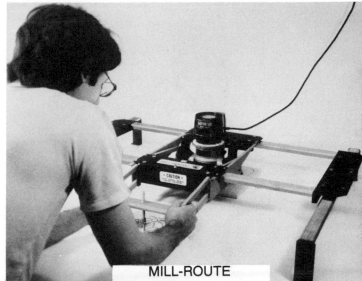

MILL-ROUTE
DUPLICATING MACHINE
BRAND: PROGRESSIVE TECHNOLOGY, INC.
PRICE: $199, router not included.

ROTO/CARVE
BRAND: ROTO/CARVE
MODEL: 210-1036
PRICE: $298
CARRIAGE: 36″
Also available, model 210-1060 with 60″ carriage, $353.

LATHE DUPLICATING SYSTEM
BRAND: TOOLMARK CO.
MODEL: 520B

LATHE DUPLICATING SYSTEM
BRAND: TOOLMARK CO.
MODEL: 3010

DUPLI-CARVER
CARVING MACHINE
BRAND: WOOD-MIZER PRODUCTS
MODEL: F-200
PRICE: $799
Also available, Model T-110, $299.

FLEXIBLE SHAFT MACHINE
BRAND: FOREDOM
MODEL: S-SC
PRICE: $158.00 PLUS PRICE OF HANDPIECE
A wide range of models and accessories is available.

DOVETAIL TEMPLATES
BRAND: KELLER
MODEL: 2400 and 3600
PRICE: $269.00 and $365.00
Everything needed to cut dovetail joints.

JOINT-MATIC
BRAND: STRONG TOOL DESIGN
MODEL: 4200
PRICE: $778
Unique machine makes a variety of wood joints, including all types of dovetails. Complete with #1604 1¾ HP Bosch router.

DOVETAIL JIG
BRAND: WOODMACHINE COMPANY
PRICE: $385

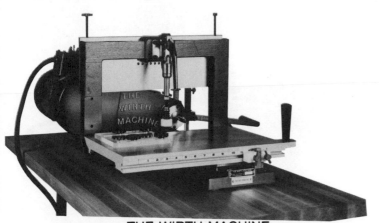

THE WIRTH MACHINE
BRAND: WOODWORKER'S SUPPLY, INC.
MODEL: 95-100
PRICE: $2,095
Makes all types of woodworking joints, quickly, easily and accurately.

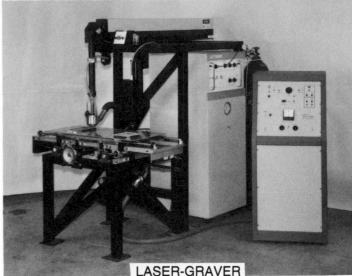

LASER-GRAVER
BRAND: LASER MACHINING, INC.
MODEL: 101
BASE PRICE: $56,900

MITER-TRIMMER
BRAND: POOTATUCK CORP.
PRICE: $235
Cuts any angle from 45° to 90°.

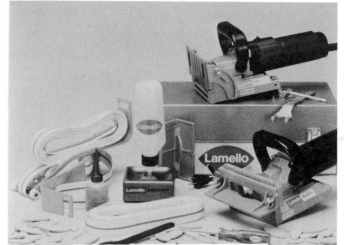

LAMELLO JOINERY SYSTEM
BRAND: COLONIAL SAW
PRICE: Various models, $350.00 to $595.00
A range of tools using a new way of joining, trimming, hinging and patching wood.

MULTI-PURPOSE MACHINE
BRAND: EMCO USA
MODEL: STAR-2000
PRICE: $795.00
Four operations in one: circular sawing, band sawing, moulding, disc sanding.

SHOPSMITH MARK V
BRAND: SHOPSMITH
MODEL: MARK V
PRICE: Varies with different packages. See mfg.
A multi-purpose machine that performs sawing, drilling, sanding, boring and turning. Offers a great variety of accessories.

WOODMASTER CENTURY XXI
BRAND: MASTER WOODCRAFT MACHINE CO.
MODEL: CENTURY XXI
PRICE: VARIES WITH OPTIONS—SEE MFG.
A 5 in 1 woodworking tool. Can be used as a lathe, table saw, disc sander, horizontal drill press, vertical drill press. A large selection of options available.

VARIABLE SPEED
MOTO TOOL KIT
BRAND: DREMEL
MODEL: 3801
PRICE: $101.95
Includes 40 piece accessory kit.

MOISTURE METER
BRAND: DELMHORST INSTRUMENT CO.
MODEL: G-30
PRICE: $200

MOISTURE METER
BRAND: DELMHORST INSTRUMENT CO.
MODEL: J-88
PRICE: $89
MEASURING DEPTH: ½"

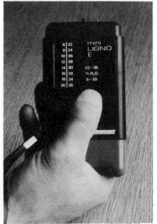

MOISTURE METER
BRAND: LIGNOMAT
MODEL: Mini Ligno E
PRICE: $120
MEASURING DEPTH: Approx. 3/16"

MOISTURE METER
BRAND: LIGNOMAT
MODEL: Mini Ligno with E12
PRICE: $175.50
MEASURING DEPTH: Approx. 7/16"

MOISTURE METER
BRAND: VALLEY PRODUCTS AND DESIGN, INC.
MODEL: TRITON 1500
PRICE: $289

BULLS-EYE
BRAND: RING MASTER
PRICE: $9.95, 2" MODEL
$14.95, 6" MODEL
New device instantly locates the center of a workpiece.

RING MASTER
BRAND: RING MASTER
PRICE: $289, without motor
$399, with ⅓ HP TEFC motor
Cuts concentric rings from flat wood.

DOWEL MATE
BRAND: RING MASTER
PRICE: $995
A dual spindle dowel hole drilling machine.

RIPSTRATE
BRAND: FISHER HILL PRODUCTS
PRICE: $66.00
Hold-down device used while ripping stock.

SHOPHELPER SAFETY GUIDES
BRAND: WESTERN COMMERCIAL PRODUCTS
PRICE: $79.50
Anti-kickback stock feeder

INVERTED ROUTER
BRAND: C. R. ONSRUD, INC.
MODEL: 2003
PRICE: STARTING AT $2,500.

OVERARM ROUTER
BRAND: BOSCH
MODEL: 93940
PRICE: $1,000
Motor not included
Pneumatic controlled.
Uses portable router motors.

SAW FENCE
BRAND: BIESEMEYER MFG. CORP.
A precision T-square saw fence system. Fits most popular table saws. Various sizes available.

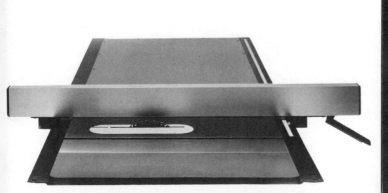

PARALOK TABLE SAW FENCE
BRAND: QUINTEC
Fits most popular table saws; wide range of sizes available.

PORTABLE SAW MILL
BRAND: SPERBER TOOL WORKS, INC.
MODEL: 22
PRICE: $1525, complete
       $525, less engine

PORTABLE SAW MILL
BRAND: SPERBER TOOL WORKS, INC.
MODEL: 18
PRICE: $995, complete
        $495, less engine

GAS LUMBER MILL
BRAND: WOOD-MIZER PRODUCTS
MODEL: LT30G
PRICE: $6,472

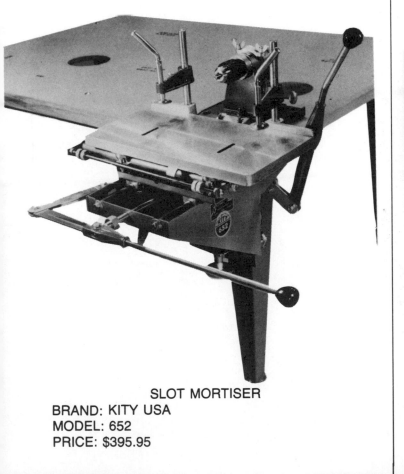

SLOT MORTISER
BRAND: KITY USA
MODEL: 652
PRICE: $395.95

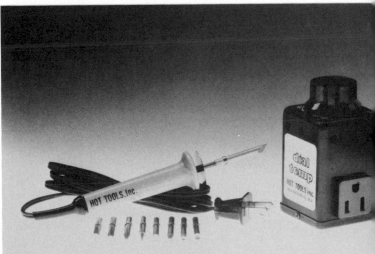

WOODBURNING TOOL
BRAND: HOT TOOLS, INC.
MODEL: WB-1, SHOWN WITH DIAL TEMP
PRICE: $17.95
DIAL TEMP PRICE: $27.50

INDEX OF MANUFACTURERS

AEG POWER TOOL CORPORATION
ONE WINNENDEN ROAD
NORWICH, CT 06360
(203) 886-0151

AMI, LTD.
P.O. BOX 312
NEW CASTLE, DE 19720
(302) 322-2226

BALDOR
FORT SMITH, AR 72902
(501) 646-4711

BIESEMEYER MANUFACTURING CORP.
216 S. ALMA SCHOOL RD., SUITE 3
MESA, AZ 85202
(602) 835-9300

BINKS MANUFACTURING COMPANY
9201 W. BELMONT AVE.
FRANKLIN PARK, IL 60131
(312) 671-3000

BLACK & DECKER, INC.
701 E. JAPPA ROAD
TOWSON, MD 21204
(301) 467-7411

BOSCH POWER TOOL CORPORATION
3701 NEUSE BOULEVARD
NEW BERN, NC 28560-9399

COLONIAL SAW
100 PEMBROKE ST.
P.O. BOX A
KINGSTON, MA 02364
(617) 585-4364

CONOVER WOODCRAFT SPECIALTIES, INC.
18125 MADISON RD.
PARKMAN, OH 44080
(216) 548-3481

C. R. ONSRUD, INC.
P.O. BOX 416
HIGHWAY 21 SOUTH
TROUTMAN, NC 28166
(704) 528-4528

CRAFTSMAN TOOLS
SEARS, ROEBUCK AND CO.
925 S. HOMAN AVENUE
CHICAGO, IL 60607

DELMHORST INSTRUMENT COMPANY
607 CEDAR STREET
P. O. BOX 130
BOONTON, NJ 07005
(201) 334-2557

DELTA INTERNATIONAL MACHINERY
CORP.
246 ALPHA DRIVE
PITTSBURGH, PA 15238
(800) 438-2487

DeVILBISS COMPANY, THE
TOLEDO, OH 43692

DREMEL
DIVISION OF EMERSON ELECTRIC CO.
4915 21ST STREET
RACINE, WI 53406
(414) 554-1390

ELEKTRA BECKUM U.S.A. CORP.
401-403 KENNEDY BLVD.
P.O. BOX 24
SOMERDALE, NJ 08083
(609) 784-8600

EMCO USA
2080 FAIRWOOD AVENUE
P.O. BOX 07795
COLUMBUS, OH 43207
(614) 445-8382

F & H MACHINERY
2433 HAMILTON RD.
ARLINGTON HTS., IL 60005
(312) 437-7110

FINE TOOL SHOPS, THE
20 BACKUS AVENUE
P.O. BOX 1262
DANBURY, CT 06810
(800) 243-1037

FISHER HILL PRODUCTS
FISHER HILL
FITZWILLIAM, NH 03447
(603) 585-6883

FOREDOM ELECTRIC COMPANY, THE
ROUTE 6
BETHEL, CT 06801
(203) 792-8622

GRIZZLY IMPORTS, INC.
P.O. BOX 2069
BELLINGHAM, WA 98227
(206) 647-0801

HITACHI POWER TOOLS U.S.A. LTD.
4487-F PARK DRIVE
NORCROSS, GA 30093
(404) 925-1774

HOT TOOLS INCORPORATED
7 HAWKES STREET
P.O. BOX 615
MARBLEHEAD, MA 01945
(617) 639-1000

INTERNATIONAL WOODWORKING
EQUIPMENT CORP
11577 A SLATER AVE.
FOUNTAIN VALLEY, CA 92708
(714) 549-3446

JET EQUIPMENT & TOOLS
P.O. BOX 1477
TACOMA, WA 98401
(206) 572-5000

J. PHILIP HUMFREY LTD.
3241 KENNEDY ROAD, UNIT 7
SCARBOROUGH, ONTARIO
CANADA M1V 2J9
(416) 293-8624

KELLER DOVETAIL TEMPLATES
P.O. BOX 800
BOLINAS, CA 94924
(415) 868-0560

KITY USA
WOODWORKING MACHINES
8188 BELVEDERE AVE. #D
SACRAMENTO, CA 95826
(916) 731-5489

LASER MACHINING, INC.
500 LASER DRIVE
SOMERSET, WI 54025
(715) 247-3285

LIGNOMAT USA, LTD.
P.O. BOX 30145
14345 N.E. MORRIS CT.
PORTLAND, OR 97230
(503) 257-8957

MAKITA U.S.A., INC.
12950 E. ALONDRA BLVD.
CERRITOS, CA 90701
(213) 926-8775

MASTER WOODCRAFT MACHINE CO.
800 SPRUCE LAKE DR.
P.O. BOX 669
HARBOR CITY, CA 90710
(213) 549-0761

MILWAUKEE ELECTRIC TOOL CORP.
13135 WEST LISBON ROAD
BROOKFIELD, WI 53005
(414) 781-3600

MINI MAX USA., INC.
3642 N.W. 37TH AVENUE
MIAMI, FL 33142
(305) 633-6372

PAASCHE AIRBRUSH CO.
7440 WEST LAWRENCE AVE.
HARWOOD HEIGHTS, IL 60656
(312) 867-9191

PARKS WOODWORKING MACHINE CO., THE
1501 KNOWLTON STREET
CINCINNATI, OH 45223
(513) 681-1931

POOTATUCK CORPORATION
P. O. BOX 24
WINDSOR, VT 05089
(802) 674-5984

PORTER CABLE
BOX 2468
JACKSON, TN 38302

POWERMATIC
McMINNVILLE, TN 37110
(615) 473-5551

PROGRESSIVE TECHNOLOGY, INC.
P. O. BOX 98
STAFFORD, TX 77477-0098
(713) 721-3351

PRO SHOP POWER TOOLS
BOX 721
ELMHURST, IL 60126
(312) 832-3803

QUINTEC MARKETING
P. O. BOX 736
NEWBERG, OR 97132
(503) 538-1875

RBINDUSTRIES, INC.
201 FIRST STREET
PLEASANT HILL, MO 64080

RING MASTER, INC.
P. O. BOX 8527-A
ORLANDO, FL 32856
(305) 859-2017

ROTO/CARVE
6509 INDIAN HILLS RD.
MINNEAPOLIS, MN 55435
(612) 944-5150

RYOBI AMERICA CORP.
1158 TOWER LANE
BENSENVILLE, IL 60106
(312) 766-1621

SAFETY SPEED CUT MFG. CO., INC.
13460 N. HWY 65
ANOKA, MN 55303
(612) 755-1600

SAND-RITE MANUFACTURING CO.
1611 NORTH SHEFFIELD AVENUE
CHICAGO, IL 60614

SHOPSMITH, INC.
6640 POE AVENUE
DAYTON, OH 45414-2591

SKIL CORPORATION
4801 WEST PETERSON AVENUE
CHICAGO, IL 60646

SPERBER TOOL WORKS, INC.
BOX 1224
WEST CALDWELL, NJ 07007
(201) 744-6110

STARMARK INDUSTRIES
3001 FULLER N.E.
GRAND RAPIDS, MI 49505
(616) 363-1033

STARTRITE, INC.
3400 COVINGTON ROAD
KALAMAZOO, MI 49002
(616) 344-3800

STEWART-WARNER CORPORATION
1826 DIVERSEY PARKWAY
CHICAGO, IL 60614

STRONG TOOL DESIGN
20425 BEATRICE
LIVONIA, MI 48152
(313) 476-3317

SUNHILL ENTERPRISES CO., THE
414 OLIVE WAY, SUITE 205
TIMES SQUARE BUILDING
SEATTLE, WA 98101
(206) 622-5775

TOOLMARK CO.
6840 SHINGLE CREEK PARKWAY
MINNEAPOLIS, MN 55430
(612) 561-4210

VALLEY PRODUCTS AND DESIGN, INC.
P. O. BOX 396, RT. 418
MILFORD, PA 18337
(717) 296-8009

VEGA ENTERPRISES, INC.
ROUTE 3, BOX 193
DECATUR, IL 62526
(217) 963-2232

WESTERN COMMERCIAL PRODUCTS
P. O. BOX 238
TULARE, CA 93275
(209) 678-7409

WILKE MACHINERY COMPANY
120 DERRY COURT
R.D. #22
YORK, PA 17402
(717) 846-2800

WILLIAMS & HUSSEY MACHINE CO.
ELM STREET
MILFORD, NH 03055
(603) 673-3446

WOODCRAFT SUPPLY CORP.
41 ATLANTIC AVENUE
P.O. BOX 4000
WOBURN, MA 01888
(617) 935-5860

WOODMACHINE COMPANY
RT. 2, BOX 227
MEBANE, NC 27302

WOODMASTER TOOLS, INC.
2908 OAK STREET
KANSAS CITY, MO 64108
(816) 756-2195

WOOD-MIZER
8180 WEST 10TH STREET
INDIANAPOLIS, IN 46224
(317) 271-1542

WOODWORKER'S SUPPLY
5604 ALAMEDA N.E.
ALBUQUERQUE, NM 87113
(505) 821-0500